I'm Not Trying To Be Difficult

EAT DOWNTOWN! *2025*

I'm Not Trying To Be Difficult

Stories from the Restaurant Trenches

Drew Nieporent
with Jamie Feldmar

GRAND CENTRAL

New York   Boston

Grand Central Publishing
Hachette Book Group
1290 Avenue of the Americas
New York, NY 10104
grandcentralpublishing.com
@grandcentralpub

First Edition: September 2025

Grand Central Publishing is a division of Hachette Book Group, Inc.
The Grand Central Publishing name and logo are registered trademarks of Hachette Book Group, Inc.

The publisher is not responsible for websites (or their content) that are not owned by the publisher.

The Hachette Speakers Bureau provides a wide range of authors for speaking events. To find out more, visit hachettespeakersbureau.com or email HachetteSpeakers@hbgusa.com.

Grand Central Publishing books may be purchased in bulk for business, educational, or promotional use. For information, please contact your local bookseller or email the Hachette Book Group Special Markets Department at Special.Markets@hbgusa.com.

Print book interior design by Bart Dawson

Library of Congress Cataloging-in-Publication Data

Names: Nieporent, Drew author | Feldmar, Jamie author
Title: I'm not trying to be difficult: stories from the restaurant
    trenches / Drew Nieporent with Jamie Feldman.
Description: First edition. | New York: Grand Central Publishing/Hachette
    Book Group, 2025.
Identifiers: LCCN 2025002456 | ISBN 9781538765579 hardcover | ISBN
    9781538765586 trade paperback | ISBN 9781538765593 ebook
Subjects: LCSH: Nieporent, Drew | Restaurateurs—New York (State)—New
    York—Biography. | New York (N.Y.)—Biography.
Classification: LCC TX910.5.N54 A3 2025 | DDC 647.95092
    [B]—dc23/eng/20250208
LC record available at https://lccn.loc.gov/2025002456
ISBNs: 978-1-538-76557-9 (hardcover); 978-1-538-76559-3 (ebook)

Printed in the United States of America

LSC-C

Printing 1, 2025

For Ann, who has stuck with me through thick and thin

Contents

Contents

Author's Note

All events in this book are recounted in accordance with my own highly subjective and potentially fallible memory. I've tried my best to tell what I believe to be the truth; although others may have different interpretations, this is the story of my life, as I've lived it.

I'm Not Trying To Be Difficult

Chapter 1

City Kids

B lame it on Muhammad Ali.

    I'm nine years old in 1964, huddled in my parents' bedroom with my father and my older brother, Tracy. The room is small—we live in an apartment in Peter Cooper Village, a massive brick complex in Manhattan for middle-income tenants—but looms large in my imagination. It's here that my mother transforms herself into a glamorous starlet for visitors; bottles of perfume and lipstick line the armoire. There are books all over, a massive rotary phone on the nightstand, silk stockings that look like snakes. My father's carved walking cane rests against the desk as he sinks his body onto the bed, gathering us tightly on either side of his bulky frame in a mound of tangled blankets.

It's February and our rickety steam heater kicks into life. There's rattling and clanging from deep within the bowels of the radiator, and I squirm. The noise is an unwelcome distraction from the reason we're all bunched around my father's radio. Howard Cosell is calling the World Heavyweight Championship boxing match between Sonny Liston and a young Cassius Clay in Miami Beach.

Clay is all of twenty-two, a fast-talking, smart-mouthed underdog from Louisville who already believes himself to be the greatest of all time. For weeks before the match, he'd been puffing himself up and taunting Liston, a bruiser with a reputation for knocking out opponents fast and hard.

The match was widely considered finished before it even started—everyone's money was on Liston—but I was not-so-secretly rooting for Clay. I loved his unabashed confidence, his verbal finesse, his absolute belief in his own abilities. I was a chubby city kid, but I was obsessed with sports and followed boxing most religiously. I kept detailed notes about my favorite players, memorizing their stats and recording each of their victories in a little notebook. It helped settle playground debates quickly.

Tracy and I wriggled around during the first two rounds, during which the fast-moving Clay boxed circles around Liston, landing punch after punch while the defending champion swung wildly. No one had thought Clay stood a chance, but in round 3, the young challenger picked it up even more, laying into Liston like he had something to prove. "Clay hurts Liston. He has Liston's eye cut open. This could be the upset of the century," the voice crackled from the radio. Tracy and I looked at each other, and I grinned. *That's my guy.* My father turned up the volume and leaned closer to the speaker.

Liston roared back to life and pummeled Clay in rounds 4 and 5, but by round 6, he was beginning to show his age. Clay floated around him, landing lightning-quick combinations to Liston's swollen face. Clay, according to the announcers, looked good and loose, while Liston was rapidly losing steam. I clapped, hollering for Cassius to finish him.

The seventh round was about to begin when Cosell took the mic. "Wait a minute—Sonny Liston is not coming out. He's... he's...out!" I couldn't believe it. Was he really staying in his corner, refusing to fight on? A minute later, I heard my answer: "I am the greatest!" shouted Clay, who was now the youngest heavyweight champion in history. "I am king of the world!" He kept chanting it like a prayer.

I jumped up from the bed, tumbled down onto the floor with my brother. My father shushed us, but he was grinning ear to ear. I knew I would never forget this moment. Through the radio alone, the man who would later become Muhammad Ali had already left an indelible impression on my young psyche. By the time I hit junior high, I had already decided that I, too, would be the best. But not as a boxer—my destiny was to open the greatest restaurants in the world.

———

My mother was my number one fan. As a cherubic-looking little girl, Sybil Krinsky (she later picked the stage name Sybil Trent) had achieved something resembling stardom as a child actress in a proto–*Sesame Street* radio show called *Let's Pretend*, which aired for more than fifteen years. A whole generation of people grew up listening to her voice, which, as she aged, grew richer and heavier, like velvet.

As a kid, Sybil was the breadwinner for her family, and her parents had no problem putting her to work. By the time I came around, she had transitioned mostly into casting work, but never lost her love for showbiz or her preternatural work ethic. She told me I could do whatever I wanted, but I should strive to be the best at whatever it was. She believed that working hard would prove your talent. Her mantra: "The show must go on."

Despite her success at a young age, Sybil had a rough childhood. As a little girl, she watched her mother die of breast cancer at the age of forty-two and would sometimes recount carrying "buckets of blood" out of her family's apartment in Hell's Kitchen. I was never sure if these were real or metaphorical buckets, but the image terrified me. Her father, my grandpa Adolph, never remarried, though he would often bring his girlfriends—who were almost unilaterally alcoholics—to our apartment. Adolph wasn't a bad guy, but I think the death of his wife shut down something in him forever, and we weren't the type of family to openly discuss our feelings.

Sybil, slender and dark-featured, was supposed to marry a guy who died unexpectedly just before the wedding. Instead, in her early twenties, she wound up with my father, Andrew Nieporent, a handsome, heavy-browed former lifeguard fourteen years her senior. I don't know much about their courtship, but I know their love ran deep; my father handwrote Sybil love poems all throughout her life.

My father was born in Paris, but his last name is a bastardized spelling of a Polish town called Nieporęt, where his Jewish family was from. He came to New York on the SS *Rochambeau* as a kid, and he grew up in the city. Andrew briefly served in the Coast Guard during World War II, and the water remained his Shangri-la; his oversized silhouette still presided over Jones Beach as a lifeguard every summer.

My mother dreamed of living on the Riviera. Andrew preferred the East River. As newlyweds, they settled in the Peter Cooper Village apartment complex, which sprawled across several city blocks on Manhattan's East Side. Dad had to beg, borrow, and steal to get us in there because there was a wait list a mile long. I think he lied about the extent of his military service.

We lived in a two-bedroom apartment at 530 East 23rd Street, the last building on the street before you hit the East River. We couldn't see the water from our second-floor unit, but you could smell it if the conditions were just right. Technically, we were at Avenue C, which got rougher a few blocks south, but Peter Cooper felt like a middle-class neighborhood, landscaped with trees and playgrounds, a self-contained world in the middle of Lower Manhattan. My dad's brother, Jean, lived a few blocks south in StuyTown, and both sets of grandparents dropped by frequently.

My dad's mother, Jennie, was a seamstress and the prototypical Jewish grandmother—she used to sit at her sewing machine with a Kent cigarette dangling from her mouth, slowly exhaling plumes of smoke through her nose as she methodically worked the pedal. She would babysit for us and make matzo ball soup and gently chastise us in her thick Polish accent. Her husband, Simon, my father's father, died when I was young, and my father made sure we saw Jennie every week so she didn't get too lonely. I still have her phone number memorized.

There was tension between Jennie and Sybil. It was the classic mother-in-law dynamic: Jennie was used to being at the center of her son's universe, and she struggled with the idea of my father dividing his attention between her and his wife.

She would always insist on us not making a fuss over her visits but then would leave in a huff sometimes when she felt slighted. I was too young to understand why Grandma would sometimes disappear abruptly. She'd call later to tell us she'd simply taken the uptown bus back home.

My father was generally mild-mannered, but an undercurrent of anger rippled just below his surface. Apparently, early in his life, he hurt someone quite badly. I was never clear on the details because he would never talk about it, but the other guy had done something to Jennie.

Andrew was not one to back down from a threat. One time, we were leaving a restaurant when a car zoomed around the corner and clipped his walking cane. The driver got out of the car, coming toward my dad with fists balled. Tracy and I were kids, but we had to physically restrain my father from getting into a fight right there on the street.

He kept rulers placed strategically around the house to smack us when we got out of line. They didn't hurt much, but every once in a while, when we were really misbehaving, he would lay into us.

Tracy and I got into a lot of physical fights—just typical brother stuff. We were roughhousing one day in the living room, where my mother had this gorgeous, elegantly curved Noguchi glass coffee table supported on two wooden beams. My brother jumped off the nearby wheeled easy chair to tackle me, and the chair went flying back, straight into the table, which promptly shattered. As we were picking our way through the wreckage, my mother came home. She saw us, saw the remains of the table, and immediately began to cry. My father arrived maybe half an hour later, and when he opened the door, the first words out of his mouth were "You sons of bitches!" Then he doled out a proper whooping.

It took him a good long while to get mad, but when he did, it was like a kettle going off. These outbursts were infrequent, but I did develop a sort of sixth sense for just how far I could push him before he tipped over. I toed that line a lot as a kid.

Tracy and I shared a bedroom and arranged our beds into an L shape. He was two years older than me, but I was always bigger than him, and people often confused me for the elder sibling. This did wonders for my ego but plagued my shyer brother, who was somewhat idiosyncratic. He didn't eat meat, loved the underdog Mets, and thought the world of Richard Nixon. In direct response, I ate anything and everything I could get my hands on, rooted for the Yankees, and volunteered for George McGovern.

I was extroverted from the get-go. Even as a young kid, I was Mr. Congeniality, holding court with the other kids in the Peter Cooper playgrounds. I was very into sports, and I loved corralling my friends into a game of touch football, all of us doing our best Joe Namath impressions.

In junior high, we'd all hang out outside at the basketball court and discuss news and politics. For a bunch of twelve-year-olds, we were pretty worldly—we had all just gotten TVs in our apartments and had watched John F. Kennedy get assassinated in our living rooms, heard the searing civil rights speeches Dr. Martin Luther King delivered. Many of our neighbors were being sent to fight in Vietnam against their will. Our parents had heady conversations late into the night, and the prevailing mood of political unrest seeped into our subconscious. I remember getting into a heated debate with one of our neighbors who loved

George Wallace, the pro-segregationist governor of Alabama. My father used to tell us, "I may not agree with what you have to say, but I will defend to the death your right to say it," and I took those words to heart. We were too young to really be hippies, but the atmosphere was still politically charged, and we were active about our beliefs. In 1972, my brother convinced me to switch sides and volunteer for Richard Nixon's campaign, which I agreed to solely for the purpose of collecting the free buttons.

At the playground, I occasionally hung out with older kids, around nineteen or twenty years old. Some of them had served in Vietnam; some of them had dodged the draft. They were aimless and mostly hung around smoking pot. I didn't want to be like them. From an early age, I wanted to latch on to something that I would do for the rest of my life. Although most of my friends were too busy being kids to think about their future careers, I decided before my first chest hairs appeared that I was going to open my own restaurant.

My dad had a civil servant job with the State Liquor Authority and helped restaurants obtain their liquor licenses. Let me be clear: My dad did not know a fucking thing about food. But he was a friendly guy, and he would make a buck on the side by taking a restaurant's application from the bottom of the pile and moving it to the top. This was in the sixties, when many of the restaurants in New York were owned by first-generation immigrants who couldn't navigate the state's byzantine licensing laws without a little extra help.

As a result, restaurant owners were always inviting my dad in to dine free of charge to thank him. I'm talking dozens and dozens of restaurants: good ones, bad ones, fancy ones, divey ones, you name it. I loved every second of it. The whole experience felt like a magic show—you walk into a room that feels like another world, sit down, and seemingly out of nowhere, hot food appears on gleaming plates. I knew, immediately, that I wanted to live in that world.

One restaurant called Headquarters was owned by President Eisenhower's former chef. You'd walk in and see a mural of soldiers erecting the flag at Iwo Jima. Headquarters served stuff like capon breast "Veronique," in a white wine sauce with grapes and pickled beets, and Lyndon B. Johnson's alleged favorite, baby shrimp in Russian dressing. There was a guy who'd circulate the dining room distributing fresh, hot garlic bread out of a giant metal container, like hotdogs at a baseball game. He was better than Santa Claus.

I wanted to try everything, and I was an equal opportunity eater. My brother was picky—he didn't like meat, but he would always order something extravagant like lobster, then refuse to let me try a bite until after he'd spent an hour pushing it around his plate.

One day we'd go to Dubrow's Cafeteria on Eighth Avenue, where the buffet had a hundred items, all of which the owner, Erwin Dubrow, would stick his finger in, and the next, we'd be eating at Café Argenteuil, chef Maxime Ribera's beautiful French restaurant, which served filet mignon and pont neuf potatoes.

French was considered the best cuisine at that time, but I was just as entranced by the eggrolls and hot and sour soup at Empire Chinese and the intricately layered Dobos torte at The Paprika, a Hungarian restaurant. I loved it when my dad came home with pounds of sliced deli meats and fat half-sour pickles from Wertheimer's on First Avenue. I swear to God, I could smell him coming home from blocks away.

One of my family's favorite restaurants was a place near Gramercy Park called Paul & Jimmy's. There was no Paul, but it was owned by Jimmy Delgado, along with Dottie Fullerton, a flamboyant woman whose husband Ray was the athletic trainer at Columbia University and a dear friend of my father (he helped us get in to a lot of Columbia sports events, a great perk for me as a kid). My dad had helped Jimmy out with the liquor license, so Jimmy helped us out with a table whenever we wanted.

The restaurant was not quite a basement, but it almost felt like one, with low ceilings and a pleasantly cramped atmosphere. Every time we went, Jimmy was there to greet us with a big toothy grin. This guy spoke almost no English, but he grabbed my face with both hands and kissed my cheeks. I squirmed to get away because he always reeked of food, and he always went in for the double kiss, which made him a weird mix of repellant and endearing. My mother found it charming, but I think she just liked the attention.

The food at Jimmy's was spectacular. The whole place, not just Jimmy, smelled like olive oil and garlic. They had a fritto misto that I can still taste, with a crunch that I've never experienced anywhere else. The antipasti were sensational, with stuffed clams and roasted peppers and all sorts of delightful snacks that amped me up even more for the main courses. I had steak pizzaiola for the first time there, and it blew my mind. How could the combination of sliced steak and crushed tomatoes be so good, and so spicy? Even Tracy wanted a bite (I shooed him away). The only downside was dessert, which was either spumoni or tortoni. The spumoni was a wash—a slab of ice cream, mostly vanilla—but the tortoni was worse, served in a paper cup with some kind of chopped nut thing on top that I didn't care for. I thought they should have at least one more option and did not hesitate to say as much.

Jimmy was jovial and hospitable, but he passed away in the late sixties and one of the waiters bought the place. The new owner was named Cosmo Azzollini, and he didn't have any affection for my father. He just didn't seem like a warm and fuzzy kind of guy, so Paul & Jimmy's slowly tapered off our roster, and I was sad to lose a place where we had been treated so warmly.

I liked to save the menus from everywhere we ate, then go home and take notes. First, I tallied up how much everything would have cost if we had paid for the meal. I was fascinated with the price of food and why some cuisines were so much more expensive than others. I'd make note of my favorite dishes and try to find recipes for them in one of the food magazines or cookbooks I hoarded from Ruby Book Sale on Chambers Street. Then, I would list out my favorite maître d's and waiters from each restaurant. I developed a roster, almost like a fantasy league, of an imaginary all-star restaurant crew.

To my young mind, the experience of eating in a restaurant felt like theater. Because my mother was an actress, we went to all the Broadway shows, and I delighted in seeing a black box of a room transform into another world. Restaurants were the same: You'd walk in, take your seat, and be completely transported. The tables and chairs were set pieces; the menus props. And behind the curtain was the kitchen, where the magic really happened. When the food arrived, I felt like bursting into applause. I knew that someone had to be directing this whole production. I wanted to know their secrets.

I loved when my father introduced me to restaurant owners. I used to lie and tell my father that I was off from school on random afternoons. Without a care in the world, he would go, "Well, son, that's great, meet me for lunch." So I'd cut class (I was never a good student anyway) and meet him downtown at The Camlet (not The Camelot, which would have made more sense), a bar and tavern overseen by the rotund chef-owner Shelly Harris. Over the course of an afternoon, guests would inevitably say, "Let me buy you a drink," to which Shelly would reply, "Rémy Martin." Round after round of brandy was sent his way, and charged to the guest. One day I asked Shelly how he drank so much without ever seeming to get drunk. He turned to the bartender and said, "Johnny, bring me the bottle of Rémy Martin." Opening the cap, he gave me a whiff: It was iced tea.

I delighted in meeting the owners, but they rarely seemed happy about their lot in life. A place on 55th Street called La Potinière was owned by a Frenchman named Albert Forgelle. My father took me to visit Albert and told him I was thinking of getting into the restaurant business. I must have been fifteen at this point. Albert looked at me woefully and, in his thick accent, said, "Young man, this is a terrible business. It is impossible to work with the waiters. It is impossible to work with the chefs. Do not go into restaurants." It wasn't the first time I had heard something like this, but instead of dissuading me, these warnings had the opposite effect: They made me want it even more. I was strongheaded, thought that, although Albert might be getting too old for the game, I was up for the challenge. Any warnings simply fortified my will.

But I did have a brief flirtation with another career path around this time. Like many young men, I got into rock and roll in a big way. It started early, watching the television in my parents' bedroom the day The Beatles came to town. Even my mother, not one for pop music, was excited about the arrival of the Fab Four. The newscasters reported that The Beatles were "invading America" as their Pan Am jet descended into JFK Airport, and I thought to myself, *What's a Beatle?* But it didn't take long for me to realize that John, Paul, George, and Ringo were going to have a profound effect on my life. I felt that their music spoke directly to me.

My brother and I started our record collection at a store called Corvette's. We shoplifted about a dozen albums—the Jeff Beck Group, Led Zeppelin, The Who. Those were the core of our collection, until we found another store on Second Avenue and 8th Street called Free Being that sold secondhand records for $1.99. Between the two of us, we amassed a record collection that grew into the thousands.

My first concert was The Doors at Madison Square Garden, where Jim Morrison famously announced, "Hitler is alive. I slept with her last night!" But my main hang was the Fillmore East on Second Avenue. Bill Graham, the venue's legendary promoter, would charge $3.50, $4.50, and $5.50 for three acts, a program, and a comfortable seat. I saw Janis Joplin, the Grateful Dead, The Who, Neil Young and Crazy Horse, Miles Davis, Steppenwolf, Elton John, and many more, unburdened by a curfew from my parents.

I used to smuggle in a Sony tape recorder in a carrying case that I'd put on my lap with the microphone out, and because there were no lights, I would try to judge when forty-five minutes were up so I could flip the ninety-minute tape. (I still have most of those tapes, a collection that is, in my opinion, nonpareil.) I was there for the music, but I also considered Bill Graham a rock star in his own right. I admired him in much the same way that I admired Muhammad Ali—both of them stood up for what they believed to be right, and I respected their integrity, not to mention their knack for self-promotion. For a minute, I thought rock and roll might be my destiny, but my passion for food won out.

It's tough to understand today, but back then, chefs were nothing. They barely saw the light of day, let alone the spotlight. Chefs were expected to be in their restaurants, chained to their stoves, every minute of every night. The great French chef André Soltner set the model at the four-star Lutèce, where it was rumored he never, ever took a day off. The front-of-house staff, the suave maître d's and captains who presided over the seating arrangements and the flow of service, were the real stars of the show. People begged and bribed the maître d' for a good seat; they could make or break a special occasion.

And though I didn't understand this at the time, the front-of-house and the kitchen staff had a serious beef with one another. The root of the tension, like so many things, largely had to do with money: Cooks don't get tips, though they often work longer and arguably harder hours than their front-of-house counterparts. But it's also cultural: The kitchen is called the back of the house, and it's a hot, cramped room filled with sharp objects, live fires, and men (and it was almost all men back then) who reveled in this pressure-cooker environment. Meanwhile, the polished, tuxedo-clad fellows up front, with the utmost decorum and a veneer of utter calm, presented a restaurant's public face to guests. The front and back of house might as well be different planets; rarely do they respect what each other does.

Despite all this, or perhaps because of it, I wanted at first to become a chef. My mother had many redeeming qualities, but cooking was not among them. She used to call herself "the snow queen"—she was great with frozen food and not much else. If we did entertain, it was with Triscuits with an onion slice and mayo, a can of sardines, or the one recipe she had mastered: roasted chicken with mandarin oranges from a can.

I, however, loved being in the kitchen. When I was in fifth or sixth grade, my mother hired a woman from Harlem named Emma Anderson to cook and clean our apartment while my parents worked. The thrill of having a Black woman in our home during the civil rights era was not lost on me, and I followed her around like a puppy, eager for a glimpse into Black life, food very much included.

Emma was an unbelievable cook. Fried chicken, stuffed cabbage, meatloaf, corned beef—she had mastered the classics and cooked entirely from feel, no recipe required. I perpetually bothered her in our narrow kitchen, which she presided over while watching the *Dinah Shore Show.* "Get out of my pots, Drew, get out of my pots!" she used to holler at me when I lifted the lids to peek inside. Eventually, she let me help with some basic kitchen tasks, and I was immensely proud of my work chopping onions. Emma was the first person to teach me anything in the kitchen.

As a teenager, I'd pick up a little spending money babysitting for other tenants in the building, and I always made a beeline for their cookbooks, poring over them like the textbooks I was ignoring in school. I devoured copies of *Gourmet* magazine and loved watching Julia Child and Graham Kerr, the Galloping

Gourmet, on TV. I used my earnings to go grocery shopping, price-comparing exotic ingredients like duck and rack of lamb for my home-cooking adventures.

I liked to cook for my family, in particular a recipe for something called chicken à la Warhol, which I cut out of a ladies home magazine. Allegedly Andy Warhol's favorite, it of course involved a can of Campbell's cream of mushroom soup. On several occasions, I almost burned the apartment down.

An early fascination with perfecting stovetop hamburgers turned dangerous when I flambéed them in brandy; another experiment with duck, dripping with hot fat, nearly destroyed the whole building. I also tried my hand at prime rib but could never nail the Yorkshire pudding. My family gamely entertained my attempts at gourmet cookery, and my mother encouraged me to keep practicing.

I thought this would be my path and dreamed of going to hotel school in Switzerland to work in some fancy European resort. But I didn't have the grades, nor did my parents have the money.

Instead, I got a job at McDonald's.

In the early seventies, a few McDonald's were scattered across Manhattan. I was fascinated by the brand and how Ray Kroc had made it so successful. And as luck would have it, the summer I turned seventeen, McDonald's announced its newest location on 23rd Street and First Avenue, down the street from my apartment. It's not like I aspired to work at McDonald's forever, but as a kid who wanted to run restaurants, I considered McDonald's a fertile training ground. If they could make a thousand dollars an hour, they had to be doing something right. I applied immediately.

It was my first restaurant job, at $2.75 an hour, and to this day, it's one of the greatest gigs I've ever had.

Our store was going to debut the brand-new Quarter Pounder. This was a big fucking deal—a whole quarter pound of meat, bigger than the Big Mac, and McDonald's was doing a ton of promotion around this thing. Commercials, billboards, the whole nine. I was proud, and a little intimidated, to be opening the store that would introduce New York to this audacious new creation.

The store was still being built during our employee training. Training was held partially at the freezing cold, dark construction site; we'd huddle around shivering while the managers drilled into us the importance of their system: "quality, service, cleanliness," or simply "QSC." It's essentially the same system employed by any restaurant in the world, but at McDonald's they have it down to a science.

Phase two of the training was held at a busy McDonald's store uptown so we could get some hands-on experience. I walked in to the gleaming white kitchen with a mixture of excitement and awe. The kitchens of my father's friends were cramped, hot, and not all that clean. McDonald's was the opposite. The equipment was polished and bright, everything was organized, no one was disheveled. On my first day there, I was so nervous working the Filet-O-Fish station that I dropped an entire brick of American cheese into the Fryolator. Somehow I was not fired, and I got with the program.

It helped that there's not a lot of actual cooking going on at McDonald's. All the hamburger meat was shipped over from some mysterious commissary, frozen like hockey pucks. The fries arrived precut, also frozen, but those we were allowed to season with salt, unlike the burgers. Things were cooked with the press of a button, and there was a system for handling a steady flow of customers. Expediting was important, and McDonald's would categorize an order of twelve burgers in a row a "run."

Here's how it worked: At the cash register, a girl named Nilda Rodriguez would monitor how many people were coming in and order the kitchen to prepare X many runs. "I need six runs!" she'd holler. I'd be in the back at the flattop slapping down six rows of frozen hockey pucks on the griddle. "Meat down!" I'd scream, and my buddy Carlos Ortiz, working the bun station, would yell, "Buns down!" meaning he was toasting the buns.

Once the burgers were ready, I'd yell, "Meat ready for dressing!" (which meant lashing it with ketchup, lettuce, pickles, and cheese—in other cities, burgers got both ketchup and mustard, but for some reason, in New York we only did ketchup). Carlos would toast the top of the buns and in a matter of seconds, we'd assemble the burgers on a tray and send them up to the expediter, who would wrap them and push them into a warming unit. If Nilda was accurate, those runs wouldn't be sitting around for more than a few minutes. It's an incredible system, designed for maximum efficiency.

I did not want to be the guy who messed with the system. That said, I could recognize that it had some flaws. Because everything at McDonald's is automated, they gave us timers to know when to flip the meat. They worked for the first few weeks, but after a few busy runs, the timers totally crapped out.

I got so frustrated with their stupid *buzz-buzz* that I just started ignoring them, flipping the meat when I saw fit. This was not part of the McDonald's protocol, but I figured it was better to improvise than ruin a run.

Another issue: Nothing was cooked to order, so if a customer wanted a modification—say, no pickles or extra ketchup—it threw the run into disarray. We called these deviations "special orders," and we were supposed to tell the customer that if they wanted a special order, they'd have to wait. But I didn't see what the big deal was. A guy wanted a plain hamburger? It took me two seconds to put a plain patty on the bun and pass it up. Boom. Done. Give the customer what they want.

Everyone at McDonald's got brought on as a general employee, with one manager who circled the joint and put you to work wherever you were needed. There was no hierarchy, so you couldn't get a big head. I thought this was a great system.

The other great thing about working at McDonald's was that I was one of the only white kids there. Almost everyone else was Black or Hispanic, and I loved hanging out with them. My classmates at Stuyvesant High School were smart, but my work friends were street-smart, true city kids.

We'd all get together and play softball after work or walk down to the East River to shoot the breeze. I even had a moment in the sun with Nilda, though it quickly fizzled when it became apparent I had no idea what I was doing.

My time at McDonald's coincided with an increased awareness about my weight. I was never a skinny kid, but in high school, the lavish meals out with my parents started to catch up with me, and, combined with my growing interest in the opposite sex, I decided to do something about it. At seventeen, while working the grill, I went on my first diet. It consisted of plain hamburger patties without the bun. It worked. The pounds melted off, and my self-confidence grew. This was the beginning of a weight loss-and-gain cycle that has followed me throughout my entire life.

My parents didn't know a thing about nutrition, and they never pressured me about my body. My father loved to eat and did so indiscriminately. He seesawed between husky and heavy for his entire life. Everything we did as a family revolved around food—going out to restaurants or getting together with the bagels and smoked fish or sliced meats my dad would bring home. I had plenty of friends at school, so I wasn't tortured by the weight, but I didn't feel great about it. The summer I worked at McDonald's, my parents went on a vacation without me (my brother was already in college), and I decided to take my proto-Atkins diet a step further. I almost stopped eating entirely.

It was my first experiment with fasting, and it worked, at least in terms of losing weight—I lost something like a pound a day. I was miserable with hunger, but I felt good about my loosening belt. At no point did I consider that this wasn't healthy or sustainable. By the time I left for college, I felt pretty damn good. But I still had a lot to learn, about restaurants and about myself.

Chapter 2

Higher Education

Getting into college was a small miracle. My dream was to go to the hotel school in Lausanne, Switzerland, widely considered the most prestigious hospitality management school in the world. Their graduates ran all of the best hotels—the Four Seasons, the Peninsula, all the classic European chateaus and estates. I'd never been abroad—I'd barely left the tristate area—but I wanted to go where the best of the best had trained.

Unfortunately, my grades and my aspirations weren't on the same page. I graduated in the bottom quarter of my class. Academia just wasn't for me—I was too busy socializing. Plus, there was no way my parents could afford to send me to Europe.

My brother had packed up for SUNY Brockport a few years earlier, and my father liked that the state schools had just a five-dollar application fee.

One day, my mother bumped into the mother of a fellow Stuyvesant classmate of mine, Willie Weissberg, and she told my mother that Cornell had a hotel school.

"Mom, Cornell is an Ivy League school. My grades are terrible. I'll never get in," I protested. My father wasn't a fan of Cornell because the application cost a hefty twenty dollars. But my mother encouraged me to apply anyway, and my best friend Lee Goldstein's father, Saul, wrote the check because he knew how much it meant to me. Thanks to that, and my dear friend Willie Weissberg (whose application I may have lightly borrowed from), I got in. No one was more surprised than me. To appease my dad, I arranged for a work-study job and applied for some scholarships to offset the tuition, a then whopping $5,000 a year. And after folding up my McDonald's uniform one last time, in the summer of 1973, I set off, via Greyhound bus, for Ithaca.

They say Ithaca is gorges for a reason. The area is home to dozens of gorges, rock formations carved by ancient glaciers, filled with waterfalls, hiking trails, and bucolic splendor. These fields and trails would prove to be excellent backdrops for my forthcoming marijuana habit, but my initial impression was that I definitely wasn't in Kansas anymore.

Right away, a reception was held for all the incoming hotel students. The first thing I noticed was that everybody in the school was from somewhere else. I was one of the only kids from New York, which is probably how I got accepted in the first place. On that first day, I met people from the Bahamas and from Greece, from Rochester and Atlanta. As a natural-born extrovert, socializing with all these far-flung new faces was heaven.

I was assigned a room in Sperry Hall, which was notable as the only dorm on campus to have alternating male and female rooms. Even the bathrooms were coed. Score! I lucked into a single room and thought for sure I was about to reenact the *Harrad Experiment*. But I didn't have much luck with girls that year (or the next year, or the one after).

It probably didn't help that I turned my room into a true college boy's den, complete with a lofted bed and Crosby, Stills, and Nash posters. I collected all sorts of crap, like ticket stubs and sports memorabilia. I was still a rock-and-roll aficionado, and I spent hours listening to Jackson Browne, Gordon Lightfoot, and Fleetwood Mac in my room with my friends.

Greek life was huge at Cornell, and I seriously considered joining a frat. My little window faced the Phi Sigma Epsilon fraternity house, and I would sometimes wake in the middle of the night to one of the brothers yelling, "Men of Cornell! Are you up? Up for...a panty raid?!" I rushed, and some of the houses wanted me to join, but at the very last minute, I backed out. I didn't like all these guys telling me I had to play by their rules.

My academic track record continued in college, though this time I was flunking classes on topics I was theoretically interested in. I say *theoretically* because I realized early on that Cornell's culinary program was a joke. I knew I wanted to run restaurants—that's why I went to Cornell to begin with. But Cornell was at its core a hotel management school, not a how-to-run-restaurants school, and it showed.

Cornell offered a "culinary arts" program that I thought would teach me how to cook. The first day was promising: I showed up to Introduction to Food Services and got my first look at the professor, Walter Herman, an older guy with a thick accent dressed in chef's whites, complete with a toque blanche atop his head. The first day, he talked us through the proper technique for making an omelet, which I knew from my obsessive cookbook reading was one of Jacques Pépin's preferred dishes for testing the measure of a young chef. *Alright*, I thought. *Now we're on to something.*

The next day, I had another culinary class in the food lab. There was a rumor that we'd be learning how to make French onion soup. I was thrilled—French food was the pinnacle of the culinary elite, and I couldn't believe my luck. I was ready to get schooled in all the classic techniques. I imagined learning how to caramelize onions and could practically smell the beef stock simmering before we even started.

Instead, each of us was handed a photocopied book of recipes. I opened to the first page, and indeed there was a recipe for onion soup—which to my astonishment read simply, "Get a #10 can of onion soup, open it, and heat. Serve with cheese croutons." I stared at the page, disbelieving. We weren't going to learn how to make onion soup from scratch? Nope. Turns out Cornell was more interested in teaching food service, steam-table stuff designed for convention visitors, not culinary arts. It felt like a bait and switch, and I was pissed.

My freshman year, I particularly liked one teacher, Vance Christian, a larger-than-life character who reminded me of Fat Albert. He ran a course called Introduction to the Hospitality Industry. But it should have been called Introduction to Vance Christian, because it was important to get on his good side to pass.

"Why are you here?" he'd boom in class. "To get an education, to learn," this room full of meek little freshmen would mumble. "What?!" he'd yell. "No, no, no. That's not why you're here. You're here for *this*," he'd say, pulling a wad of bills from his wallet and flapping them around. "You're here to make money!" I perked up when he said that. Professor Christian was speaking the truth, and he was one of few authority figures I listened to. His other favorite lesson was that the most important thing in hospitality was to gain professional knowledge through experience and to have confidence in your ability to do things correctly. Professional knowledge, experience, and confidence—that stuck with me.

I did not like many of my other classes: Food chemistry, which everyone hated because it started at eight in the morning, was taught by a professor who flunked almost everyone; Intro to Sanitation was useful, but boring as hell; Intro to Accounting I failed and had to take again the next semester.

My second year, Walter Herman was on a consulting trip in India when he suddenly died. As a result, a few other teaching assistants in his culinary class and I were promoted to teach his course. This was big for me—I finally had some authority to do things the right way in the kitchen.

As part of the culinary curriculum, students had to come up with a theme with a matching menu for the student dining hall. One of my classmates chose "Italian night." We devised a whole menu of dishes with red sauce, eggplant parm, the works. Maybe ten minutes before dinner was supposed to start, he grabbed me in the hall. "There's something wrong with my tomato sauce," he said, panic rising. I went back into the kitchen and saw his tomato sauce in these huge stock pots, all of it flecked with little black spots. I took one taste and immediately knew that the spots were not pepper. This poor kid had burned the bottom of the pans and then stirred the burnt bits into the sauce, ruining the whole batch.

I sprang into action, grabbing a fresh pot and calling out like a surgeon: "Olive oil. Garlic. Canned tomatoes." I whipped up a new sauce from scratch. The students watched as I stirred together a huge batch of the stuff, with just minutes to spare. Nobody taught me how to do that—it was just me thinking on my feet.

Outside class, I worked overtime on the social front, making it my business to know everyone. You could say I was a bit of a politician, but I considered it an essential part of my education. I had lots of friends, though I never had just one clique. I had some buddies I'd drink with, some I'd smoke joints with, some I'd go skinny-dipping near the waterfalls with. I joined the student-faculty committee and became a resident advisor.

Every year, the students would take over the facilities for an event known as Hotel Ezra Cornell, a three-day conference conceptualized and run by the student body. The idea was that we would show off our skills for alumni and visitors. One year, I was elected director of the food and beverage program. It was a big deal to run the show and my first real taste of managing a restaurant. I selected other students for various jobs and oversaw the entire process.

For one event, two students, Larry Reinstein and Michael Kogen, were in charge of a dinner for about two hundred people in the main dining room. They made a very classy meal, stuffed Lobster Newberg in this creamy white sauce, and for dessert, something called Ice Coupe Baumanière. I was in the dining room when they sent out the desserts. Everyone oohed and aahed over the ice cream, presented in vintage coupe cups with a delicate white topping crowning each scoop.

A minute later, one of my classmates pulled me aside and hissed, "Did you taste the dessert?" I grabbed a coupe from a student waiter's tray and took it back to the runner's station for further inspection. One bite in, I knew something was off. The ice cream tasted almost savory. It wasn't quite bad, but it wasn't quite right, either. It took me a minute to figure out that they'd put the Lobster Newberg sauce on top of the ice cream.

I ran into the kitchen and saw the culprit, a classmate named Don, who had been "hired" as the dessert cook. He was stoned and had a big shit-eating grin on his face. He had no idea he'd done anything wrong. "What the fuck did you do?" I threw my hands up, exasperated with the lack of professionalism in our mock restaurant. But it was an important lesson—anything can go wrong, and you have to be on top of everything, at all times.

My father was in the dining room that night. I went over to him, feeling sheepish about our mistake, but before I could say anything, he patted me on the back and said, "Son, that dessert was delicious."

———————

I was introduced to marijuana my freshman year. I got stoned plenty at Cornell, or at least that's my memory of it, but it wasn't like I was some crazy party guy. It was the seventies, and that's just what we did after class.

One day I tried LSD. It was my freshman year and I was with a few of my friends. We went to a guy's house off-campus, and I remember he had these two beautiful Irish setters. Just as the drugs were starting to kick in, he started playing this cruel game with the dogs. He'd hold back the male and throw a ball for the female to chase. She got a ten-second head start before he'd let the bigger male go, who would inevitably overpower the female and get the ball first. I was transfixed by these two dogs running through the open yard and could see the humiliation of the female trying and failing to get the ball. I was devastated for her. I found the whole thing very hard to watch. That day, I decided that LSD was too powerful for me, and from then on stuck with marijuana.

One of my major accomplishments at Cornell was being inducted into the Quill and Dagger Society. It's an honor society, but it's not all about grades—students from all parts of Cornell are "tapped" for their distinguished efforts in the community. Because of my contributions to the food and beverage program, I was able to furnish the society's clubhouse room with some select alcoholic beverages. The room was private, overlooking a beautiful part of the campus, and I was happy to provide booze in exchange for having a place to try to impress girls.

I made many lasting friendships during my time at Cornell, some in unexpected places. One spring break, I hitched a ride down South with a classmate. The plan was to stay with my friend Bobby Isaacson, a southern boy who had grown up in Atlanta. We had scored tickets to Opening Day and were eager to see if Hank Aaron, who was on the verge of breaking Babe Ruth's home run record, would indeed make history. Then we'd drive over to Daytona Beach to meet up with Bobby's roommate from Sperry Hall, John Lombard.

In Atlanta, the baseball stadium was crackling with anticipation, packed to the brim with fans rooting for their hometown hero. But the Braves were losing on their own turf. At the bottom of the fourth, with the score 3–1, Aaron faced off against Dodgers pitcher Al Downing. Aaron looked intensely focused as the ball flew toward him, and he took a hot, heavy swing. He connected. The ball went up, up, and away, gracefully arching over the left-field wall.

When I tell you that the crowd went wild, I cannot even begin to express it. People were screaming, crying, hugging each other, swinging beer into the air. Aaron rounded the bases, fireworks exploded, and two fans somehow ran onto the field to congratulate him. I captured it all on my little 8 mm camera, my own personal Zapruder film.

(Years later, a customer of mine introduced me to Hank. I told the athlete, in his seventies at the time, that I'd been at his record-breaking game. He looked at me dismissively and said, "Everybody says they were there." But because I keep everything, I was able to show Aaron my wrinkled program from that historic day, which softened him up right away.)

At school, I was developing friendships that would last a lifetime, but on campus, I developed a bit of a reputation among the faculty, and it wasn't always favorable. I was very social, and very involved with the student government, so for better or worse, I was pretty well known at Cornell. I had certain strong beliefs about my education, and reheating canned soup wasn't what I signed up for. I was paying $5,000 a year to be there, and I wanted to get value for every dollar. I wasn't trying to be incendiary—I really thought the faculty should know that they could do better—but my conviction did not endear me to the staff. They thought I was a loudmouth and a troublemaker, and in one case, my outspokenness almost cost me my degree.

I'm Not Trying To Be Difficult

Every winter, the hotel show takes over the New York Convention Center, where Cornell has a booth. My senior year, the faculty decided that instead of a booth at the show, they would have a hospitality suite at the Sheraton Hotel. In truth, the hospitality suite was just a place for the professors to hang out and drink all day. They'd bring students down from Ithaca and we all had to work a few shifts in the suite as part of the trip.

On the day of my appointed shift, one of my professors, who seemed like he'd had a few too many, approached me. "Your buddy Lombard didn't show up for his shift today," he said. "You guys really think you're hot shit, don't you?" he sneered.

I was confused. "I'm here," I said. "I don't have anything to do with Lombard. Maybe you'd like to step outside? You're making a scene."

His eyes narrowed. "Are you asking me to go outside because you want to fight me?" he said at the top of his voice.

I turned away, but the next thing I know, someone shoved me from behind, pushing me halfway across the room. I glanced around and saw my professor glaring at me. The mood in the suite was tense—everyone was staring at us, waiting for the first swing. *I gotta get out of here*, I thought, and made my way to the exit.

The next morning, we were due to depart by bus at seven to visit the Anheuser-Busch beer factory in Newark, New Jersey, and then return to Ithaca. I was in the hotel lobby checking out when one of my classmates, this Norwegian guy named Al Iveland, asked me if I could loan him twenty bucks to check out. "No problem," I said. "I'll see you on the bus."

As I stepped onto the bus, the first person I saw was the professor who had pushed me the day before. I greeted him, and as I proceeded to my seat, he turned to the bus driver and said, "Close the doors, we're leaving."

"Wait a minute—Al is on the checkout line inside, give him a minute," I protested.

"I don't care. We're not waiting for him. Let's go," the professor replied. And at that moment, the driver closed the door and started the engine.

I yelled: "Open up! This guy doesn't have any money! He's from Norway!" The driver heard me pleading and opened the door. I burst out and ran into the Sheraton looking for Al.

Scanning the room, I saw out of the corner of my eye that the bus was pulling away without me (and Al, for that matter). It was the dead of winter, and I sprinted outside to the middle of Seventh Avenue, chasing after the bus. I would have run to Ithaca to get that fucking bus. I trailed after it for a full ten blocks and finally got in front of it, screaming, "Let me on!" The driver opened up and I stumbled inside, panting, yelling at my fellow students, "You're all a bunch of cowards!" They were half asleep.

When we arrived at Anheuser-Busch, we waited for an hour before anybody took us on the tour. It turned out that six students were missing from the bus that morning because the professor hadn't bothered to do a head count before we took off. And yet, somehow, I was the one who got in trouble for inappropriate behavior.

Back at Cornell, the repercussions were swift. Dean Beck, the head honcho, was on sabbatical, and the assistant dean, Colonel Guarnier, was in charge. I had met with him a few times already. "We're stripping you of your position on the student-faculty committee, and we're reviewing your record," he said. He told me that because I had allegedly started a fight with a professor, I was on the brink of expulsion. Maybe, he suggested, I was suffering from a mental illness and should go to the Gannett Clinic to get checked out.

I was stunned. I didn't feel I had done anything more than stand up for my friend. I had a reputation for being outspoken, but I didn't go out of my way to poke the bear. I went to Professor Christian for advice. I can still hear his voice in my head. "Drew, Drew, Drew," he said in mock falsetto. "Turds and cream float. If you're really upset about this, you should go to the campus ombudsman." I had no idea what that was, but it turns out it's a judicial administrator, someone you can state a grievance to who will investigate the situation. I pled my case, and the professors involved in the Sheraton scuffle rescinded and offered me an apology. I'll never forget the assistant dean saying to me, "You took it like a real man." It was like they were busting my balls for sport—the first, but certainly not the last, time I'd find myself in this position.

Suffice it to say that when I graduated a few months later, Dean Beck (back from sabbatical) was onstage to hand me my diploma. He pointed at it as he passed it to me and said, "Congrats—you sure talked enough for it."

Because I found the curriculum at Cornell somewhat lacking, I needed to supplement my education in other ways. One day, a posting was tacked to the bulletin board outside the dean's office. It read: "Looking for six students, experienced in Russian service, to sail to the following ports: Dublin, Leningrad, Oslo, Bergen, Stockholm, Copenhagen, Amsterdam, etc."

I was eighteen years old, and I'd never been abroad. I also had zero experience in Russian service, which is a very formal, fussy banquet style of serving that was at the time considered the peak of sophistication. My only restaurant-related job up to this point had been at McDonald's. I called the number anyway. It belonged to a German upperclassman named Uwe Christensen, and I told him I was the man he was looking for, "with plenty of experience." Apparently, I sounded convincing enough because Uwe hired me for my first waiter job on the SS *Vistafjord*.

I ran over to John Lombard's dorm room, panting with excitement. "It's the opportunity of a lifetime! Sail around the world!" I hollered. John said he already had a job at the Rochester Country Club. But his roommate, Bobby from Atlanta, immediately piped up: "I'll do it!" Bobby wasn't even in the hotel school, and he knew nothing about restaurants, but he was as excited about the prospect of traveling as me. Soon, he too fabricated some bogus references and called Uwe about the job.

The *Vistafjord* was a big, beautiful ocean liner owned by the Norwegian America Line. It sailed its maiden voyage in 1973, and I came aboard a year later. At the time, the *Vistafjord* was one of the most luxurious cruise ships in the world, with food as a major selling point. The kitchen, which was manned almost exclusively by Austrian cooks, turned out a massive selection of Continental fare for six hundred passengers three times a day, seven days a week. A typical menu might include lobster ragout with truffles, prime rib with all the fixings, and cold fruit soup with "finger bisquits." For a food-obsessed kid who wanted to see the world, and maybe sneak a few bites of caviar, waiting tables on the *Vistafjord* was like dying and going to heaven.

There was just one problem: I had no experience. This became immediately apparent when, on the first day after embarking from Lower Manhattan, I showed up to the dining room in a light-blue shirt for all sixty waiters to see. Everyone else, per dining custom, was dressed in crisp white.

The next forty-two days were a crash course in all things hospitality. If Cornell was attempting to teach me food chemistry and basic accounting, the ship was where I learned how to work a dining room. It's also where I got my first glimpse into the inner workings of a professional kitchen, and where I learned that the front of house was my real calling.

But first, I had to learn how to be a waiter. The other guys all knew what they were doing—most of them were a few years older than me and had gone to fancy European hotel schools. They knew their jobs and took them seriously. My only advantage was that I spoke English, which made me popular among the American guests, most of whom were older and had saved up their money for this big Baltic trip.

In front of the guests, it was all very professional. We carried gleaming silver trays loaded with caviar and its accouterments, poured French wines with a deft twist of our wrists, and kept our uniforms (white button-up shirts, black bowties, navy jackets) immaculately pressed. We also oversaw the sprawling buffet tables, groaning under platters of cured meats, open-faced sandwiches, pickled vegetables, dips, and more.

There was one waiter for every ten people, and we were taught to accommodate their every whim, no matter how ridiculous. One guest wants kippered herring for breakfast? No problem. A special request for reindeer medallions? Of course. They were entitled to whatever they wanted, whenever they wanted it, no questions asked. We worked seven days a week, breakfast, lunch, and dinner, plus an occasional tea service and midnight snack. As waiters, we were assigned to the same guests for the entire six-week cruise, which made the guests feel almost like family by the end of the trip (unless, that is, the guests forgot to tip, at which point their bags would mysteriously go missing when they disembarked).

Behind the scenes, it was distinctly more chaotic, though in a generally cheerful way. While the guests were enjoying their spacious cabins upstairs, the staff was crammed two to a room belowdecks in bunk beds. At the end of dinner service, everyone would retreat downstairs to drink, smoke, and blow off steam. There was always a lot of room swapping going on, as tends to happen when you cram a bunch of hormonally charged young people together in an enclosed space.

This was all well and good, but the system (or lack thereof) between the front of house and back was more problematic. There was no logical setup for orders to be received in the kitchen. No handwritten tickets or dupes to keep track of things—you would just go from the dining room to the kitchen and order what your table needed from the chefs.

As a result, it was common for the waitstaff to sneak in extra orders of filet mignon or other expensive items for ourselves. We technically had a staff cafeteria where we were supposed to take our meals, but no waiter was ever hungry. We brought the extra food to our cabins at the end of the night, hidden in a napkin, and ate like kings. I probably gained thirty pounds on that first cruise alone.

The second issue was that whoever designed the ship did not understand the physical requirements of a kitchen serving a dining room. The dining room held six hundred passengers, but the kitchen was a level below, accessible only via a single narrow escalator. For diners, it was magical to see dozens of jacketed waiters materialize from the bowels of the ship carrying trays of shrimp cocktail and veal chops. But for us, the escalator was a nightmare.

Getting trays out from the kitchen was nearly impossible. One time, I was attempting to bring a tray of hors d'oeuvres upstairs—creamed herring, sardines, cucumber salad, and so on. The more experienced waiters could carry a twelve-plate tray over the head with two fingers, but I wasn't that good. I was hoisting this thing waist-high with both hands. As I went up, I felt the escalator narrowing, and I tried to lift the tray in time, but all twelve plates went crashing to the floor. The grinding of herring across the steps was bad enough—but the worst thing was going back to the garde-manger to ask for twelve more of the dishes that dropped. The kitchen crew already had it out for waiters, but after a drop they wanted to fucking kill you.

Even if you could successfully get your dishes out of the kitchen, the next challenge was getting them back in. If you had just cleared a table and were descending to the kitchen for the next course, you'd have to put your tray in lightning fast, because right behind you was another guy trying to do the same thing. This led to a lot of accidents. Sometimes you'd be forced to put your tray on the ground, and dirty dishes piled up on the floor.

Silverware was also a constant issue. Ideally, you'd set your table at the end of each night to be ready for breakfast the next morning. But there was never enough silverware to go around. Even if you were lucky enough to rummage up the required number of forks in advance, you'd show up in the morning only to see that some other waiter had stolen them. And if they really wanted to spite you, they would pour maple syrup on your table, just to fuck with you. Eventually, we started taking silverware back to our rooms, which meant waking up even earlier to set the table for service each morning.

None of this really bothered me because I was nineteen years old and getting paid to travel around the world. After I learned the basics of waiting tables during that first Baltic cruise, I went back to work at the cruise line all through college, working other routes on my Christmas and summer vacations. I traveled across Europe, the Caribbean, and North Africa (where you could get hashish the size of golf balls). I loved the travel but also the camaraderie of the crew. Even after a brutal dinner service, with guests demanding special treatment and the lot of us piling up on each other in the kitchen, we'd all crack jokes and a beer after hours, watching the water from the crew-only deck.

Bobby and I were two of the few Americans on the ship. He smoked a lot of pot and was always getting into trouble. They gave out condoms for free onboard ship, and we'd go into town and resell the rubbers, along with American cigarettes, to pay for cab rides. We were docked in Leningrad one day and wandering around the main square in town when we were approached by some black marketeers who wanted to buy our blue jeans. Apparently, they were worth big bucks in Russia. I was game. Bobby and I got into a busted-up car with these three shady guys, who drove around in circles to ensure no one was following us. They took us to a run-down apartment on the outskirts of town, and there, spread out on a mattress, was a selection of icons—ancient religious paintings on blocks of wood decorated with gold leaf. They were almost certainly stolen and illegal to own. Bobby's eyes lit up. He was convinced they were worth millions.

In exchange for my jeans, I picked up a little icon. I had brought overalls to wear back, and I chose an icon small enough to fit in the front pocket, near my chest. Bobby, however, bought the biggest icon they had, with nowhere to hide it. They dropped us back in the main square and we made our way to the ship.

When we were docked at a port, we couldn't just come and go as we pleased—security checked everyone before you were allowed back onboard. As we walked up the gangplank, I grew increasingly nervous. The security guy was patting down a fellow waiter ahead of us. They peeked under his jacket and, lo and behold, found his pilfered icon, undoubtedly from the same sketchy guys we'd seen. Two Soviet officers lifted him by his armpits and carted him away to God knows where.

I was sweating bullets. I shoved my icon further down the front bib of my overalls and prayed it wouldn't be found. Bobby shoved his icon down the back of his pants and draped his corduroy jacket over his back to cover the obvious bulge. They must have been distracted by the fuss with the other waiter, because they waved us through, and we ran back to our cabin and stowed the stolen artifacts under our bunk beds.

Much like I did on campus, I made it my business to get to know everybody on the ship. Although most of the waiters ignored the back of the house, I made inroads into the kitchen. On these ships, the entire menu was written in culinary terms. I learned that *Soup du Barry* was cauliflower, and *Consommé*

Celestine meant a julienne of crepes. You had to memorize all these culinary terms and be able to explain them to the guests. I excelled at learning the intricacies of the food. (And tasting all of it, too.)

I wanted to know how the food was made, so I'd show up to the kitchen early and ask the cooks questions. The Austrians rolled their eyes at first but eventually humored me, I think because they could tell I actually cared. At this point, I still kind of thought I wanted to be a chef. But as I started developing confidence in my culinary knowledge, guiding guests toward the best possible meal, my attitude shifted. Professor Christian had always said that you will be successful if you know what you're talking about. I didn't really, not yet, but I was starting to put the pieces together.

I loved the energy in the kitchen, the adrenaline in the air as hot pots and pans flew across the room. The cooks could be loud, boisterous, and rude; they were the kings of their private domain. But upstairs in the dining room, a very different, guest-facing social dynamic played out, and the ability to move between the two worlds with finesse was required.

I realized that the front of the house was where the action happened—you had to deal with all different kinds of people, hear what they liked and didn't like, learn how to please and appease them. For an extroverted guy like me, working the dining room just made sense. And so my professional ambitions moved away from cooking toward everything else it takes to make a restaurant great.

Chapter 3

Warner LeRoy and the Three-Ring Circuses

Prior to graduating from Cornell, I interviewed with Westin International, Hyatt, and Rockefeller Resorts and didn't get a single job offer. Whether that was because they asked for references from the professors I didn't get along with or some other reason, I'll never know. The rejection stung. I had slogged through four years at the country's best hotel school specifically to land a job at the country's best hotels.

I was happy to be finished with college, but one dark cloud hung over my otherwise celebratory graduation. Just a few days before the commencement ceremony, my father had suffered his first heart attack, and my parents weren't able to come up to Ithaca. I was plagued by the thought that I had caused them distress. They were aware, to a certain extent, of my challenges at Cornell; they knew that I was nearly kicked out.

For a long time, I felt very guilty about the stress that this had caused them. I thought I had finally gone too far and had pushed my father to the edge. I carried the weight of that guilt for years.

I decided to work one last cruise after graduation—a Mediterranean route, which took me to ports I'd never seen. But as much as I loved the job, I saw it as a pit stop en route to my ultimate goal of opening restaurants in New York City. I had a chip on my shoulder about the professors who didn't believe in me and was determined to succeed on my own terms. This was the beginning of a pattern in my career—someone would doubt me, and I would use that as fuel to prove myself.

I still had a lot to learn, though, and I knew it. I focused on finding a position where I could work my way up the ranks in New York. I was living with my parents when I got a call from Tom Gneiting, the general manager at Maxwell's Plum on 64th and First Ave. He was a Cornell graduate who had seen my work at Hotel Ezra Cornell, and he liked what he saw. He hired me as assistant restaurant director.

Maxwell's Plum was a three-ring circus. I've never seen anything like it. It was owned by Warner LeRoy, the son of Mervyn LeRoy, the Hollywood producer who made *The Wizard of Oz*. LeRoy had showmanship in his blood. The restaurant was flamboyant, crammed from floor to ceiling with tchotchkes, crystal light fixtures, and Toulouse-Lautrec paintings on the way to the bathroom. We would inflate hundreds of balloons every weekend for brunch. There was an enclosed sidewalk café in the front, and the more exclusive dining room in the back was modeled after Maxim's in Paris. It had this amazing ceiling made of Tiffany glass, illuminated by hundreds of tiny light bulbs, and celebrities like Warren Beatty, Dustin Hoffman, and Barbra Streisand dined there, away from the hoi polloi.

Maxwell's was ground zero for the singles scene in New York City, complete with an enormous mahogany bar smack-dab in the middle of the dining room where eligible bachelors and bachelorettes could camp out and flirt all night. We called the young women who went to the bar alone looking for a free meal "dinner hookers," though more than a few professional call girls made their way in as well.

The bar was perpetually packed. So was everywhere else—Maxwell's had 250 seats and served up to a thousand people a day. At the time, it was one of the highest-volume, highest-grossing restaurants in the city, raking in $5 million annually, much of that from booze—the perfect place for me to level up my skills after my basic training on the cruise ships.

The menu was enormous, and the food was far better than it needed to be. Somehow, this tiny kitchen cranked out everything from roasted duckling to footlong hot dogs, every dish perfectly executed. John Canaday, the restaurant critic at *The New York Times*, gave it four stars, a distinction only five other restaurants in the city held. I already had a keen interest in the critics—this was before Yelp and Resy and Instagram, and the *Times* critics might as well have been God. I cut out the reviews every week and kept a close eye on them.

I was making only $300 a week, but at the end of each shift, I was privileged to sit down and have a meal on the house. That alone was worth its weight in gold. The buttery sole almondine, crisp with toasted breadcrumbs and served with lemon, and calf's liver with sage butter and bacon were my favorites. I camped out at the bar at the end of my shift, watching the bartenders wipe away all the drips and spills from another night of revelry.

Most restaurants have a general manager who oversees the operations of the whole place. The chef rules the kitchen, and the maître d' runs the floor, but the GM is above both of them, watching over everything from a cramped back office. When you work in restaurants long enough, you realize that they are run from either a front-of-house mentality or the back, depending on the background of the GM. These days, most chefs don't want someone from the front of the house telling them what to do, even if that someone has the title of General Manager. Chefs tend to do what *they* want to do, and therein lies the crux of the main tension in the restaurant industry.

Maxwell's Plum was a little different. The push-pull between front of house and back of house was there—that's pretty much a given. But because the whole place was such a production, there was an unusual position called the restaurant director, which I thought was just about the greatest thing in the world. All performances need a director, and though I was the lowly assistant director (meaning I spent much of my time on the floor helping with service), the idea of having one person running the show—and casting all the other roles—took root in my brain.

The front-of-house team at Maxwell's was huge and all over the place. Many of the waiters were European and gay, and they had their own factions and rivalries among themselves. The more experienced worked in the formal back room, wearing red jackets with gold buttons. Others were aspiring actors and artists who had recently moved to New York and needed a flexible job between auditions—these were funneled to the more casual café up front, dressed in loud floral-print shirts with pink ties.

The bar staff were a charismatic lot who poured weak drinks and pocketed extra change whenever they could. Bloody Marys were popular at the time, and the head bartender at Maxwell's was famous for waving a handle of vodka across the bar to top off a whole row of tomato juices. This little act was quite popular until *New York* magazine sent a sample of one of his Bloodys to a lab and the report came back that almost no alcohol was in it.

It seemed like everyone in the restaurant was trying to line their pockets with a little something extra. One waiter had a friend who worked with Andy Warhol at The Factory, and he had access to certain posters that had fallen off the back of a truck, if you will. He sold them on the side, real hush-hush. The waiters were always jostling to get assigned to a "good" table, one with presumed big spenders who'd leave a nice tip. I was in charge of making their schedules, no small feat with the whole staff vying for prime times and tables.

Van Ribblett was the maître d' of the back room, a position that held a lot of power at a restaurant like Maxwell's, where getting seated at the right table was its own form of social currency. Van was a six-foot-six former hairdresser and self-taught painter who presided over the Tiffany-encrusted back dining room like it was his own private Idaho. Although it was common practice in those days to palm the maître d' a twenty-dollar bill to ensure you got a prime seat, Van took things further, instructing the reservationists not to book the room full so that he could sell tables to walk-ins for the highest price. We all knew it was happening, but nobody confronted him.

One day, the restaurant director, a debonair British man named Robin Hollis, decided he'd had enough. He instructed the reservationists to book every table in the room. "Fill it up," he barked. Van was in the habit of showing up about five minutes before we opened the room for dinner, so that night, he walked in, saw the reservation sheet, and his expression was priceless. He didn't know who had set him up, but eventually his eyes landed on me, and he summoned me from across the room with his enormous finger. "What the fuck am I supposed to do with this?" he hissed.

"You'll figure it out, Van," I said and walked away.

He was let go the next week.

Everyone had a big personality at Maxwell's, and navigating them all was part of the job. Warner LeRoy didn't come around that often, but when he did, it was like Elvis entering the building. He'd sweep in wearing these over-the-top outfits (gold lamé suits, a jacket with epaulets in the style of Sergeant Pepper) and make his demands. We had an eight-track player in the restaurant. One day Warner busted in and cornered me: "What's that noise?" he demanded. "I don't want any more music!" He stormed off. I did as he asked.

A few hours later, the general manager, Tom Gneiting, came in, looking perplexed. "Why isn't there music playing?" he asked. I explained what happened with Warner, but he said, "I told you to put on the music, play the music, dammit!"

So I did as he asked. Maybe an hour later, Warner storms back in, swinging his overcoat and heading straight to me. "What the fuck did I tell you about the music?" he growled.

"Warner, I'm sorry, Tom told me..." I trailed off, but it didn't matter. Warner was already past me, moving fast for a man his size, dead-eyed on Tom, whom he took into the office and slammed the door. We could all overhear what came next. I believed deep down that some of Warner's outbursts were for show, but they certainly kept us in line.

I was working so much I practically lived at the restaurant, though technically I had moved to a tiny walkup apartment on 64th and York, complete with a bathtub in the kitchen. I liked to take the elevator up to the fifth floor in the neighboring tenement, then jump over one rooftop to my building to avoid walking up the stairs.

At the end of one particularly busy Sunday brunch service, I spied a familiar face lingering at one of the tables—a wide mouth twisted into a smile that looked like a scowl, a prominent nose, and a head full of thick dark hair. I knew immediately who it was: Bill Graham, the rock-and-roll promoter I had idolized as a teen. The Fillmore East had closed several years earlier, but here he was, sipping the last of his coffee at a two-top along the rail. It was already my job to say hello to everybody, so I did just that, introducing myself and jabbering about my time at his theater. He was polite, a little reserved, as cool a cat as ever. You have to be careful not to overstay your welcome at the table, but he didn't rush me along, and I went home that night feeling certain that I had the best job in the city.

That said, much of what I learned at Maxwell's was how *not* to run a restaurant. I still wanted to open my own place eventually, and I kept a running list in my head of things *not* to do.

The enormous menu was one head-scratching example, especially with a kitchen the size of a postage stamp. A smaller menu allows you to control food costs, prep work, and the timing of cooking and service. The expediter at Maxwell's used to stand in the kitchen with a microphone barking, "Pick up! Pick up!" and waiters would scramble to grab all the plates they could at once. It was sloppy. I couldn't understand why we didn't just streamline things, but I was a lowly assistant and it wasn't my call.

Another setup I didn't love was the waiter system—most high-end restaurants have a captain to advise diners on the menu, a waiter to deliver the plates, and a busser to clear them. Maxwell's had captains only in the back room; everywhere else, waiters were responsible for everything, so they ran around frantically and ignored their tables in the process. *When I open my own place*, I thought, *I'll have runners*—people whose sole job was to bring the food, piping hot, from the kitchen to the table, so that the waiters could remain on the floor, managing their stations and attending to the guests.

Let me be clear: I loved the job. I was working at arguably the hottest restaurant in Manhattan, navigating big personalities, and eating like a king. I would have happily stayed there, working my way up to the all-powerful position of the restaurant director, had Tavern on the Green not come calling, a siren song too powerful to resist.

Tavern on the Green was originally a sheepfold smack-dab in the middle of Sheep Meadow in Central Park. It was converted into a restaurant in the 1930s, but years later, it had lost some luster, and *The New York Times* described it as a "rustic little money-losing pub." In 1974, while I was at Cornell, Warner LeRoy took over the Tavern's lease and closed the restaurant for a two-year, then-unheard-of $10 million facelift. When it reopened in 1976, in typical LeRoy fashion, it was a completely over-the-top production.

LeRoy doubled the seating to eight hundred, added a glass-enclosed Crystal Room overlooking the gardens, plus a bunch of private drinking rooms, and draped every square foot with yet more Tiffany glass, Art Nouveau mirrors, and sparkling chandeliers. His daughter once said that he wanted the interior to look like "the inside of a wedding cake," and I'd say he succeeded. It was one of the busiest restaurants in the country, and when management offered to transfer me over from Maxwell's, promote me to restaurant director, and bump my weekly salary up to $550, I couldn't refuse. Where else could I serve a thousand people on a Saturday night, then wake up a few hours later and do fifteen hundred covers for brunch?

If Maxwell's was a madhouse, then Tavern was pandemonium. It was host to a regular parade of rich and powerful guests, yet the reservations system was a total catastrophe. We had eight people crammed into a little room upstairs answering the phones and a wall covered with handwritten sheets showing reservations for the next thirty days. They were booking deuces (tables for two) ninety minutes apart and four-tops two hours apart. At a restaurant like Tavern, where everyone wanted a prime seat and everyone wanted to linger, that simply wasn't enough time to turn tables (i.e., get one party successfully cleared out and another seated at the same freshly set table). The result was a logjam of angry guests, harried waiters, and a backed-up kitchen.

Each night, the reservationists would deliver the handwritten reservation sheet for the following day to the host stand up front. One busy Saturday, we lost the sheet. I cannot even begin to explain what a crisis that was; it meant that hundreds of people were on their way in, and we had no idea who they were, how big their party was, or where they were supposed to go.

I volunteered to work the door to meet the crisis head-on. I knew there would be some VIPs, and I thought I could maintain a veneer of calm while attempting to figure out what the hell to do with them.

As I'm checking people in, I look up to see none other than Tom Landry, the coach of the Dallas Cowboys, who had materialized in the cramped front room where everybody funneled in and out of the restaurant. I recognized him instantly, thanks to his signature fedora.

"Good evening, Mr. Landry. How many in your party, sir?" I asked, trying to play it cool.

"Eighteen," he drawled.

Alarm bells started ringing in my head. Where the hell was I going to find room for eighteen hungry Texans? Visions of my impending job termination danced through my head, but I was determined to not let it show and, more importantly, to not let Landry wait. "Of course, Mr. Landry," I said. "We're setting the table right now."

I smiled at him and tried not to let him see me break into a sprint as I scoured the Crystal Room for enough six-tops to hastily fasten together to seat them all. Somehow, and I have blocked out most of the details, I made it work on the fly, and Landry was an exemplary guest, leaving a massive tip before he left.

I was beginning to learn that in most restaurants, the inmates run the institution. Even if the boss—be it the owner, manager, director, whoever—sets forth certain rules, they're not really the ones in control. As soon as that boss turns their back, the employees will devise their own way of doing things.

Here, too, we had a maître d' with slicked-back hair, Ray Garcia, who looked like Robert De Niro in *New York, New York*. Garcia controlled the Crystal Room. He'd allow customers to palm him a bill for a good table, then "accidentally" drop it on the floor to see how big it was before deciding where to seat them. If a guest asked if he could have a window table, Ray would look them dead in the eye and respond, "That's entirely up to you, sir."

I thought that captains should make the Caesar salads tableside with a fresh dressing. The process, as I saw it, was very simple: Put an anchovy in a wooden bowl with a tiny bit of garlic and mash it around. Put the greens on top, add a little olive oil and lemon juice, plus a coddled egg. With two spoons, mix it all up, add the cheese and croutons, plus a touch of black pepper, and present it with a flourish. Voilà. A Caesar salad made à la minute. The customer loves the showmanship, and it saves the waiter from making a trip to the kitchen to get a gloopy, premade, mayo-laden dressing.

I thought it would be a slam dunk. But I swear to God, every captain in the place tried to circumvent my new system. They preferred to dump the premade dressing onto the salad at their stations, out of sight from the guests. They would even go as far as to get the dressing in advance and hide it in our beautiful silver coffee pots.

The chefs, too, operated in a sort of alternate universe divorced from the front of the house. Warner LeRoy was a great showman, and though he claimed he wanted the best chefs in the world, he went about hiring them all wrong. He relied on headhunters, but the problem with hiring people based on their résumés alone is that you get varying degrees of bullshit. The headhunters would send the names of guys who had done stints in fine restaurants in Europe and New Orleans, but the chefs were often past their prime by the time they landed at Tavern. Many were too slow to keep up with the relentless pace; several were simply too drunk.

We used to host these big corporate luncheons. One day, we had executives from a luxury car company—Mercedes-Benz, I think—come in for lunch. There were seventy-five people total. Our chef at the time was a Swiss old-timer named Berthold Widmer, and the menu that day called for strip loin of beef as the entrée. I was in the kitchen when the cooks started to slice the beef for plating, and I noticed that the meat was blood rare, borderline mooing. Now, as restaurant director, I generally had better things to do than micromanage the plates coming out of the kitchen, but I was also responsible for ensuring the plates were up to a certain standard. So I said, "Chef, don't you think that's a little rare?"

"Shut up! I'm the chef! I know what I'm doing! I know the German people, and they like their meat rare!" Widmer roared, eyes blazing.

I backed off. The plates went out. I watched as the car execs poked at their bloody meat, frowning. After everyone was served, Jordi Dobbs, the captain that day, in the middle of the room, with a theatrical flourish, asked, "Is everything all right?" Seventy-five plates were immediately sent back to the kitchen. Old Widmer was so outraged, I thought he was going to explode.

I learned two important lessons that day: One, chefs will always be difficult, so I better find some way of dealing with them if I want to run a successful restaurant. And, two, never ask the guest, "Is everything alright?" That question implies that something might be wrong, and you should be able to *know* if something is wrong. Instead, say, "Is there anything you need? Is there anything I can bring you?" It's phrasing I've taught to all of my servers since.

After a few months of chaos, I began tweaking the system. I streamlined the reservation-taking process and spaced-out seatings to a more reasonable two hours, which enabled us to turn tables more efficiently. (Here's some simple restaurant math for you: fewer pissed-off customers = more revenue.) I pruned the bad wood, letting go of the slick-palmed maître d's and personally hiring and training new ones.

During orientation, I told all new employees to never say no. Guests might show up asking to sit on the roof. Still, the answer is not no—it's "Let me see if that's possible. I'll speak with a manager." That simple phrasing makes the guest feel like they're being heard—even when their request is unattainable. It enables you to come back with, "I'd love to take you upstairs, but unfortunately we aren't seating on the roof tonight. Let me offer you the next best thing." You can laugh about it later.

I made other changes, too: When I'd arrived at the Tavern, no one had ever bothered to set up the outdoor dining area known as the Garden properly. I laid out a new floor plan with the appropriate number of deuces and four-tops, installed a bar so customers didn't have to wait on drinks from inside, and drafted a new "garden menu" that was limited to the dishes the staff could get in and out of the kitchen quickly. Boom. Triple the revenue within a year for that seating area alone.

I then directed my attention to private dining, which was big business at a restaurant like the Tavern. Think about it: one room, one night, hundreds of people, with a guaranteed minimum. The catering director, a real loudmouth, looked like Michael Douglas in *Wall Street*, with slicked-back hair, fancy suits, the whole nine. When I got to the Tavern, his attitude was that everything about the restaurant sucked except for him. But as I whipped the whole operation into shape, he started singing a different tune, wining and dining guests who were considering booking a private event, and it was a major vote of confidence in me. Lo and behold, for the low cost of one comped dinner in the Crystal Room, fathers of brides were easily convinced to book their 250-person weddings with us.

One night, I was making my rounds, when I noticed a small, impish-looking guy scoping out the restaurant. I recognized him as the chef of Ma Maison in Los Angeles, Wolfgang Puck. I was impressed that this guy would come all the way to Tavern on the Green just to check us out. I greeted him, and he was stunned that I knew who he was. I asked him to come with me and gave him a full tour of the kitchen and all the dining rooms, and thus began a friendship that would last many years.

Slowly but surely, I gained the respect of the staff (though they still never made the Caesar dressing the way I wanted). I stayed at Tavern for about four years, helping the restaurant's annual revenue grow from $15 million to $32 million. It was one of the most incredible periods of growth any restaurant had ever seen. And I learned how to operate in one of the fastest-paced, highest-volume dining rooms of all time, developing a skill set that would later prove to be invaluable.

———————

I worked crazy hours at Tavern, too, but somehow managed to date one of my first real girlfriends during this time. She was a few years younger than me and finishing her senior year at Cornell while I was working at Tavern. She was a sweet girl, and I was nuts about her, but she came from a religious family who didn't appreciate the fact that I was Jewish. I didn't appreciate her desire to save herself for marriage, so perhaps we weren't meant to be.

Nevertheless, I used to take the bus up to Ithaca on my days off (I'm a city kid; I never learned how to drive and to this day still don't have a license). During one of my visits, a fellow Cornellian named Tony Zazula came running up to me on the street. I knew Tony a little bit from school; he was quiet and struck me as a bit of a nerd, given that I'd only ever seen him in the library. He knew I was working at Tavern and barraged me with questions about it. He told me he'd seen an ad in the paper that the restaurant was hiring; he was hoping for a good word so he could land the job.

I thought to myself, *This guy's not gonna get hired*—Tony was nice, but he lacked that oomph, that extra edge that would set him apart at one of the busiest restaurants in New York. I wished him luck and we parted ways. When I made it back to New York, a big winter storm was brewing, and very few people turned up to work. So imagine my surprise when Tony Zazula came walking in, in the middle of this blizzard, for his job interview. This so impressed our general manager Hugo Ralli that he hired him on the spot.

Tony was a snazzy dresser and quickly became a pet of Hugo, himself a very stylish man. The two of them used to sit out in the garden at the busiest times during the middle of service and have a cocktail. This was against my way of doing things—guests were in need of service! But Tony was sucking up to Hugo, and we at one point nicknamed him "The Clone." After several months, Hugo tried to promote Tony to be his assistant, which would have meant I was reporting to him. I called Warner LeRoy and told him if that happened, I would leave. Tony didn't get promoted.

———

Despite a little professional rivalry, Tony and I became friendly. Warner LeRoy had a dining incentive for his managers. The deal was, each manager got $250 a day to eat at ten Michelin three-star restaurants abroad. Earning three Michelin stars is a huge, huge deal. There is no fourth star—three is the highest honor and designates that a restaurant is virtually perfect and "worth a special journey." The idea was that we'd experience the best food and service the world had to offer, then bring those techniques to Tavern on the Green. In 1980, Tony and I decided that we would travel together, pool our resources, and eat at twenty three-star restaurants.

We flew into Paris, picked up a rental car, and spent three weeks crisscrossing France and Switzerland. Our first meal was at Maxim's—not technically three stars, but probably the most elegant restaurant in Paris. It was famous for its stained glass ceiling, absolutely exquisite. (Maxwell's Plum had basically ripped off the motif for its back room, but Warner LeRoy had used Tiffany glass instead.) We were so jetlagged that I don't remember what we ate, but I do remember that when we asked for the check it was comped. So, of course we thought we'd eat for free everywhere after that; I was soon proved very wrong.

We got in the car to travel to Mionnay, outside of Lyon, to visit the restaurant run by Alain Chapel, considered a founding father of nouvelle cuisine and one of the greatest chefs in France. As soon as we were seated, the power cut out. The staff hurried around to light candles and get on with the show, but Alain looked like he was just about to die. He paced around the dining room, devastated. Miraculously, maybe half an hour later the electricity came back on, and the color returned to his face. The dinner proceeded, and I was stunned by the dessert. It was au courant in many French restaurants to bring desserts out on a rolling cart called a *chariot de dessert*, but at Alain Chapel, they enlisted two poor waiters to hand-carry this enormous silver platter groaning with profiteroles and Napoleons and all the rest. I had a flashback to my time on the cruise ships; I really felt for the waiters.

Of course, Paul Bocuse was the chef's chef, and we went to his restaurant near Lyon, too. There was a saying at the time, "All signs point to Paul Bocuse," but we couldn't find the restaurant. We showed up late but were received beautifully and got a taste of his already-iconic soupe aux truffes noires Valéry Giscard D'Estaing—so named for the president of France—a clear soup with truffles adorned with a giant puff pastry dome.

More incredible meals followed—at Auberge du Père Bise, Moulin de Mougins, Maison Pic, and more. I'll never forget Jean and Pierre Troisgros leading us into the kitchen at their restaurant in Roanne, an ultra-modern space with red laminate and mirrored surfaces (it was the eighties). Jean pulled a perfect, glistening lobster out of the walk-in. "Theeese iz your dinner tonight," he drawled with obvious delight, as the lobster writhed and twitched. These guys were serious about ingredients, and I was seriously in awe of their devotion to the craft.

This is not to say that everything went off without a hitch. There was one restaurant we were both dying to get to—the eponymous establishment of the renowned Swiss chef Frédy Girardet. His restaurant was in Crissier, about ten minutes from Lausanne, where I had dreamed of going to hotel school. We had arranged to visit Girardet for lunch on the last day of our trip. We'd had a lot of incredible meals by this point, but still, Tony and I were like two schoolboys, chattering about our grand finale.

We spent the night before in Nice, dining at Jacques Maximin in the Hotel Negresco, and woke up before dawn to make what we thought was a five-hour drive to Crissier. As soon as we got on the road (with Tony driving, naturally), we knew we were in trouble. Although the line between Nice and Crissier looked straightforward in the atlas, the roads themselves were all switchbacks, rising up and winding us around the mountains. It was breathtaking scenery, but there was no way in hell we were going to make it to Girardet by 1:00 p.m., even with Tony driving like he was in the Grand Prix.

At two o'clock, panicked, we pulled into the restaurant. Frédy Girardet was standing outside waiting to rip us a new asshole. "Do you know how many people want to make a reservation here, and you couldn't even be bothered to show up?!"

he screamed. We tried to explain, but he wasn't having it. He banished us back to our car, and we slunk away.

Planning on being there only for lunch, now we had nowhere to stay in Lausanne. After eating our way across the finest restaurants in Europe, we'd be reduced to renting a last-minute room in some flea-bitten motel while we figured out our next steps. Tony was basically catatonic, and in his fog, he managed to get us into a minor car accident. We abandoned our rental on the side of the road.

Still, I was determined to eat at Girardet. We hadn't come this far to accept defeat. I started calling around. I reached the headmaster of the Lausanne hotel school and begged him to put in a good word for us. He refused. I asked the concierge at the Beau Rivage to help us out. No dice.

Finally, I called the restaurant directly. I said, "Listen, we work in a restaurant in New York where we serve a thousand covers a night, and even when we're fully booked, if we really want to accommodate somebody, we figure out a way to make it happen. We're going to come by tonight at nine and I'm sure you'll take care of us." I hung up the phone without even waiting for a response.

That night, we took a cab back to Girardet. When they saw us, they led us to a table immediately, and we sat for one of the most exquisite meals I've ever had in my life—mussels lined up in a pinwheel with a Provencal sauce, fish decorated with zucchini that resembled scales, foie gras everywhere. I felt I had accomplished a monumental feat, and I was grateful for the chance to redeem myself before this great chef.

That trip was where I learned what hospitality looks like at its highest level. The amount of attention that is lavished on you at a Michelin three-star restaurant in Europe cannot be over-stated. They will do anything for you, and they will do it with grace. Dishes were finished tableside with great finesse; the plating itself was performance. I had never experienced anything like it. The servers exuded hospitality from the very center of their being. I knew then that I wanted to capture the essence of that experience.

But in typical fashion, I wanted to do it my own way.

Chapter 4

A Tour of the Le's and La's

By 1983, I felt I had learned enough to leave the Tavern on the Green and pursue my ultimate goal of opening my own restaurant. There were just a few issues: I had no space, no money, and no chef. On the flip side, I was arguably in the best physical shape of my life—training for the New York Marathon. I spent hours running in Central Park and working out at the New York Athletic Club. There, I would sometimes see Paul Kovi, one of the owners of the Four Seasons, reading his Italian newspapers by the swimming pool and think to myself, *I want to be that guy one day.*

One day that winter, I took my mother to lunch at Le Périgord on East 52nd Street. Le Périgord was about twenty years old at that point and had cemented its reputation as a sort of genteel clubhouse, serving haute French cuisine to well-heeled New Yorkers. Bathed in soft light and staffed by well-choreographed

European waiters, it was overseen by a smooth, tuxedoed Swiss man named Georges Briguet. He came over to our table to say hello.

Briguet asked where I was working and I confessed that I was between jobs. He told me that a friend of his was opening a new restaurant a few blocks over and looking for waiters. "Oh, no, Drew is a manager, not a waiter," my mother interjected, but I was interested. I decided to walk over to 49th Street and Fifth Avenue to meet Jean Louis Missud, an affable Frenchman who had just left his job at another classic French restaurant, La Côte Basque. He offered me a job as a waiter at his new place, La Reserve. I countered by telling him I should come on as captain, the one who oversees the waiters. He agreed. And so I dusted off my tuxedo and began what I call the Tour of the Le's and La's, a two-year whirlwind at some of New York's most venerable French restaurants.

At the time, New York fine dining meant only one thing: French. Places like La Côte Basque, La Grenouille, La Caravelle, and Lutèce were all direct or spiritual descendants of Henri Soulé, who ran Le Restaurant Français at the 1939 World's Fair in Queens and then opened the legendary Le Pavillon. Many of Soulé's acolytes opened their own spots in the 1960s and continued to rack up critical acclaim for decades after. At these restaurants, there was a formula: The proprietor was always in the house, captains were dressed in black tie, waiters were expertly trained, and the food was very traditional. Dishes like whitefish quenelles in Champagne sauce and blanquette de veau were presented in elegant dining rooms, often from beneath large metal cloches. The style of service was fussy, formal, and frankly condescending if you didn't abide by the restaurant's rules. Prices were high, dress codes were strict, and guests paid for the privilege of being talked down to.

My very first day at La Reserve, I worked a double shift, and midway through dinner, it started snowing heavily. By the time service ended, the streets were blanketed in snow and eerily quiet. The weatherman called it a blizzard and advised people to stay home. I had to walk the forty blocks home to my apartment. The next day, I was scheduled to work lunch. I woke up to three feet of snow on the ground and, again, no traffic on the streets. But we had reservations on the books, so I pulled on my coat and trudged back to La Reserve. One cook showed up that day, plus me. Two people came in for lunch. The show must go on.

It was highly unusual for a French restaurant to hire an American as a captain. Almost all the staff at such establishments were European and had honed their skills for years in restaurants overseas. Naturally, they hated me. Part of it had to do with money—waiters and captains were always fighting over the tip, which was supposed to be split 15 percent to 5 percent, an arcane guideline that few diners were aware of. At one point, American Express printed separate tip lines for waiters and for captains on credit card slips, but most customers had no clue who did what, and they just left one tip for the staff to battle over later. At La Reserve, the captains would confront diners after they had already paid their bill and beg for a separate tip, an awkward scene for all involved.

But, really, what the waiters hated most was that I was an outsider, an interloper, breaking in to their highly codified, highly French little world. They expressed their distaste through a series of pranks. For example: One of the captain's jobs was to sauce certain dishes after they were set in front of the guest. A waiter would hand me the sauceboat, and as I began the tableside performance, I'd find I'd been handed a fork instead of a spoon. Quite funny, but petty nonetheless. Their attempts at sabotage were useful, in a way—I couldn't break a sweat in front of guests, no matter what, so I figured out how to maintain my own facade pretty damn fast.

Still, I got mine where I could. I was teaching myself about fine wine and was desperate for a taste of the then-revolutionary Opus One. I convinced Missud to order a case, knowing that guests often didn't finish their bottles. Soon enough, one of my regulars ordered the Opus (at my suggestion) and at the end of their meal, with about a third of the bottle remaining, generously told me to keep the rest. After dinner, I excitedly went to retrieve the bottle from the pantry where I'd stashed it, but it had disappeared. I asked the busboys what happened. They looked at me and whispered, "Michel." Of course. Michel was one of the French waiters, and a total prick, with a bulging red vein in his forehead. I approached him and asked where my wine was. "Pfft! I don't have your fucking wine!" he snarled and stomped off indignantly.

I said nothing, but the next day at lunch, a table ordered a cheap bottle of Mouton Cadet. I poured the wine, and once again at the end of meal, there was a little bit left. I took the bottle into the bathroom downstairs and pissed into it, then placed it in the same pantry. Back to the dining room I went, until one of the busboys signaled to me. I scampered back to the pantry, and sure enough, there was Michel, swirling the liquid in his glass and frowning. I had exacted my revenge.

Aside from squabbling with the French waiters, I tasted everything I could. I considered it all a part of my education. And because I was responsible for taking orders, I was learning a certain vocabulary about how diners wanted their food: "I'd like my lamb pink." "I want the duck crisp." It was all these clichés, but that's how they ordered, so I filed those descriptors away for later, for when I would design my own menu.

Georges Briguet and Jean Louis Missud were in business together and often exchanged staff, so I put in stints at both La Reserve and Le Périgord. One day, after their meal I took a party at La Reserve down to the kitchen for a brief tour, standard procedure for VIP tables. But shortly thereafter, this group opened a restaurant in Houston and stole our pastry chef. Briguet blamed me for this incident, and I was let go (though we eventually made up and remained friends).

In 1984, I went to work for a newly opened French restaurant in the luxurious Hôtel Plaza Athénée on the Upper East Side. The chef there was an up-and-coming young Frenchman named Daniel Boulud. He had a stellar reputation. Combined with the prestige of the Plaza Athénée name, Le Régence was one of the most anticipated openings in the city.

While the guests in the dining room enjoyed nouvelle cuisine presented on gleaming rolling carts, in the back, the young Daniel was a tyrant. I mean a world-class yeller. He would do all the classic stuff: scream at the cooks and throw their plates in the trash if one little sprig of parsley was out of place. One time he took apart this poor garde-manger. I asked the kid, "Why do you take it from him? You should stand up for yourself." "Oh no," the cook said, "he's the chef, I can't do that." He was deeply entrenched in the brigade way of thinking and couldn't imagine questioning the authority of the chef.

One time, Daniel came after me—I can't even remember what he was upset about—but I fought back. "Fuck me? No, fuck you!" I yelled. The waiters were aghast. This did not happen in a French kitchen. But guess what? Daniel stopped disrespecting me after that. We became friends. Over time, he learned to control his behavior, and today, Daniel Boulud is one of the most successful chefs in the world.

Daniel Boulud introduced me to a significantly influential figure in my career, Jean-Louis Palladin. Jean-Louis, who resembled a poodle, with his mop top of curly hair and oversized eyeglasses, was the visionary French chef behind Jean-Louis at the Watergate in Washington, DC. He was something of a prodigy, having been the youngest chef in France to receive two Michelin stars. Unlike the stuffy French chefs of the old guard, Jean-Louis was fascinated by American ingredients and went to great lengths to procure the best of them. His cooking melded classic technique with the freedom of his adopted hometown. It was amazing to watch a French chef treat the American palate like an equal.

I went to visit Jean-Louis at the Watergate in the fall of 1984 for lunch. I still remember the pumpkin soup with foie gras poured tableside. He came out to chat, and we hit it off right away. He looked at things differently, and I was fascinated by his approach to cooking. He talked a lot, but he also listened, and liked to challenge himself in the kitchen. This was the beginning of one of my most cherished friendships; Jean-Louis eventually became a trusted confidant and travel buddy.

I also met a sharp young man named Daniel Johnnes at Le Régence. He had been hired as a waiter, and though he didn't have a ton of experience, he spoke fluent French and sounded like a native. Johnnes was developing a keen interest in wine, just like me. I kept him in mind for the restaurant I knew I wanted to open someday.

A few months in, I went running in Central Park on my lunch break. When I did this, I hung my tuxedo outside of my locker at the New York Athletic Club so it wouldn't wrinkle. This day, I returned to the locker room a sweaty mess and noticed a handsome man around my age eyeing my tuxedo, a dead giveaway that I was in the biz. He introduced himself as Charles Masson Jr., the proprietor of La Grenouille, an early pinnacle of classic French restaurants. Charles had taken over operations at the tender age of nineteen, when his father passed away, but he was serious about maintaining the exceptionally high standards. After we chatted for a bit, Masson recruited me to work for him. I couldn't turn down the opportunity to work at a four-star restaurant.

At La Grenouille, classic French food was executed with style and service to boot. There were lavish floral compositions and plush ruby banquettes in the dining room, and the kitchen turned out buttery Dover sole with mustard sauce and cooked-to-order soufflés that kept their cloudlike consistency right up until their inevitable meeting with a spoon.

As a captain, I really had to step it up. I was used to carving a roast duck tableside at the other French restaurants, but at La Grenouille, the duck was a wild Canadian bird, and therefore much tougher to slice. In addition, it was listed on the menu as duck aiguillettes meaning very thinly sliced off the breast. At the other Le's and La's, it was enough to simply carve the breast off and plate it with the leg, but here we were to slice the meat and arrange it neatly on the plate like a fan. Each time I tried to slice the Canadian duck gracefully, I wound up crucifying the poor bird. I prayed that people wouldn't order it on my watch.

But the same level of care was not lavished on all things at La Grenouille. I remember a solo diner who asked for a bottle of Cristal Champagne, to be followed by a bottle of Petrus '61, which at the time cost about $600. I poured the red wine. He swirled it, tasted it, and nodded his approval. But a minute later he called me over and said, "Listen—I'm not saying the wine is bad. But something seems funny with it. Is there an expert here who could come taste it for me?" We didn't have a dedicated sommelier. I called over our maître d', Jean Benjamin, who didn't know good wine if it hit him upside the head, but this was all part of the act. He swirled, sniffed, and sipped the Petrus. "It's delicious, simply delicious!" he exclaimed. The big spender seemed satisfied. But he barely touched the wine and had already finished his entrée. The souffle was about to arrive, and I asked if he would like me to clear his drink.

"Yes, please do," he said. I was thrilled—I now had a half decanter full of '61 Petrus to taste with my colleagues. I brought it back to the kitchen with some wine glasses, eager for a taste. I took a sip, expecting nirvana, and nearly spat the stuff out. It was dead. Totally shot. Disgusting. There was no temperature-controlled wine storage at La Grenouille, and this amazing bottle had been stored in a warm room, where it spoiled. The guy shouldn't have even been charged for it, but most diners didn't know jack about wine, and we got away with some shady stuff in the name of fine dining. I vowed I would never pull the wool over my guests like that again.

I was always taking notes in my head. Whereas Maxwell's Plum and Tavern were big, bustling spectacles that trafficked in high volume and turning tables as quickly as possible, meals at the Le's and La's were different. Guests there were often a little older and more refined; they couldn't be rushed. The dining rooms were civilized and spacious, with soft lighting and acoustics conducive to actually hearing your date. I saw that curved banquettes naturally lent themselves to more intimate conversations and that offset lighting helped avoid harsh reflections off the gleaming plates. I didn't love the haughtiness that went along with the whole production, but I did file away certain touches that could create a transportive environment.

Something else happened around this time that contributed to my desire to go my own way. I ran the New York Marathon in November 1983 and finished in four hours and seven minutes. The very next day, while I was nursing my sore legs, I received a call from Tom Margittai, one of the owners of the Four Seasons, about a potential job opportunity.

The Four Seasons, under the command of Margittai and his partners Paul Kovi, Alex Von Bidder, and Julian Niccolini, was the most powerful restaurant in the city. An elite squadron of politicians, publishing-world impresarios, and socialites gathered there for refined takes on a newly coined cuisine called "New American." There were few restaurants I wanted to work at more. The Le's and La's had their own sheen, but the Four

Seasons, along with a small handful of peers like Joe Baum's Windows on the World, was doing something different, new, and exciting. I wanted in.

So, when Tom Margittai called me, I was exhilarated. He explained that, as part of the hiring process, I would talk to everyone, and all four partners had to agree for me to be hired.

I had planned a trip to California for later that week as a sort of postmarathon reward. So, I rushed to interview with everyone at the Four Seasons before I left, and I thought I had it in the bag. After grueling stints at some of the city's best restaurants, I had the knowledge and the confidence to back it up, just like Professor Christian had preached. I talked to everyone except Julian Niccolini, but because we'd crossed paths while I worked at Tavern on the Green, I figured he'd already tacitly given his stamp of approval.

Off I went on my California vacation. The whole time, I was expecting to come home and start working at the Four Seasons. Instead, when I returned, Alex von Bidder called and said, "As you know, Drew, everyone has to be on board with hiring you and there's been some disagreement. Unfortunately, we're not going to be able to offer you the job."

To this day, I still don't know who didn't like me, though I suspect it was Niccolini. Sometimes you'll just never know why someone has it out for you. There's nothing you can do except stand up for yourself. But in that moment, I was not so sanguine. I was shocked that I didn't get the job. Pissed.

When I put the phone down after that call, all I could think was: *I'm gonna show these motherfuckers.*

Chapter 5

Redefining Downtown and the Birth of Montrachet

The whole time I was burnishing my résumé at the Le's and La's I had an end goal, the same one I'd been working toward as a kid: to open my own restaurant. But I didn't have a European restaurant in my mind while I was working at all these French joints. Instead, I had a vision for a New American restaurant, the most cutting-edge cuisine of the day, paired with then-up-and-coming California wines. I had a name for my fantasy project: the Silverado Trail, named for the historic route in Napa County. I even printed up business cards for it.

In between departing from the Tavern on the Green and before starting at my first Le, I had briefly managed a restaurant called 24 Fifth Avenue, located on, as its name implies, lower Fifth Avenue.

I hired a woman named Leslie Revsin as the chef. Leslie, who was the first female chef at the Waldorf-Astoria hotel, was a brilliant creator of nouvelle American dishes like Roquefort beignets on apple purée. I admired her skill and decided to print her name on the menu each night, an unheard-of move intended to put her talent on full display. But Leslie was, like many chefs, also hot-tempered and mercurial. She would spend an inordinate amount of time fussing over dishes before sending them out, leading to long delays between courses, and she would occasionally decline to show up for work entirely, causing me no end of headaches.

I didn't work there for very long, but a few important things happened during my brief tenure at 24 Fifth. One was that Mimi Sheraton, then the critic for *The New York Times*, reviewed us. Mimi, tough and very smart, was particularly feared because she was known not to pull punches in her critiques. She had a tendency to come in on slow nights, like Sundays, which was dangerous at a restaurant like 24 Fifth, where the chef's attendance was somewhat unpredictable. Fortunately, Leslie deigned to show up the day that Mimi came in unannounced. Unfortunately, Leslie also decided to spend way too long tending to each dish before allowing it to leave her sight.

In her two-star review of 24 Fifth, Mimi included this line: "The frequent slowdowns between appetizers and main courses seem to be the fault of the kitchen, even though the restaurant was less than half full on each of our five visits." It was one small note in an otherwise positive review, but it was monumental for me—this was the first time that a critic noticed that it might not be the front of house's fault the food wasn't showing up in a timely fashion. *Hey, maybe the kitchen is fucking this thing up.*

This one critique wounded me personally; it was a crack in the facade, and I vowed that I would never let that happen again.

I was twenty-seven years old at this point and already an unrepentant workaholic. I worked eighty-hour weeks, nights and weekends very much included. Although I was surrounded by beautiful women at the restaurants, I didn't have much time for dating. And whatever professional hubris I possessed, my confidence when it came to the opposite sex was lacking. I'd had a few girlfriends in college and a drunken hookup on the cruise ship, but there was nothing serious to speak of in the romance department. I wanted a family someday, but I was so focused on my career that the prospect of pursuing a relationship was practically a joke.

Still, I wasn't completely blind. So, when a group of three attractive young women came in to 24 Fifth one night, I took notice, particularly of the petite brunette dressed in all white.

I seated them at a prime table, right by the window. Two of my waiters, one of them French, immediately descended on them and started flirting. As the manager, I wore a dark suit and tried to keep some professional distance from the floor staff since I was theoretically in charge of them. But in this instance, I did pull one of the waiters aside. "Try to get their numbers," I said. He winked at me.

The women finished dinner and were getting their coats. The French waiter told me they had all agreed to meet for a nightcap at a nearby restaurant, Texarkana. "Join us later," he said, and disappeared.

I was always one of the last people to leave the restaurant at night, long after most waiters had clocked out. That night, after everyone had left, I made my way to Texarkana, but the women (and the waiters) were nowhere to be found. As I nursed a drink alone at the bar, the bartender said I had a phone call. A phone call? That couldn't be right. He shrugged and passed the phone to me.

"Where are you?" said a mysterious female voice on the other end of the line.

"I'm at Texarkana. Where are *you*?" I asked.

"Oh, we left, but we're right up the street," she said. "Come meet us at this address. Tell the doorman 'LiPuma 3C.'"

I raced over to the apartment building up the street and blurted out "LiPuma 3C" to the doorman, who eyed me suspiciously. But he allowed me up, and there was the cute brunette, greeting me at the door.

It was late. One of her friends had gone home with the French waiter, and the other friend was already asleep on the pullout sofa. She poured me a glass of wine. She was twenty-three, right out of college, and working at *McCall's* magazine. She was from a big Sicilian family in Rockland County that loved food, the kind who always made their dinner reservations before booking their hotel rooms on family trips. She grew up coming into the city to eat with her parents; she paid attention to all the new restaurants. Turns out, she'd actually had a reservation somewhere else that night, but her two friends, visiting from Montreal, were delayed and they'd had to give up the table. So, 24 Fifth was a last-minute plan B, based solely on the fact that it was across the street. I couldn't believe my luck.

We also talked about my parents, Cornell, working at Tavern on the Green. I was excited that she recognized the names of some of the restaurants in France I admired. I told her I wanted to open my own place one day, hopefully soon. She asked a lot of questions and seemed highly engaged while I ran my mouth about my big plans. But I could not bring myself to make a move. She was beautiful, but I wanted to be a gentleman. After talking for more than two hours, I started making motions to leave. "Well, it was nice to meet you," I said. "Can I call you sometime?"

She stared at me. "You don't even know my name," she said. "Sure I do," I replied. "LiPuma 3C."

Ann's and my first official date was seeing Robin Williams in *The World According to Garp* and eating at the famous Coach House restaurant. We got serious quickly. I met her family, who planned an evening at the Russian Tea Room and a Frank Sinatra concert at Carnegie Hall. Her parents, Sal and Vera, loved food, so they took to me right away. Within a year of meeting, though I technically had my own apartment in Stuyvesant Town, I was basically living at Ann's place.

Ann accompanied me on my trip to California. We spent two weeks from San Diego to San Francisco eating our faces off at the restaurants that were just starting to define what we now call "California cuisine." I was overwhelmed by the beauty and the space in the state; I still had visions of the Silverado Trail coming to fruition.

We met all sorts of characters on the West Coast. I was particularly excited to try Wolfgang Puck's food, especially because he had visited the Tavern on the Green. I couldn't wait to check out his new place in Los Angeles, Spago. There, I watched him move across the open kitchen with grace, wearing a baseball hat instead of a toque and draping thin-sliced smoked salmon across a wood-fired pizza, of all things. No one was doing stuff like this in New York. Here was a French-trained chef throwing out the conventions of fine dining and doing it his way. He looked like he was having fun.

The next day, we went to Santa Monica to visit Michael's, named after the young, tousled owner, Michael McCarty, who, in the middle of telling me I simply *must* go visit Hearst Castle, stepped aside to take a phone call from Julia Child. "Julia, baby!" he exclaimed exuberantly, like they were old friends.

Our last day was in San Francisco, we had plans for lunch at Sutter 500, which a colleague of mine had urged me to check out. "You've gotta check out this chef there named David Bouley," he said. "He's doing really incredible stuff." Bouley was American but had worked under masters like Roger Vergé, Joël Robuchon, and Frédy Girardet in France. My interest was piqued.

We arrived at the restaurant with tempered expectations— I wanted to get in and get out quickly and save my appetite for dinner at Campton Place, whose chef Bradley Ogden was greatly renowned. As soon as we sat down, David came out to greet us. I'll never forget that first meeting. He was young— around my age—tall and attractive, with a mop of curly dark hair and penetrating green eyes. Despite his good looks, there was something a little off about the way he presented himself— it was almost like he couldn't make direct eye contact, and he mumbled when he spoke, shifting his weight awkwardly from foot to foot.

He planned to prepare a special menu for us. Ann and I shot each other a look, but it was no use. Bouley had already disappeared into the kitchen, where he was clearly more comfortable. In short order, he sent out some of the best food we've ever had in our lives. His beautiful bass en barigoule, which is a classic stew of artichokes sautéed in olive oil with onions, carrots, tomatoes, and white wine, is burned into my brain forever. The fish was plated over the barigoule, and Bouley had folded in this vibrant fresh herb pistou at the last second. It was astonishing. His command of flavors and textures, even then, was next level—it was almost like he was speaking directly to the ingredients themselves, coaxing them to perform at their highest level.

We were so floored that I can't even remember the dinner we were so looking forward to that night. I didn't know exactly what to make of this talented and eccentric chef David Bouley, but I knew I wouldn't soon forget his cooking.

Back in New York, I felt it was time to get serious about turning the Silverado Trail into a reality. Freshly scorned by the Four Seasons and invigorated by the nascent California cuisine I'd tasted, I began browsing *The New York Times* Business Opportunities section on Sundays. Pretty soon, a three-line ad caught my eye: "1500 square feet, $1500/month, Lower Manhattan restaurant space," along with the address: 239 West Broadway.

Fifteen hundred dollars a month was a great deal—something even I might be able to afford. (To put things into perspective, commercial real estate in Manhattan now is closer to $150 per square foot.) West Broadway in Lower Manhattan was charming and had just started to pick up, a great location for a restaurant. A few buzzy spots had recently sprung up in the area, including Chanterelle and the Odeon, taking advantage of the low rents. I decided to jog down and check out the space.

I quickly realized that West Broadway is indeed charming as it cuts through SoHo on its way south to Grand Street, but there the appeal abruptly stops. One block south of Grand is Canal Street, the loud, gritty thoroughfare that bleeds into Chinatown and the Holland Tunnel. And somewhere below Canal Street is where this West Broadway address was, surrounded by... absolutely nothing. It was empty. I mean desolate. This was 1984, and TriBeCa had yet to become an actual neighborhood, let alone a desirable one.

I walked into the space, a former art gallery, and felt my heart sink. It was completely raw—no kitchen, no dining room, and no air conditioning. Everything would need to be built from scratch, and all that cost money. Plus, the neighborhood (or lack thereof) was a problem: There was no foot traffic, no built-in clientele. Even the address itself was confusing, wedged into this weird little corner of Lower Manhattan. The space went against everything I'd been taught at Cornell about opening a restaurant, where they'd preached: "Location, location, location."

But still, that price: $18,000 a year was within my extremely limited budget, and the handful of other restaurants nearby were gaining notice. I met with the landlord, John Matera, who had a canvas business a few blocks over on Lispenard Street. He was an older guy, gruff, but decent. The ten-year lease itself was short and sweet, maybe eight pages, with just a few notes hand-written along the margins.

A ten-year term is fairly standard, though most restaurants don't manage to stay open for that long. It's important to remember that the rent only goes one way from signing—up. So every year or two years or whatever the terms are, your rent will increase by 2, 3, or sometimes even 4 percent. That's a bad formula for restaurants, which are like the movies: They usually do most of their box office opening weekend, not months or years down the line. I don't know who created this system, but hats off to them—the landlord always wins.

Still, I was twenty-nine years old and had been working toward my own space for the better part of a decade. It felt like now or never.

I signed the lease.

I was still working at La Grenouille when I found the space, so I knew my days there were numbered. One night, I was serving a table of VIPs in the cream-colored dining room. They ordered a bottle of Louis Latour Montrachet, perhaps the greatest wine in the world. As I was pouring the wine, I felt something warm in my hand. I looked down and it was like the bottle was glowing, literally. I was either having an LSD flashback, or it was a sign from God. I looked at this wine and the thought came into my head: *Why are you trying to reinvent the wheel? Just open a French restaurant. But do it your way.*

"My way" would combine elements of everything I'd learned up to that point: The food, first and foremost, had to be amazing. The service did, too, but not in the pretentious, exclusionary style of the Le's and La's. The menu would be written in English, not French, and unlike most French restaurants, which made a sport out of gouging diners, I'd offer good value for the money.

I had eaten at Joël Robuchon's Jamin in Paris. The lunch prix fixe there was 185 francs, or the equivalent at the time of about $18.50. If no less than Joël Robuchon could price his menu at $18.50, I could do him one better: Mine would be a flat $16.00. And there would be a small but carefully considered (and equally affordable) wine list, with a then-unheard-of mix of French and California wines.

The West Broadway space, obviously, was far removed from the sophisticated trappings of the Upper East and West Sides. I resolved to strip away every pretense of fine dining—the snooty maître d' who metered out access to the "good" tables, the dress codes for guests, waiters in white jackets, the wildly inflated price tag. I saw myself as a director casting people in different roles. I knew I would need help with the accounting and paperwork, which were not my strong suits. I'd need servers who had experience but who weren't too steeped in the old system. And, of course, I needed an exceptional chef, someone with the vision to build something new and the talent to back it up. One name kept coming back to me: David Bouley, whose meal in San Francisco still haunted me.

I also needed more money. Sure, the rent on the space was cheap, but I had all of $50,000 to my name, and I'd need a lot more than that to install a kitchen, deal with permits and fees, buy the food and wine, and actually pay people to work for me. A million things can kill a restaurant. A *New York* magazine article that came out a few years before we opened said 65 percent of restaurants in the city failed in their first year. Those that did last a year rarely made it to five. The causes, the article said, were usually not enough start-up money, infighting among operators, and lack of experience. I had no money, but I staked my claim on plenty of experience. The infighting would come later.

The first person I approached about going into business together was Tony Zazula. He'd come a long way from his nerdy library days at Cornell and had demonstrated himself to be a confident, capable wingman at Tavern on the Green. Plus, he was better with behind-the-scenes admin work than me; he was meticulous with paperwork and accounting. I wanted to have a capable partner, like Tom Margittai and Paul Kovi at the Four Seasons. Tony agreed to match my $50,000 investment in exchange for equal ownership. We were partners.

My next influx of cash came from Michael Chin, whom I had worked with at 24 Fifth. He was a banquet manager, around the same age as me, and a very capable guy. One night, stepping off the Fifth Avenue bus, I saw him outside. I explained that I had found a space of my own and asked him to please keep me in mind if he knew of any potential investors. He immediately said, "I'll do it." I was shocked and grateful. Fifty thousand later, Michael, too, was a partner.

My father, a child of the Depression, didn't know the first thing about investments. He held on to the first dollar he'd ever made and wasn't about to spend it on my burgeoning scheme. At this point, Ann and I had been together for a few years, but I couldn't fathom getting married until I had made something of myself. So, though her family liked me well enough, they weren't about to put up any cash for a guy who wouldn't even propose to their daughter. That left my mother, Sybil, who had always told me to follow my dreams. She agreed to invest $25,000 of the money she had made in theater all those years ago. And we secured another $50,000 from the Small Business Association—which was a feat unto itself—bringing our grand total to $225,000.

This is, in the realm of restaurant budgets, chump change. These days you couldn't build a bathroom for that money. And I would never advise anyone with more than a bean for a brain to pour all their life savings into a venture as risky as a 1,500-square-foot affordable French restaurant in a misbegotten corner of Lower Manhattan. But this was what I had been working toward for my entire young life. I had everything to prove. I was equal parts confident and fearful and had no idea if I could really pull this off. But at least I had the name settled: Montrachet.

Bouley readily agreed to work with me. He was tired of California and ready to come back to the East Coast. We were both young with wild ambitions. I had been around the block and recognized that Bouley was a seriously talented chef, turning out plates that were on par with what I'd eaten in Europe and way beyond everything I was eating (or serving) in New York. With his food, I figured, we'd do fantastic.

At Ann's apartment, over Chinese takeout and cheap beer, we dreamed up menus and concepts. At first, Bouley wanted to name the restaurant after himself. This was before Daniel or Jean-Georges had their eponymous empires—the only restaurant named after a chef at the time was Joe's Pizza. I reasoned with David by telling him that if the restaurant was a flop, he'd never be able to use his name again. Eventually, he relented.

Bouley had an amazing vision for the menu. I enjoyed our brainstorming sessions, even if some of his ideas were a little out there. In the early eighties in New York, no one was talking about organic farming or local produce, which Bouley championed passionately. Other ideas were less successful: At one point, he commissioned a buddy of his to custom-build a rotisserie for the kitchen. He called me to see if I could receive a cord of firewood, which is about eight hundred logs. When we put two of the logs in to test the rotisserie, the kitchen filled with smoke because the exhaust fan wasn't strong enough. So many neighbors called the fire department that we quickly put the kibosh on the rotisserie idea.

I kept pushing Bouley to give me a draft of his menu, and he kept putting me off. After weeks of back-and-forthing, he finally showed me what he'd been working on; it was riddled with typos and grammatical errors. But the dishes themselves were compelling. Squab stuffed with foie gras painstakingly rolled in cabbage and braised until it was so tender it almost fell apart. A cold lobster salad plated with several dots of herb pistou. I had seen similar dishes on my travels in Europe—the lobster dish, for example, is a Joël Robuchon signature—but no one, and I mean no one, was cooking like this in New York.

One night, after a marathon session with Bouley in our little studio apartment on 9th Street, Ann looked at me wearily. "You're going to have a hard time dealing with this guy," she said.

"What are you talking about?" I asked.

"He's difficult," she replied. "You can't control him."

I brushed her off. He had his eccentricities, to be sure, but I was so focused on the food that I saw no cause for alarm. As usual, however, Ann's predictions would prove true.

In the meantime, construction on the space had started. The original lease of 1,500 square feet could seat about sixty people. A few weeks later, an adjacent woodworking shop became available for lease. I pounced on it. This enabled us to have three distinct dining rooms, though the layout was awkward. There was no basement to prep or store food, so everything had to be designed to be self-contained. The architect I hired, Paul Dennis, assured me that he would build a restaurant just as beautiful as, if not more than, La Grenouille. This was a tall order considering how raw the space was, but Dennis drafted a plan that made me believe it could be done.

There was some drama with the original contractor, a hard-drinking Irishman named Bill Pittman I knew as a sort of jack-of-all-trades from my Tavern on the Green days. It's the nature of the beast for a contractor to hire subcontractors like plumbers and electricians and to pass on the cost, but one day, Bill left his invoices on the table. I looked at his numbers and realized the guy was completely ripping us off. My partner Tony, never great at confrontation, asked me to do the dirty work of firing Bill, who immediately threatened to sue us. That never came to pass, and in typical keeping-it-in-the-family fashion, to finish the job I wound up hiring another builder I knew from the Tavern named John Gaul. John was an honest guy who managed to pick up the pieces, proof that there are some good people in what can be a very dirty business.

All kinds of hidden expenses and unexpected delays can arise when you're building out a restaurant, but amazingly, Montrachet proceeded without too many hitches. Our plans were approved by the Buildings Department and our food-handling and sanitation permits were all in order. My father, though he had retired a few years prior, was able to call in a favor at the State Liquor Authority to help move our license along, an enormous help that probably saved us months of administrative headaches. We did have some trouble with ConEd refusing to turn on our gas until the last possible second, without which we couldn't cook a thing, but I've since learned that that's normal, nothing special.

I can be a little neurotic about things I don't know how to do. The food I understood. Contracting, less so. I used to sit with John at the Square Diner and over countless ham-and-egg sandwiches hammer him for details about the construction. I wanted to know how everything worked, and I wanted every-thing to be built perfectly. I became obsessed with banquettes and spent hours picking out the right mohair fabric for them, insisting that they be built with springs, the right way, not just filled with stuffing. John humored me, though I suspect he wished I'd back off and let him do his job.

We went to a liquidation auction at a shuttered restaurant in Yonkers called Cooky's Steak Pub to see what they had. It was a wild scene—freezing cold, no heat inside, the terrible smell of vermin because the place had been closed for months and the landlords had left it untouched. The guttural auctioneer gamely raffled off everything that wasn't nailed down, from glasses to silverware to tabletops, at a tenth of their normal price. I was bundled up in my long green army coat, scarf wrapped around my neck, and I fell in love with the sturdy tabletops that were going for five dollars apiece. John teased me for measuring and remeasuring them a thousand times, but there was a method to my madness.

If you want to maximize the seating arrangement, especially with deuces, you need tabletops that measure, ideally, 26 by 30 inches. You can maybe get away with 24 inches if you're really cutting it tight, or 30 by 30 if you want the flexibility of making it into a three-top, but 26 by 30 is a perfect deuce. Cooky's Steak

Pub had dozens of tables exactly that size. When I got them back to Montrachet, I discovered hundreds of pieces of chewed gum stuck to their bottoms and spent hours razor-blading them off.

I had almost no money to play around with, but I desperately wanted a beautiful table setting on those tabletops. I scraped together enough to buy Christofle silverware from France and Hutschenreuther plates from Germany. By the time the buildout was done, there wasn't a budget for artwork or other decorative touches. The press would label us "minimalist chic," but the reality was, we couldn't afford any extra flourishes.

As we inched closer to opening, Bouley auditioned cooks for his kitchen, and I set about making front-of-house hires. Having worked just about every role on the service side, I had some intuition for who would make a good waiter. It's hard to describe, but sometimes you can just sense empathy in a person. And knowing our shoestring budget, I was also looking for staff who weren't afraid to jump in and get their hands dirty. This was not going to be the highly codified world of French waiters and captains—I needed people who would see a napkin on the floor and bend down to pick it up, no matter their official title.

It wasn't difficult to find staff; I had a deep Rolodex from my stints at Maxwell's and Tavern, downtown Manhattan was cool, and I was promising a different kind of work environment from the staid uptown old guards. I wanted service to be smooth and professional, yes, but also approachable—the goal was to impress diners without intimidating them. Most of my hires were around my age, meaning the front and back of the house were infused with a youthful energy. Instead of the traditional white shirt and black pants that had been the unofficial waiter uniform for decades, I outfitted everyone in simple black shirts and black pants, a minimalist downtown uniform to match our minimalist downtown space.

All the busboys were guys I knew from Tavern, easily lured by the promise of better pay. (Always be good to the busboys!) A young, ambitious Cornell grad named Jennifer Schiff, who had followed me like a puppy from Tavern to 24 Fifth, took no convincing whatsoever. Daniel Johnnes, the Francophile and burgeoning wine whiz, wanted out of the uptown scene and his hotel job. I hired everyone at the same level and split their pay (including tips) equally—another decision that went against the norm, but one that I felt was more democratic to a staff who were all-hands-on-deck.

However, I kept in my back pocket one seasoned waiter no one knew. Ciro Santoro was Italian by birth but had spent most of his career working as a server in fine restaurants in Paris. He spoke fluent French, slicked his dark hair back with a comb, and moved with the grace of a ballerina. About a year before I opened Montrachet, Ciro had been my waiter at Le Pré Catelan in Paris. I was so impressed with his effortless service that I gave him my card and told him to call me if he ever found himself in New York. Much to my surprise, a few months later, I got a call: "Hello, it's me, Ciro. I am in New York and I need a place to stay." In short order, I gave this suave Italian man the keys to my apartment and the promise of a job when Montrachet opened.

Once the team was hired, I drilled home a few points during training. You're entitled to bread and water even if you're in prison, I'd say, so get both those things (complimentary, of course) onto the table as soon as the guest sits down. Make sure the water glasses stay full, and the wine glasses, too, but don't pour more than three ounces of wine at once, lest you run out (a standard wine bottle holds around twenty-five ounces, or enough for a four-top to each comfortably get two glasses). Most importantly: Take the order. The only way to make the numbers work for a restaurant in New York City is to get *at least* two seatings per night. Table turnover is crucial. If you book a table for 6:00 p.m., you have to get it back at 8:30. Book at 7:00, time's up at 9:30. Every minute a guest hems and haws between the chicken and the fish is precious money slipping away. Take the goddamn order—politely, of course.

I was spending my nights working at La Grenouille and my days downtown putting the finishing touches on Montrachet. I started bringing my tuxedo down to West Broadway with me because La Grenouille was a straight shot uptown on the E Train from Tribeca. One afternoon, I got a call from a cocaptain at La Grenouille. In a panicked whisper, he told me that Bryan Miller, who had recently succeeded Mimi Sheraton as the restaurant critic at *The New York Times*, had come in for lunch. I asked how they knew it was him—anonymity for critics was a huge deal, and though restaurateurs were always on the lookout, few among them could make a positive ID. Critics made reservations under fake names, paid with bogus cards, and occasionally went so far as to disguise themselves with wigs or glasses. Miller was brand-new to the job, making his appearance and dining habits especially unknown.

"We didn't," my coworker explained. "But he came in with Pierre Franey, who we did recognize." Pierre Franey was a French chef and frequent collaborator of the *Times*'s most distinguished food editor and critic, Craig Claiborne. Miller might be new to the job, but Franey was an old hand and wielded enormous influence over the section, even if he wasn't technically the one writing the review. "Where did you seat them?" I asked. *Table 102.* I winced. Table 102 was one of the worst seats in the house, all the way in the back. The pervasive attitude— especially at power-dining restaurants like La Grenouille—was that where you sat was just as, if not more, important than what you ate. It was all about the mood, not the food.

I was perplexed about this choice of seating, but it was too late for me to do anything about it. "What name was the reservation under?" I asked. *Benson.* Knowing that critics make three visits to a restaurant before filing their review, I told him to call me immediately if he ever got Benson on the reservation sheet again.

A few weeks later, I was downtown when the call came. "Drew—we have Benson coming in for lunch." I changed into my tuxedo as fast as I could and jumped on the subway. I wasn't scheduled to work that day, so the staff was surprised to see me rush in after lunch service had started.

I brushed their murmurs aside and stationed myself along one side of the dining room, where I could clearly see "Benson," tall and thin, sitting on a banquette with a young woman. I studied his every move, committing his face to memory, but I also had a tiny little camera stashed in my pocket. As his meal came to a close, I followed him outside—from a distance, of course—and trailed him for about ten blocks, hiding between parked cars, crouching down to try to get a clear picture of the most wanted man in restaurants. When I got the film developed, I saw that I had managed to snap about twenty photos of the back of Bryan Miller's head. Not one single clear shot. But it didn't matter—I would never forget the face of the man who controlled my destiny.

Montrachet officially opened on April 15, 1985. Our first night, we did thirty-seven covers. That's nothing to brag about. It was mostly friends and family. My parents came—my dad shuffling on his cane, my mother radiant, surrounded by her theater friends. Ann's parents, too, some of Tony's and my old Cornell cronies, and a ragtag collection of industry friends who had heard me boast about opening my own place for years.

Night two, we were down to eighteen covers, and I was convinced we were done for. But within a week or two, word of mouth traveled, and we were starting to fill out to a healthier fifty or sixty covers a night. Some regular customers from Tavern and the Le's and La's were curious about what exactly I was doing all the way downtown. I was proud to have built a following, and I did everything in my power to make sure they had a good enough time to come back.

It's every ambitious restaurateur's dream to be reviewed by *The New York Times*, but you have to wait for the critic to come to you. I sent a letter to Pierre Franey, a sort of proto press release outlining Bouley's experience (and mine). "Our objective at Montrachet is to create an intimate restaurant . . . serving the high cuisine we have always been associated with," it read. "We hope to synergize our experiences and energies by offering a repertoire of original dishes and an intelligently chosen and fairly priced wine card." I thought that Franey, having the ear of the critic, might plant the seed that we deserved coverage.

Artists and designers from nearby SoHo, such as Geoffrey Beene and Willi Smith, started trickling in with their friends. Joel Dean, who a few years earlier had founded the trailblazing grocery store Dean & DeLuca a few blocks up, was an early fan. Regular Joe Schmos looking for a hot meal came in, too— that's the beauty of having a sixteen-dollar menu.

The food, right out of the gate, was extraordinary. The opening menu had a version of that same impeccable bass en barigoule I had fallen for in San Francisco, a smoky eggplant and red pepper terrine, and boneless chicken thighs stuffed with fried sweetbreads in a delicate parsley sauce. Bouley was in charge of the kitchen, but I was always poking my head in, much to his annoyance. Most restaurant owners steer clear of the kitchen except when absolutely necessary, but I would check on the cook's mise en place, ask questions about the dishes, and taste everything. Some might call it micromanaging, but to me, the food has always been the most important thing, and I wanted to make sure it was up to my standards. Does this piss chefs off? Absolutely. Has it come around to bite me in the ass? Perhaps. So what, though? It needs to be done.

As we inched up in covers, I noticed a little slowdown on the kitchen side. People were waiting a beat too long between courses. I like my food to come out boom, boom, boom. Guests are fed, tables are turned, rinse and repeat. I couldn't figure out the source of the delay. I had worked on cruise ships and at Tavern on the Green—massive operations that efficiently cranked out a thousand meals a night. Surely our ninety-seat restaurant couldn't be that hard to keep up with?

I went back to the kitchen to see what was up. The first course—often a salad or cold dish—came out in a timely fashion, thanks to the garde-manger who assembled it. But then... nothing. Bouley wasn't firing the entrées until the waiters had completely cleared the appetizers from the tables. He wanted to see whether they had finished everything. And if they hadn't, he would ask why they didn't lick the plate clean.

After appetizers, the next course takes fifteen to twenty minutes to cook, then it needs to be plated, then that plate needs to be married with all the other plates going out at the same time. Now the table has been sitting for half an hour, guests shifting uncomfortably in their seats, waiting for more food to arrive, while the orders pile up in the kitchen. It's like a highway during rush hour—everyone is stuck in place and increasingly pissed off about it.

I was concerned, but I didn't make a big fuss. Bouley's food was still fantastic when it did manage to come out, and I was running the front of the house, juggling reservations and working the door. At the time, we had no online database of guests. The database was my brain, and my brain was working overtime as more and more people sought us out.

When you're taking reservations by hand, as we did back then, there are a million ways to fuck it up. You can put it on the wrong day, at the wrong time, with the wrong party size. There was no real way to check the veracity of someone's reservation, and people often tried to take advantage of the system. So I stationed myself at the door, screening the customers and tracking their every move. We had one guy who would sit only at table three; if it wasn't available on a given night, he'd simply reschedule. I took notes on everyone, filing away wine preferences and anniversary dates. I kept all this information inside of my head while simultaneously running the floor and occasionally checking in on the kitchen.

The first few weeks were a blur; I was operating on pure adrenaline. I missed one service in one hundred, for a wedding, and swore it would never happen again. Sure, it was a lot of work, but it was my work, my way, just how I liked it.

And if I thought it would get any easier, less than two months in, I was proved wrong. Very, very wrong.

Chapter 6

The Review
(and Its Aftermath)

We'd been open for about a month, and I was making my usual preservice rounds when the phone rang. I always answered.

"Hello," said the caller. "I'd like to come in on Thursday for two at eight o'clock."

I looked at my reservation sheet. No dice. "I'm sorry," I said. "I can only take you early, at six or six-fifteen."

There was a pause, and then, "Okay, I'll take it."

"Great," I replied. "What's the name?"

"Benson."

My blood ran cold. There was only one Benson in this town.

"Could you hold on for just a moment?" I sputtered. I held the phone away and counted to five. With a deep breath, I went back to the line: "Actually, sir, we've just had a cancelation at eight. Looking forward to seeing you."

Click.

And with that, the critic who held my fate in his hands was booked.

Now, there are various schools of thought on how to treat a critic. Some places really overdo it. Some kitchens make two of every dish during their review period just in case the first one isn't perfect. I think that's bullshit. If you get the staff too amped up, they'll fuss over every little thing. It's better to do things right from the beginning, so you can just be yourself. A critic wants to be anonymous, so let them.

Of course, I wanted to make a good impression, but there's only so much you can do on short notice. You can't transform into a new restaurant overnight. Despite my concerns about Bouley's pacing, I felt confident about his food. It was cutting-edge and fantastic, beautiful and complex, and not too fussy. A young Bill Yosses, who later became the pastry chef at the White House, was on dessert duty, and even back then his creations were impeccable. I don't know what was going through Bouley's head in the days leading up to Miller's reservation, but I don't recall going overboard to prepare—we had as much as we could dialed in; everyone knew how much was on the line.

I did, however, strategically book the room on the night of Miller's first visit. He had a deuce, so I seated him and his date on the banquette, flanked by (unbeknownst to him) my mother on one side and Ann on the other. I seated a few other trusted confidants nearby. The idea was to surround him with friends who could alternately rave about their meals within spitting distance and eavesdrop on what he was saying. Ciro was their waiter. Ciro specialized in swift, gracious service, and I knew he wouldn't overstay his welcome. I kept my eye on the proceedings from across the room, not wanting to be noticed.

Mid-course, Miller and his wife, an elegant Frenchwoman, stepped outside for a cigarette. I snuck over to my mother. "What are they saying?" I asked, desperate for intel.

"It's the damnedest thing," she replied. "They're speaking all in French." My seating plan was rendered useless.

Over the course of his three visits, Miller wasn't particularly savvy about changing his fake name, so we knew each time "Benson" reappeared.

I wasn't sure how many stars to expect. I knew four was out of the question—that's rarefied air, reserved for only the finest of fine-dining temples. Montrachet was never built for four, and I didn't want it, anyway, because there's only one way you can go from the top. I was hoping to avoid one star, which can sink a restaurant, but I would have been happy with two. I thought we were serving three-star food, but with our stripped-down environs, bargain pricing, and lack of dress code, I wasn't expecting *The New York Times* to group us with the three-star Le's and La's.

The week before the review came out, Miller called Bouley to fact-check, so we knew judgment was imminent. At the time, restaurant reviews were published on Fridays, meaning the paper was printed on Thursday nights. That Thursday, after the last diners had left the restaurant, Bouley and I took the subway together up to the *Times* office on the West Side. We were both quiet on the ride up, nerves jittery. The freshly printed papers in those days were delivered to the lobby around 10:00 p.m., and we paced anxiously in front of the building.

The papers hit the stand. I tore through the pages, still warm off the press, heart pounding. David was pawing through his own copy, brows furrowed. I whipped to the food section. There, the headline: "New and French in Lower Manhattan." And printed in a breakout box beneath our name and address (with the note "It's advisable to ask directions if driving"), three black stars.

Restaurants | Bryan Miller

New and French in Lower Manhattan

AFFORDABLE French restaurants are as rare as air-conditioned subway cars these days. And when you find one that is as charming and enterprising as Montrachet, a seven-week-old venture in TriBeCa, there is ample reason to celebrate.

Montrachet is a handsome, low-key place housed in one of those high-ceilinged former downtown industrial spaces. It has been tastefully redone with a polished mahogany-and-onyx bar, pale green walls, pinkish-rust banquettes and soothing lighting. David Bouley, the 32-year-old chef, has put in time at some of Europe's most renowned restaurants as well as at Le Cirque and

Le Périgord in New York. He does not tread any particular culinary trail; his repertory is diverse, personal and well-conceived. One evening you can enjoy a homespun French dish of braised cabbage rolls stuffed with foie gras and squab meat and flanked by squab legs. Another time it could be an au courant preparation such as red snapper with tomato-coriander sauce and fresh pasta.

Appetizers fall in the $4-to-$10 range, while entrées average about $15. One of the better deals in town has to be the $16 prix fixe dinner, which includes a deliciously smoky eggplant and roasted red pepper terrine, savory roast duck flanked by wild mushrooms, leeks and pearl onions in a heady red wine sauce tinged with cinnamon, and a first-rate crème brûlée.

If you prefer à la carte, a highly recommended appetizer is boneless chicken thighs stuffed with sweetbreads. The sweetbreads are firm, succulent and perfectly cooked, and the refined Italian parsley sauce is a wonderful foil. Other good bets are the moist and gamy duck terrine on a bed of mâche salad, and the assortment of smoked and fresh fish: cured sturgeon, delicate raw marinated salmon, and buttery smoked salmon wrapped around a creamy mousseline of sevruga caviar. Tasty little cornmeal madeleines were an unusual and satisfying foil to the sautéed fresh duck liver.

One of the few starters that fell flat was the chunks of rich lobster meat in an even richer crème fraîche sauce punctuated with tiny balls of apple and tomato. It was a lovely tableau; so are butter sculptures, but I wouldn't want to eat one. It also lacked seasonings. The only soup sampled sounded far better than it tasted: littleneck clams with saffron, artichokes and celeryroot. Once again, it was overly rich—and clamless. The bib lettuce, watercress and endive salad was spoiled one evening by acrid, burned morsels of garlic.

At 95 percent of the restaurants I visit, bread is not worth writing about; most of it comes from the same three or four commercial sources. Montrachet's bread, which also comes from the outside, is exceptional—thick-crusted, earthy and with a little crunchy "lid" giving it the appearance of a tiny soup terrine.

The intelligent and generally moderately priced wine list has something for everyone and complements the food nicely. Among whites, some of the best selections for the money are the fresh and delicate 1983 Semillon from Clos du Val ($15), the lush and fruity 1981 Sonoma-Cutrer Chardonnay ($22), and the equally pleasing bargain-priced 1982 Silverado Chardonnay ($19). Good red choices are a Fixin ($16), a 1982 Georges Duboeuf Fleurie ($18) and the 1982 Ridge Zinfandel (Paso Robles, $18). Drew Nieporent, the owner, a former captain at La Grenouille, Le Périgord and other French restaurants in town, is both a highly personable host and accommodating sommelier. His waiters scurry around the room in black shirts, pants and ties looking like a team of cat burglars, but they provide prompt, professional service.

Chef Bouley does not try to overwhelm guests with an encyclopedic menu. His card carries about 10 items and a few daily specials. A standout on the permanent roster is the red snapper, in which the fillet is skillfully broiled until the skin is parchment crisp and the meat moist and flaky. It is presented atop the zesty but not overpowering coriander-tomato sauce and garnished with baby carrots, asparagus and crackly deep-fried parsley. A small portion of al dente spaghetti in a fragrant pesto sauce rounds out the dish.

Another winning seafood selection is sea bass "en barigoule." The meaty fillet is poached in broth and served

with slivers of fresh artichoke, asparagus, mushrooms, carrots and herbs in
a clear white wine sauce. An individual
rack of lamb—two chops and a small
loin steak—is cooked to rosy succu-
lence, enhanced by a lustrous stock
and port wine sauce. One is tempted to
say that this dish, accompanied by buttery mashed potatoes, is as soothing as
the one mother used to make, except
mother never diced the zucchini with
tomatoes and placed them in puff pastry as a side dish. Veal steak with baked
garlic cloves and a Rhone wine sauce
was chewy on one occasion, tender and
flavorful the next. Whatever Mr. Bouley prepares, it is always colorfully presented. The veal came with a palette
of green sugar snap peas, glistening
sautéed spinach and an orange cloud
of delicious carrot purée.

Desserts maintain the kitchen's high
standards. The most extravagant is
the combination of two hot soufflés—
raspberry and pear with chocolate—
inflated disks bursting with fruit
essence, dusted with sugar and draped
in fresh strawberry sauce. As if that
is not enough, you are given a ball
of superb vanilla sorbet as a cooler.
Crème brûlée is the real thing, with a
glassy caramelized crust enclosing a
dense, eggy custard. A slice of layered
hazelnut ice cream topped with Grand
Marnier truffles and a coffee sauce is
beyond resistance. A tarte tatin of pear
and apple, with a thin, buttery crust
and caramel sauce, melts in the mouth.

If you are too impatient to let it cool,
Calvados sorbet comes to the rescue.

Montrachet, with its alluring food,
relaxed atmosphere and reasonable
prices, is destined to be one of the most
popular spots in this up-and-coming
part of town.

Montrachet

239 West Broadway, 219-2777 (It's
advisable to ask directions if driving.)

Atmosphere: Casually elegant dining
room with soft lighting and rust-
pink banquettes.

Service: Friendly and efficient.

Recommended dishes: Boned chicken
thighs stuffed with sweetbreads,
duck terrine, assorted smoked
and fresh fish with caviar mousseline, fresh foie gras, sea bass "en
barigoule," squab with braised cabbage rolls, snapper with tomato-
coriander sauce, rack of lamb, veal
steak with baked garlic cloves, hot
raspberry souffle and chocolate pear
souffle, crème brûlée, hazelnut ice
cream, pear and apple tatin.

Price range: Appetizers $4 to $10;
entrées $12 to $17 (prix fixe meals,
$16 and $26).

Credit cards: American Express.

Hours: Dinner only, though there are
plans to open for lunch soon. Dinner Tuesday through Sunday, 6 to
11:30 P.M. Reservations: Suggested.

It's hard for me to recall exactly what I said or did in that moment. I was stunned. I think I bought every copy of the paper in the place and brought them back down to the restaurant, where my staff was nervously awaiting their fate. Bouley and I must have hugged, but I really don't know. Champagne was probably popped. I'm sure I looked elated; what I remember most was feeling terrified.

Why? Think about it. Most people have to work a lifetime for that kind of recognition. I got it right away. I knew, even in that celebratory moment, that the real work started *now*. From that point onward, I would spend every waking moment trying to live up to my three-star rating. I felt like the heavyweight champion of the world—and when you're on top, there's always someone fighting to knock off your crown.

The effect of the *Times* review was immediate. Suddenly, everyone in New York City wanted—no, *needed*—a table at eight o'clock, and they were willing to beg, borrow, and steal to get one. When I say the phones never stopped ringing, I mean it. The *buzz-buzz* haunted me in my sleep. It escalated to the point where I had to set up a recorded message because I couldn't answer all the calls at night. "Thank you for calling Montrachet, it's five o'clock and we have to go to work now. Please make your future reservations between 10:00 a.m. and 5:00 p.m. when we are able to assist you." It was nonstop, full-on, every night, no time for questions.

I could have sold out Shea Stadium, that's how many people wanted to come in. We opened the unfinished third dining room in the back, which featured a glamorous wall-mounted

AC unit that dripped on the floor. There was no shortage of customers, but I was determined to hold back. There's an art to not overbooking, even at the hottest restaurant in town. Stacking reservations too tightly led to chaos in the kitchen and hungry, pissed-off guests. Even though every person we turned away meant less revenue, I kept tables evenly paced, aiming for two solid turns a night. This, theoretically, gave the kitchen enough time to cook, the servers enough time to serve, and the guests enough time to enjoy their meal and decide to come back.

Theoretically.

In reality, problems escalated in the kitchen. Put simply, Bouley couldn't get the food out. What had started as a slight delay between courses had blossomed into a full-on shitshow. Following the review, Bouley grew exponentially fussy with his food, and guests were now waiting a half hour to an hour between each course. The three-course meal could take three hours, and diners were not happy about it. Neither was I—more people than ever wanted to come in, but service wasn't running the way it should.

I felt enormous pressure to keep operations running smoothly, but Bouley was making it impossible. Our reputation was on the line, along with the very real financial need to turn tables. Bouley knew how crucial that second seating was to our ability to keep the lights on, but that didn't seem to bother him. He was the master of his domain but forgot that his domain was one part of a larger organism.

I remember when he took the whole kitchen staff out for a celebratory lunch at Lutèce following the review. Every table at Montrachet was booked that night. Didn't matter to Bouley. His lunch with the cooks went so long that no one even showed up to start prep work until 5:00 p.m., well lubricated from all the wine at lunch. There was nothing I could do about it. He was their boss, and what the boss says goes.

Meanwhile, our reputation just continued to grow. Seemingly, everybody wanted a piece of Montrachet. One night, Michael Tong, the owner of Shun Lee Palace and a frequent customer, called me and said that Craig Claiborne, the influential *New York Times* food writer, was in the hospital. Michael was asking his restaurant friends to deliver some meals and asked if Bouley and I were up for it. We were, and we set about devising a special menu.

The night of the delivery, it snowed so hard that we closed the restaurant. Closing was unheard of, but we knew no one would be making it in that night.

Bouley and I had both gotten to the restaurant early, however, so we decided to stick with our plan to feed Craig Claiborne. We arranged a meal on a beautiful tray with our Christofle silverware and Hutschenreuther plateware and wrapped the whole thing in plastic. I somehow managed to get a cab to take me all the way up to the hospital on York Avenue on the Upper East Side and maneuvered myself over snowdrifts with the oversized platter in hand.

When I got to his room, Claiborne was lying in his bed, glasses on his nose, reading. He barely acknowledged me but motioned for me to enter and pointed at a little countertop where I could put the tray down. We had maybe two minutes of small talk—he was polite, and thanked me for the delivery, but clearly was not up for schmoozing.

I left his room and was waiting for the elevator, thinking about how the hell I was going to make it back downtown in this snowstorm, when Craig shuffled out of his room with the tray in his hands and signaled to a nurse. He handed her the tray and said in his deep southern drawl, "Can you take this? I can't eat this shit."

So much for his beautiful three-star meal, hand-delivered in a blizzard. I was crestfallen, but bigger concerns were brewing back at the restaurant.

Tensions between Bouley and I were coming to a head. The way I saw it, we had achieved the seemingly unachievable *together*. Two young men, early in their careers, earning three stars from *The New York Times*. I loved Bouley's food and believed in it. I'd given him a stage where his talents could shine. But he didn't seem committed to ensuring Montrachet remained successful and earned its stars. In fact, it seemed like what he really wanted was to take our three stars, put them in his pocket, and move across the street.

People sometimes ask if we tried to work things out. But talking to Bouley was a nonstarter. Like me, he was proud and convinced of his own superiority. During service, when temperatures and tempers flared, he would look at me with those piercing green eyes, with an expression that said, *Are you a fucking idiot? Do you think I don't know how to cook?* You couldn't say anything to him, especially after the review had lavished praise on his culinary skills. He never came to me to discuss things, either; we grew more and more estranged by the day.

I started hearing through the grapevine that Bouley was entertaining other offers. When a chef earns three stars at a restaurant they don't own, there's always someone trying to poach them. Investors and real estate bigwigs start sniffing around, offering them something bigger and better. It's flattering for their ego. But being skilled in the kitchen is not the same as being skilled at managing a restaurant. I'm not saying there aren't good chef-owners. But I am saying that if you can't get the food out of the kitchen in a restaurant the size of Montrachet, chances are that other operational issues will follow.

The rumors only fueled my resentment further. I felt like Bouley was trying to claim everything we'd worked for together as his own, cutting me out of the picture entirely. He couldn't share the spotlight. One night a few months after the review, a group of my friends were eating at the restaurant. Bouley came out of the kitchen and sat down at the table next to them, where they could clearly overhear him discussing funding a new deal with someone. My buddy tipped me off to the conversation, and I watched the whole thing play out right in my own dining room.

I went into the kitchen and grabbed Ray Bradley, the sous chef at the time and a close friend of David's. I had a feeling a confrontation was brewing, and I wanted David's cooks to see what he was doing with their own two eyes. I pointed to the table where Bouley was sitting and said, "Ray, I just want you to know that, if anything ever happens here, that's the reason why." I felt totally disrespected. Bouley didn't even take it outside!

All I can compare it to is the feeling of finding out your partner is cheating. Even if you know that things haven't been going well, it's still a punch to the gut. My pride was wounded, and I couldn't understand why Bouley was so desperate to get out. We may not have been getting along, but I felt like we had built an incredible business, and we were blowing it—the success of the place was going to be its demise. It broke my heart.

For as far back as I can remember, I've had a righteous streak. My parents taught me that there's a right way to do things, and the politics of my generation instilled a willingness to fight for those things. Muhammad Ali, my role model, was outspoken about his beliefs. My indignation had flared at Cornell when I felt my professors weren't doing their jobs, and again at the Le's and La's when the European staff tried to sabotage me. Seeing Bouley double-dealing at Montrachet, with everything on the line, I was hot with resentment.

The personal tensions were one thing—I probably could have sucked it up if the restaurant itself was running smoothly. But what really upset me was that we were suffering because of Bouley's selfishness. The waiters were exasperated, the guests were being neglected. His ego was going to hurt the business, and that was the one thing I couldn't stand. Montrachet was the culmination of everything I had ever worked toward, and though Bouley was integral to its initial success, he was also at risk of causing it to fail. It felt like a question of life or death.

I had no choice. I had to kill the goose that laid the golden egg.

———

As an operator, I'm inherently risk averse. I don't care if my restaurant doesn't make money, but I do not like to *lose* money. So I always have a plan before making any major decisions, such as replacing my head chef.

I wanted zero lag time between firing Bouley and installing someone new in the kitchen. So, a few months earlier, I had begun quietly putting out feelers to a small circle that I was interested in meeting new chefs. I wasn't looking to revolution-ize the menu—I felt I understood Bouley's food and wanted someone who could capture its essence and its quality, minus the drama. Someone who could keep the ship upright. I wasn't so much looking for a three-star chef as I was looking for a friend, someone trustworthy.

My answer came in the form of Brian Whitmer, a tall, laconic chef I knew from our mutual stints at Tavern on the Green. Brian was a Kansas boy trying to make it in the big city and a hard worker by nature. He understood the assignment and had confidence in his ability. I trusted him to execute.

But getting him on board only solved part of the problem. I needed someone who could hit the ground running, and that meant training somewhere for at least a few weeks beforehand. Once Bouley was out, much of the kitchen staff would go with him. And I couldn't afford to shut down for a few weeks while we staffed up, nor did I want the guests to suffer while we mud-dled through a wonky transitional period. The whole point of going out to a restaurant is to be taken care of—not to be some kind of guinea pig while the staff gets its act together.

I quietly asked my friend Charlie Palmer, the chef at the River Café in Brooklyn, to let us use his kitchen as a secret train-ing compound for Montrachet's new staff. It was a big ask, but Charlie and I had a wonderful friendship and a mutual respect for one another's work, so he agreed. It was a tremendous leap of faith on his part, for which I am eternally grateful.

I secretly met with Brian for weeks to develop a new menu that he would practice in the River Café under lock and key. The plan was somewhat insane, but I had enough hubris—and enough on the line —to believe that it would work.

I called Bouley in for a meeting at the New York Athletic Club on a Sunday, when the restaurant was closed. The night before, I had rented a van and packed everything he had at the restaurant into it. At our meeting the next morning, I told David that things weren't working out and that he would no longer be the chef at Montrachet. He was surprised, even though we both knew he'd been planning his own departure. I didn't want to linger—I told the chef that all his things were waiting for him in a van outside the restaurant.

Bouley didn't take that well. He shot downtown and burst into the restaurant during prep, only to find an entirely new staff installed in the kitchen, happily chopping away. Needless to say, he flipped out. He couldn't believe I'd engineered a complete kitchen swap without him knowing. I could barely believe it myself.

The front of house had my back. They were the ones who had suffered the most because of Bouley's antics—the ones on the front lines, dealing with angry customers. They tried to ply guests with more bread and water, but carbs can only get you so far. I recall the mood at our first post-Bouley service meeting as relieved. The faces in the kitchen (except for one person who stayed) were all new, and everyone just wanted to get back to business as usual.

When we opened for service that night, I intercepted a regular, Penny Trenk, as she was walking toward the kitchen. "Is everything alright?" I asked. "Oh yes, I just wanted to thank David for an exceptional meal tonight," she said. I told her he had the night off for his birthday. "Please pass the message along!" she chirped. "It really was the best meal I've ever had!"

Chapter 7

After the Storm

Montrachet earning three stars so early on was like winning the lottery without being able to collect the cash. Sure, Bouley was gone, but now, I had to defend those three stars with all my might. Now the real work began.

Brian was a capable chef, though he lacked the European training of his predecessor and had a less precise approach. His mise en place was often a mess, changing every day, and he struggled in the swampy heat of the un-air-conditioned kitchen. I wasn't too worried, because we had a strong team of sous chefs to back him up, and most importantly, he was willing to listen to me. Finally, with the kitchen stabilizing, I began to feel like I was getting my restaurant back.

But even with things returning to baseline, it wasn't like I could sit back and relax. As a restaurateur, I woke up every day wondering what would go wrong. And beyond the usual day-to-day headaches at the restaurant itself (clogged grease traps, a chef passing out from heat stroke, deliveries running late, etc.),

I knew that Bouley was cooking up something of his own. It didn't take long for my recently departed chef to announce his grand plan: a flagship restaurant, named (of course) after himself, just a few blocks away from Montrachet.

New York magazine had a fall preview issue with this full-page photo of a smirking Bouley in front of a huge wooden chest overflowing with glistening live lobsters and whole fish. The article said his food would be "like his food at Montrachet, only now he will have a freer hand to create more dishes." It made me want to scream. It was reported that he'd be flying in his fish daily to Tribeca. My question was, Where were they going to land the fucking plane?

To rub salt in the wound, Bouley had taken several former Montrachet staffers with him: a half dozen cooks, which was to be expected, but more crushingly, he also took Ciro. Ciro, whom I had given an apartment and a job when he landed in New York and whose dignified demeanor helped service flow night after night at Montrachet. I had heard rumors he might have been going with Bouley, but he didn't have the balls to tell me to my face. One night, after service, he and I took a long walk through Tribeca. We sat down on a park bench in front of the space where the new Bouley restaurant would be.

"Ciro, life is about forks in the road," I said. "You have to make a decision—are you going to go work for that guy, or are you going to stick with me?"

Head in his hands, he started weeping and thanked me for all I'd done for him. But he had made his decision. After that, I lost touch with him, though I later heard he'd been fired. Losing Ciro to Bouley stung, but that wasn't the first time or the last that I'd feel betrayed by one of my own.

When Bouley (the restaurant) opened in the fall of 1986, anticipation was high. The space he had leased on Duane Street was stunning, with vaulted ceilings, antique furniture from France, and a lush terrace out front. The press ate it up. When the Zagat survey came out that year, Montrachet's review referenced Bouley's departure and said "see Bouley."

I was livid and called Tim Zagat directly. "You're telling people to go to Bouley in *my* paragraph!" I screamed. I wanted Montrachet's review to stand on its own.

Tim was very quiet but then said, "Normally, when I get a call like this, I listen, put the phone down and say 'fuck you.' But in this case, I'll change what it says in the next edition of the survey." True to his word, Bouley's name was removed from Montrachet's blurb the following year.

I had no problem calling Tim Zagat or any food critic, for that matter, if I had a problem with something they had written. At some point in the eighties, it became common for restaurateurs to hire a publicist to handle all their press interactions. The flack would create all these milquetoast talking points and serve as a barrier between the journalist and the operator. It never occurred to me to outsource publicity to someone else. I've always cultivated personal relationships with writers. I have a lot of respect for what they do, but I'm also not afraid to stand up for myself. And as with most things, I think it's better to handle it on my own.

Behind the bluster, I was anxious about Bouley opening around the corner. I saw it as a competitive move. As the hype machine kicked into full gear, I was a little nervous that we were about to get killed. I tried not to let it show, didn't raise an eyebrow when my customers asked about his new place. Calm and collected was the image I was going for—no cracks in the facade. But inside, I was still smarting.

My fears turned out to be unfounded. When Bryan Miller finally reviewed Bouley a few months after it opened, he said it had "the potential for greatness" but made more than a few missteps. He awarded it just two stars. What I wouldn't give to have been a fly on the wall at Bouley the day that review dropped! (A few years later, Miller revisited Bouley and found it had worked the kinks out, and he granted it an exceptional four stars, but for the brief period that Bouley had two stars and Montrachet had three, I felt utterly vindicated.)

That said, I have always and will always believe that Bouley, despite his eccentricities and the challenges of working with him, was an incredibly talented chef. There's no arguing with that. We both went on to do many great things that had nothing to do with each other or Montrachet. I believe that when two people part ways, the number one thing is that they each prove they can succeed without the other. And we did, for better or worse.

After about a year at Montrachet, Brian handed over the reins in the kitchen to his sous chef Debra Ponzek. Debra was a sharp young woman from New Jersey, who had worked her way up under this renegade chef named Dennis Foy. Still in her twenties when she came to Montrachet, she was a natural talent and a sponge for new information. The fact that she was a woman made no difference to me; I hired on talent, and she had it in spades. Her first year, Debra was nominated for Rising Star Chef at the James Beard Awards, alongside Bobby Flay, and she won. Later, the two had a romance that resulted in a beautiful wedding at the Rainbow Room, but the marriage was rather short-lived.

I loved working with Debra. I would read about these obscure French dishes, things I'd never even tasted, like gar-bure, a hearty soup with cabbage and confit. Debra would go research them and make her own version, which was inevitably delicious. Her cooking was refined yet rustic, precise, eloquent. I don't think she ever made a bad dish.

Debra was a ball of energy and very driven; the cooks respected her work ethic and no-nonsense style. There was a real sense of camaraderie—the cooks would hang out and play stickball on West Broadway before service; the whole staff got together to make parody videos for me on my birthday under the name Hose Productions. (Back then, I was fond of saying "Don't hose me," "You're a hose man," or "I just got hosed.") In them, Debra would be goofing around in the kitchen, mak-ing dishes she knew I hated, or the waiters would be guzzling Champagne straight from the bottle. It was all in good fun; I loved receiving these tapes.

Most importantly, Debra wanted to work with me, not against me. She wasn't trying to conduct the show; she wanted to play music together. When she started, she was green and, even after a year, I was still sensitive about the upheaval with Bouley. I had a lot of ideas for how to make things right, and she, being young and hungry, was happy to execute them. Debra was no pushover—she voiced her opinions, but they felt like respectful disagreements rather than emotional war-fare. As she gained confidence and experience of her own, I trusted her more. I wanted—and expected—her to make her mark on Montrachet, and she did. We had a long and fruit-ful partnership; she stayed at Montrachet for nearly eight years, fostering talent like Traci Des Jardins, who, in 1994, I was happy to put in charge of the kitchen at Rubicon in San Francisco.

At the same time, Daniel Johnnes was also coming into his own. Though he had been hired as a waiter, his interest in wine was growing, and his talent with the guests was undeniable. Most diners were intimidated by wine, and few restaurants—especially affordable downtown ones—had a dedicated wine director or sommelier. But Daniel had a way of getting people interested in wine that felt friendly, not scary. He was into everything—fine French wine, yes, but also weird New World stuff that no one had heard of. He was just so enthusiastic it was hard *not* to want a taste of whatever he was raving about. And he wasn't interested in making a list with crazy markups, which fit with my value-first ethos.

Our wine list, under his watch, soon grew from a few dozen to a few hundred and would eventually surpass a thousand. We had so many bottles we had to store them in the banquettes. People came in and completely put themselves in Daniel's hands. He built his own following and is responsible for Montrachet developing several talented sommeliers and becoming a major destination for wine lovers.

———————

Having the restaurant in good hands enabled me to—to the extent that such a thing is possible while clocking sixteen-hour workdays—get on with the rest of my life. At this point, Ann and I had been dating for four years. I wanted to get married and start a family, but I felt like I couldn't until I'd made a name for myself. I didn't have a pot to piss in—I'd invested my entire life savings into Montrachet, and if it didn't succeed, how could I provide for a family?

With the restaurant's three stars secured, it was time. Ann and I got married in April 1986, a year after Montrachet opened, at the Sleepy Hollow Country Club in front of some two hundred people. Ann and I had been together for long enough that she had no illusions about what she was marrying into—she knew the life of a restaurateur demanded eighty-hour workweeks, and she never gave me grief about it. I, in turn, never gave her any reason to worry; this mutual trust has built a marriage that's lasted nearly forty years.

A few months after our wedding, I was awakened around four in the morning by a phone call. It was the day before Christmas Eve and the whole city was feeling festive. On the line was my mother, calling from my childhood apartment in Peter Cooper Village. She told me, in a frantic whisper, that my father—who she was next to in bed—wasn't breathing. Ann and I raced over (our apartment was only a few blocks south), but by the time we got there, there was nothing left to do. Andrew Nieporent had died in his sleep at the age of seventy-four.

My father never knew how to take care of himself. In the years since his first heart attack when I was graduating college, he'd suffered several more. In his later years, he was perpetually weak and out of breath, and he never changed his diet for the better. I, having yo-yoed through a few diets myself, never knew how to talk to him about it. In his late sixties, he'd had a pacemaker put in but later complained to his doctors that he was having trouble sleeping. He started taking sleeping pills, which sped up his heart rate, and ultimately killed him.

On the day he died, it took forever to load his body into the hearse. My mom was in the apartment filling out paperwork for the funeral home, and I kept staring out the window to where the hearse was parked below. Carjackings were common in those days, and I remember being concerned that someone would steal the hearse with my dad's body in it.

We got him buried right away. I went back to work the next day—Christmas Eve is a busy night for restaurants, and I'm not one to wallow in grief. I think my staff was a little shocked to see me, but what else was I going to do? I had to get back to work. It was my own way of processing.

My father was an enormous influence on me. He was deeply devoted to my mother, brother, and me, and it showed. He'd taken me out to a million meals and instilled in me a deep love of food. No question about it—he is the reason I'm in the restaurant business. Did I ever tell him that? Not directly, but I think he knew.

When I'd left Tavern on the Green, he thought I was insane. I'm not sure he totally believed I could pull off my own restaurant. But when Montrachet opened and we earned those three stars, he was so, so proud. He used to come down in the afternoons just to watch me conduct our preservice meetings. "Don't mind me," he'd say, perched in the window seat with his cane across his lap. He was just happy to be there, and that alone made me feel like I'd succeeded.

That year, we made it through the busy holiday season and lurched into January, a notoriously slow month for restaurants. I was still working every day and tending to my mother, who wasn't as stoic with her emotions. It was a weird few weeks, with the city cold and quiet, me trying to keep the reservations tight at the restaurant, and trying not to think too hard. Then one day, barely three weeks after my father died, and six months after we'd been married, Ann pulled me aside. "I'm pregnant," she said shyly, "with a baby boy."

We decided to name him Andrew.

Chapter 8

Bob and Building Tribeca Grill

Robert De Niro, who I later learned to call Bob, was dating Willie Smith's sister around this time, a beautiful model named Toukie. They'd come in a few times—Toukie a chatterbox with a megawatt smile, Bob silent and glowering. He liked to sit at the last table with his back to the room. This was just a few years after *Raging Bull* came out; he was already one of the most famous actors in the world.

It was maybe their third time in when Toukie called me over. *Something is wrong*, I thought nervously. But Toukie beamed as I approached the table: "Bob wants to know if you'd ever want to do another restaurant in Tribeca," she said sweetly. I tried to play it cool, but inside I was doing backflips. Robert De Niro asking *me* to go into business? This was beyond my wildest dreams.

I wanted to know what kind of place Bob had in mind. A man of few words, he instead invited me on a walk to go check out the then-vacant warehouse that he planned to transform. I remember thinking, *Holy shit—this is huge.* Bob was contemplating taking over the former Martinson Coffee Building on Greenwich and Franklin, just a few blocks down from Montrachet. He lived nearby and wanted to stake his claim in the neighborhood with a big, splashy project. He wasn't just envisioning a restaurant—he wanted to build a full-blown, multistory, multiuse complex. He'd call it the Tribeca Film Center, a place where writers, directors, producers, and, yes, actors could fine-tune their craft. But all creative geniuses need to eat, so De Niro wanted a restaurant on the first floor.

Bob had grand visions for the film center, but his plans for the restaurant were vague, at best. A gathering place for the film-world cognoscenti, nothing too fancy, good food. That was about as far as he'd gotten. I asked him if perhaps he wanted it to be like La Coupole in Paris, the famous brasserie and artist's den. Yeah, yeah, he said, like La Coupole, sure. That was the extent of his creative direction.

But I didn't need Bob to help me conceptualize the restaurant, and in fact, I preferred that he stay out of it. This was a huge opportunity for me, and—unlike Montrachet, which hardly anyone knew existed until after the review—there was a lot more pressure baked into this opening. A huge space with a celebrity owner—what could go wrong? I felt up for the challenge. Even though running Montrachet took up my every waking hour, I knew in my heart that I wanted to open multiple restaurants. I had lots of ideas, and it was the only way to survive in the industry. Not that I was *planning* for my second restaurant to be in partnership with Bob De Niro, but what a phenomenal opportunity.

For years, I'd admired Joe Baum, the legendary restaurant impresario who created the Rainbow Room, the Four Seasons, Windows on the World, and countless others. Baum lavished attention on each concept, sparing no expense, and perfectly cast the designers, chefs, and servers to bring his visions to life. Going to eat at a Joe Baum restaurant wasn't just dinner but also a Broadway-style production. Those restaurants delivered, night after night, with impeccable food, high-touch service, and a finesse that made it all look easy. It was a model I was keen to emulate.

Although Bob (or rather, Toukie) had approached me for my expertise, I still had to jump through hoops to get the gig. Bob sent me to his accountant, Bert Padell, a wrinkly little man with an office crammed floor to ceiling with sports and music memorabilia. He was an accountant and business manager for many stars, including Run-DMC, Madonna, and De La Soul. Visiting his office was like going to a museum.

Bert was good with numbers but knew nothing about the restaurant industry. Still, he was the only person Bob seemed to trust to make the deal. Bert was skeptical of me and thought Bob should hire someone else. He suggested Eddie Schoenfeld, another young front-of-house guy who was making a name for himself with a bunch of high-end Chinese restaurants. Nevertheless, I got the gig. Regardless of whether Bert thought I wasn't up for the job or just didn't like me, it complicated things.

Bert and Bob's team second-guessed me on just about everything, which would become a running theme in our partnership. I didn't understand why they'd bothered to hire me if they were going to minimize my input. I hired a lawyer to negotiate my deal and he did a remarkable job. He got me ownership of both the restaurant and the real estate, which is where the real value is.

Officially in business as the Tribeca Grill, I set about bringing my vision to life. A straightforward menu, a kitchen that could pump food out, a big bar to drive up sales. This would not be fine dining, although I still demanded that the food and service be first class. I had a three-star reputation to uphold, and there was no way I was letting Tribeca Grill fall into the trap laid by other celebrity-backed "restaurants" that were opening at the time. I put the word in quotation marks because Planet Hollywood, which opened a few months before Tribeca Grill, had nothing whatsoever to do with a traditional restaurant. It's about selling branded jackets and throwing lavish parties. I wasn't interested in that.

People thought that because De Niro was involved, it would naturally be an Italian joint. Too obvious. This was 1989, and New American food was the hot thing. Now it's a cliché, but back then, people were excited to break out of the Eurocentric mold. Chefs were touting local, seasonal ingredients for the first time and freely mixing and matching techniques from all over the world. Béchamel and fussy garnishes were out. Sun-dried tomatoes and baby vegetables were in. I knew that a New American menu was the right fit; it wound up being one of the few decisions I didn't have to fight over.

I hired a chef, Don Pintabona, who had cooked at River Café (I had asked my old friend Charlie Palmer if he could recommend an up-and-comer in his competitive kitchen). De Niro took an instant liking to Don, and though the menu we developed was far from red-sauce classics, I think the fact that he was Italian didn't hurt. New American cuisine gave chefs a lot of leeway, and Don, who had traveled extensively in Asia, had a deft hand incorporating those flavors into his American menu—shrimp rolls and rice noodles with a sesame and soy dressing. I let him do as he pleased, so long as the dishes fit the grill concept.

With the idea for the restaurant settled, we could start to run some numbers. Risk averse as ever, I put forth the worst-case scenario. If it did really well, the sky was the limit. Underpromise and overdeliver, and you'll never be in the red.

When you're building projections, you start from the inside out, and base calculations on the size and the seats. You think, We can run two hundred covers a day, seven days a week. Add in lunch. The average check will be, say, $50. Add that all up, and there's your initial projection for gross sales. Let's say it adds up to $5 million a year. Hey, that could be a profitable restaurant! Then you back out from that number, because the size of the space will determine how much it costs to build. At the time, it cost around $200 per square foot; today it's more like $1,000 a square foot or more. But circa 1990, a 13,000-square-foot restaurant at $200 a square foot would run you about $2.6 million to build, plus a little extra for all the unforeseen problems that are guaranteed to pop up. Keep in mind that I had done Montrachet for $225,000. This was a whole different ball game.

One thing that wasn't hard: raising the money. For what De Niro lacked in vision, he made up for with famous friends, many of whom thought it would be fun to own a little piece of a restaurant. He tapped Bill Murray, Sean Penn, Christopher

Walken, Ed Harris, Mikhail Baryshnikov, and Lou Diamond Phillips. Bert Padell brought in Frank DiLeo, who was Michael Jackson's manager at the time; he'd played Tuddy in *Goodfellas*. Two up-and-coming producers, Bob and Harvey Weinstein, who had rented space upstairs, came on board too. I brought in Penny Trenk, who had passed on an earlier chance to invest in Montrachet and wanted to make up for it here. Barbra Streisand was interested, but dropped out at the last minute because she didn't want her name on the liquor license. Then there were Paul Wallace and Stewart Lane, who had sold Bob on the premise to begin with. Bert Padell put together all the investors under the name Homeboy, a nod to his rap-world connections.

Out of the forty-plus restaurants I've opened in my career, Tribeca Grill was the easiest money to raise. It wound up having one of the fastest returns on investment of any restaurant in New York, with most investors earning their money back in just three years. That's practically unheard of in this business.

The investors were settled, but more battles ensued over the buildout. I know enough to know I don't know everything, but the things I *do* know—namely, how to build a restaurant—I don't like to be second-guessed on.

Bob De Niro employed this guy named Bob McDonald, who seemed to take a perverse pleasure in disagreeing with me. Every time I opened my mouth, he argued with what I said. If I said black, he said white. I'd suggest something as simple as putting an electric panel on one wall; he'd immediately point at another. I began to think he was doing it for sport, but he had De Niro's ear and was starting to become onerous.

Still, a part of me understood where McDonald was coming from. With a buildout of several million dollars, chances are someone is trying to rip you off. Contractors and subs see Robert De Niro's name attached and they charge the absolute maximum. You can never get a straight answer about where exactly the money is going, but you feel it in your gut that they're full of it.

The press was champing at the bit for months in advance, calling Tribeca Grill the next hot ticket. People were calling me personally for reservations before we even had a phone. This writer from *New York* magazine tried to stir the pot with a preview article detailing all the alleged delays and blown budgets. It felt like they were rooting for us to fail before we even got a chance to begin.

It didn't help lower expectations that we hosted a private party for Liza Minnelli and Mark Gero before opening to the public. ConEd hadn't even turned on our gas at the time, and we didn't have running water, but we had this fabulous event with little Sterno burners and passed apps. The paparazzi was there and the party got massive publicity, all contributing to the sense that we were building something big, and we better not screw it up.

———

The architect Bob had hired was named Lo-Yi Chan. Bob liked his elegant and quiet style. I did too, but I didn't understand how he got the job; he had never designed a restaurant before. The thing about working with celebrities is, they tend to surround themselves with people who say yes to them. Bob himself didn't express a lot of strong opinions, but he kept this wall of insiders around him at all times to carry out his wishes, and Chan was not the type to pick a fight with the top brass.

I let Chan do his thing, but the one thing I really pushed for was a bar in the middle of the dining room. It was an audacious request, but I had been at Maxwell's Plum and seen how well it worked. A bar set the scene, created the mood. It made the room—in this case, an enormous, industrial-looking one—feel warm and alive. Guests love hanging out at a central bar. There's action radiating in every direction, which turns every table into a good table. The people-watching from a central bar is unparalleled—an important consideration for a celebrity-backed restaurant that was sure to attract gawkers—and it has the added benefit of bringing in additional cash.

Maxwell's Plum had closed and was up for auction. As luck would have it, the original bar was available. But neither of the Bobs saw my vision. No one else has a bar in the middle of the dining room, they said. That was exactly my point! I wanted to set us apart; I had seen its success firsthand.

I went so far as to mock up a model bar and put it in the middle of the space so the Bobs could see how it would look. Finally, after weeks of hostility from McDonald and passive aggression from De Niro, I managed to get my way. It was a victory, but a hard-fought one, and all the second-guessing was wearing me down. I just wanted to get the damn place open.

I put up with it for a few reasons. I was teaming with Robert De Niro, you know? Come on. That's a relationship you want to make work. He hired me to do a job that he knew I could do well. I had to push for things, but I stood up for myself, like I always have, even when it gets me into trouble. At this point, I had not yet learned the value of letting go. I felt my entire reputation was on the line, and I clung to any semblance of control I could get.

I'm always thinking about the design of a restaurant. In the front of the house, I like to offer different types of seating—banquettes, booths, and tables with chairs. I gravitate toward banquettes because they line the perimeter of the restaurant and allow you to see the whole room. And—this might seem like a small thing, but it's an important detail learned from my tour of the Le's and La's—I like to curve the banquettes. People love to cozy up in the curved "corner" of a banquette; it makes them feel intimate.

I also always pay attention to lighting. Lighting in a restaurant should be like the lighting in a theater on a stage. It should pick up nicely both skin tones and the food, a nice warm light that bathes everything evenly. A lot of restaurants have these pinpoint lights that only highlight one small part of the table at a time. I like it when you don't see the bulb—a nice recessed light behind the banquette is much prettier.

A lot of people with a front-of-house mentality never think about how to set up the kitchen, but front and back are two parts of a whole, and they need to work together. Best-case scenario when you're opening a restaurant is that the chef is on board and involved in designing the kitchen from the beginning. It never fails to amaze me just how clueless architects can be about the kitchen; they treat it like an afterthought, when it's the engine of the whole restaurant. They often make it too small or forget that you need to include storage or don't think about the countertop real estate needed to lay out dozens of plates during the dinner rush. It's not always possible, but we had the luxury of building out a raw space, so Don and I worked together to make things efficient.

Where you put the kitchen is hugely important. It's usually in the back, but you don't want to create what I call a bowling alley effect, where a central corridor leads to the abyss, with waiters and food runners scurrying to and fro. You want your waiters to be on the floor so they can see whether the guests need another drink or changed their mind about something.

When you're designing a kitchen, it really depends on the menu and the chef thinking about what stations they need: cold food, hot food, garde-manger, pastry, and so forth. If you know you're doing an intense volume, you need to space out the activity in the kitchen. You don't want to wind up having three cooks on the hot line who are responsible for doing 90 percent of the cooking à la minute. You need to work with the chef to keep things balanced. And no matter what, I firmly believe that you need to put the dish pit in the front of the kitchen so runners can drop off dirty dishes immediately. I learned that one the hard way, way back on the cruise ships.

The kitchen at Tribeca Grill is about one thousand square feet, and we had about a dozen people cooking in there at once. That was way bigger than the kitchen at Montrachet but with only a few more people because the food was less intricate.

We cooked a lot of things over the grill, obviously. Looking back, if we could do it all over again, we should have done some kind of wood fire, which is a very primal, romantic way of cooking. But wood fire is really difficult because wood is expensive and can be challenging to work with. So instead we got a gas grill, which we've had to replace several times over the years, but it gets the job done, gets the grill marks on there alright, and you know what? It works. It worked for thirty-plus years, and maybe it doesn't have a whole beautiful backstory like they do at a place like Asador Etxebarri, but we pumped out four hundred covers a night on it and that's beautiful in and of itself.

At the big restaurants I came up in, systems had been developed to handle volume but often at the expense of the food's quality. At Tavern on the Green, for example, if you were a waiter with four tables, you had to go into the kitchen and wait for all the food for all four tables to be ready before returning to the dining room. Since everything came out at different times, waiters would put a plastic cover over the plate or shove it under a heat lamp, which ruins the texture, temperature, and flavor. Then, to top it off, when all the food is finally done, they'd pile up twelve plates on a tray and rush out to the dining room, where they'd been ignoring guests all night.

I knew there was a better way. At Tribeca Grill, I banished heat lamps and plate covers from the kitchen. I hired a fleet of food runners who were responsible for physically taking the food from the kitchen to the table the moment it was hot and ready. There were no giant trays being precariously tiptoed across the room. The waiter was always within eyesight of the guest, should they need to flag them for anything at all. These things not only helped create a better experience for the customer but also helped improve front-of-house and back-of-house relations, because there were more hands on deck all working toward a common goal—getting the food out hot and fast. These techniques are now commonplace at restaurants ranging from Eleven Madison Park to Applebee's, but Tribeca Grill was one of the first high-volume establishments to employ and perfect them.

When we finally opened, it was full-on, even more than I expected. I told Don I thought we'd do three hundred covers a day—two hundred for dinner and a hundred for lunch. But we were slammed from the second we opened. Don was stressed—he'd yell at me, "*You said it would be three hundred covers!*" We regularly did four hundred or more for dinner alone.

And I could have booked even more covers. But like I did at Montrachet, I tried to keep it manageable so we could still reliably deliver the goods—that's the only way to survive after the opening buzz dies down.

I was inspired by the Tadich Grill in San Francisco, a legendary old-fashioned fish grill. In the beginning, we had a lot of seafood. We'd list all the fish, and you could order it grilled, sautéed, or poached. That slowed down Don and his team, so we changed the format and streamlined the dishes. That's the nature of the beast—you either adapt or perish. Turns out, the more options you give people, the more ways there are to fuck it up. It's better for the chef to decide how the food should be cooked. It's their job for a reason.

Don was working like a dog, but he was resilient. He had a good team of cooks, guys like Pat Trama, Brad Stillman, and Gerry Hayden, all of whom went on to become notable chefs in their own right. Overseeing the exceptional wine list was David Gordon, whom I had worked with at Cornell and Tavern on the Green. I was developing a farm system, keeping the good workers in the family, and wound up hiring most of those guys to run the other restaurants I'd open in the next few years.

We also quickly added a second kitchen upstairs for private dining. De Niro and McDonald didn't want it at first. We'll just get a dumbwaiter, they suggested.

"Why do you think they call it a dumb waiter?" I pushed back. "I'm not putting the food in an elevator. It ruins it. Hot food needs to be served hot."

Oh, the waiters will just bring it up and down the stairs, they countered. Another terrible idea. I fought like hell and finally got my way. We installed a second kitchen upstairs, where we did banquets for $150 a head, and in the first year we made a million extra dollars as a result.

The first few weeks, the crowd was a little rough. De Niro's name attracted a lot of wannabe tough guys, Jersey boys styled out in ridiculous suits and slicked-back hair. (That started to die down when they realized the menu wasn't Italian.) With so many celebrities attached to the space, people were coming just to try to catch a glimpse of someone famous, and they'd camp out for hours waiting, which went against my turn-the-tables MO.

The rubberneckers usually got lucky, especially in the beginning, when the Grill really was a hangout for the downtown film scene. There were the actors who had invested, obviously, but plenty more came in to see and be seen, too. Madonna wanted to come by but was concerned that her ex, Sean Penn, had a piece of the place. She thought maybe he'd put something in her food, and I had to assure her, no, no, Sean doesn't go into the kitchen. Tony Danza got mad at me for "burying" him at a table toward the back, which happened to be where De Niro liked to sit.

When Nelson Mandela made his first visit to New York after twenty-seven years in prison, Tribeca Grill held a fundraiser in his honor. It was an absolute who's who of an event, with limousines and flashbulbs and a police barricade to keep Mandela insulated from an enormous crowd outside. De Niro was in the house, along with Eddie Murphy, Spike Lee, Cyndi Lauper, Robin Williams—and Joe Frazier, which was the most exciting to me.

It was a sit-down dinner, and all the money went to the African National Congress. The room went silent when Mandela, a boxer in his youth and lifelong boxing fan, stood up to speak—and called Joe Frazier up to join him. As Mandela spoke about his time in prison, Smokin' Joe began to weep, and I swear to God half the room did too. It was a momentous occasion, which cemented our reputation as *the* spot to be in 1990.

One night, Don Johnson came in. It happened to be the same night that Naomi Campbell, who had dated Bob, was having a private party upstairs. The paparazzi were all lined up for her, but Mr. Miami Vice thought I'd tipped them off to his presence. He berated me, accusing me of calling the photographers on him. *Don't flatter yourself, Don,* I thought. Of course he wanted to sit at a prominent table near the front. As he was finishing his meal, I offered to escort him out through the kitchen to avoid the photographers. "Oh, it's alright," he said. "They already got me." It was all I could do to keep my eyes from rolling a full 180-degree rotation inside of my head.

My wife started calling me "Forrest Gump" because of all the celebrities I'd wind up with in pictures. At a certain point, I asked myself, *Is there anyone famous I haven't met?* I never got starstruck, though—I had a job to do, and I took that job seriously. And despite all the VIPs pouring in, I still worked hard to ensure that we treated the noncelebrity guests well, too. We treated everyone the same, delivering good service consistently. That's how you keep people coming back. And there is no magic trick to making that happen except to be really fucking good at your job, over and over and over again.

Okay, I admit there was one time I was a little starstruck.

Bruce Springsteen had a manager named Barbara Carr. Barbara's daughter, Kristen Ann, had died of sarcoma, and Bruce was playing a charity concert in her honor at Madison Square Garden. The president of the Garden, Bob Gutkowski, had arranged for the afterparty to be held at Tribeca Grill. I went to the show—watching Bruce is always epic—and I'd informed the restaurant that he would probably play for three hours, so we should be ready to go around 11:00 p.m.

At midnight, Bruce was still onstage, not even thinking about finishing. I must have found a payphone, because I called down to the restaurant to tell them that it would be a late night. Bruce eventually made it down after one in the morning, and he and his entire posse hung out until the sun came up. Tribeca Grill hosted a lot of famous faces over the years, but that's a personal highlight for me.

———

By 1992, I had really hit my groove. Montrachet and Tribeca Grill were only about a block apart, so I spent my nights darting between them. Tribeca was just coming to life, and I knew everyone in the neighborhood. I liked to set up a makeshift office outside the Grill with a table and my cigar and take calls during the day, then proceed to work the door at either place at night.

Nowadays, online reservation systems like Resy and Open-Table offer a complete database of your guests at a glance, how many times they've come in, whether they have any dietary restrictions, if they're celebrating a special occasion, all that. But back then, I did it all myself. I have a freaky photographic memory for my customers, and in seconds I could identify the regulars and know whether they were there for an anniversary or if they hated shrimp or had tipped well last time. I also have a compulsive need to know who's coming in every night. I once took a fax machine with me on a family vacation in Florida so that I could physically see the reservation sheet each night. My wife and mother-in-law, Vera, were not amused. But there's no such thing as work-life balance when you own a restaurant. You're always on, always there, even if you're not physically present.

It took a lot of effort to develop a system that worked for seating the room in a restaurant as large as Tribeca Grill. People are obsessed with getting a "good" table, and my whole goal with the layout was to create no bad ones. Yet no amount of planning can prepare you for the diner who isn't happy with where you put them. People pull all kinds of bullshit to get the table they want. They yell, they bribe, they cajole.

I developed a very polite way of saying no when people requested a table they couldn't have. I always offered them another spot, but nine times out of ten, I guarantee, they'd pick a worse table than the one you led them to initially. Sometimes you set them up for it: "Oh, Table A. Right this way, sir." They're thinking, *Fantastic, Table A,* then you bury them. It's basic psychology. My theory is that you should actually seat your best tables first. Why? Because then you get them back.

At the Grill, even when we were completely slammed—and we pretty much always were—I insisted on honoring reservation times. It's disrespectful to the guest to make them wait when they've planned their whole night around you, and it's also bad for your bottom line; you can't turn a table if you don't seat it.

One night, we had a party of five scheduled for 9:30 p.m. But the previous seating was still at the table, taking their sweet time, and it was obvious they weren't going to be done by 9:30. The lingering group was a party of four, so if I could get them to switch seats to a four-top, I could seat the party of five at that table with no problems.

I knew I would have to offer them something in exchange for this minor inconvenience. I walked over and introduced myself. Pardon me, I said, but if you'd allow me to move you to this table—I pointed to the four-top right behind them—I'd be glad to buy you all desserts. They said yes, and I felt I had solved the problem. Maybe a minute later, I walked past the table again and one of the men grabbed me by the arm: "That was the fucking rudest thing anybody's ever done to me in a restaurant," he announced. My reaction was knee-jerk: "Great, then get the fuck out."

The other people at the table stood up to defuse the situation, explaining that their friend had had too much to drink, that they'd had a great time tonight, that they would be happy to have dessert at the other table. I took a deep breath to calm down, they switched seats, everything was cool.

Maybe twenty minutes later, one of the waiters was trying to get my attention. The party was getting up to leave and, apparently, they weren't paying the check. I confronted them, and the same belligerent guy gets back up in my face: "You told us to get the fuck out, so we're getting the fuck out," he said.

"Come on," I said. "I said I'd buy you desserts, not the whole meal." He pushed past me and bolted out the front door, flipping me the bird and yelling from the street. I went after him and yelled right back, but eventually I let him go; sometimes it's not worth the fight.

When I came back inside, I sat down at a table with Frank DeLeo, one of our partners. As I was explaining the situation to Frank, a busboy came over with something in his hand. "Drew, I found this on table thirty-five," he said. A wallet. On the table of the party that left without paying.

At that very moment, a woman from that same table came back in the restaurant, looking sheepish. She approached Frank and me and said, "I think we left something at the table."

"Oh, really?" I said, feigning innocence. "What is it you left?"

"Um . . . a wallet," she said.

"A wallet? Really? Wow." I smirked at her. "Well, we're very honest people here. And if you left something here, I'm certain that if you pay the bill, and we find the wallet, we'll return it to you immediately."

Frank, an intimidating presence, scowled at the woman, and lo and behold, the bill was paid. The next day, the wallet was returned, and I continued to see that woman, who lived around the corner, walking her dog outside every day for years.

The pressure in any restaurant in America is not the first seating; it's being able to do a second. These days, it's common practice on Resy to have a little disclaimer, something from the restaurant that basically says, "We need the table back in two hours." It might also say, "We have a grace period of fifteen minutes, and if you're late, the table might be given away." The reservation system might even make guests enter a credit card number to reserve a table as a way to guarantee they actually show up. In the early nineties, though, guests basically had free rein to show up late (or not show up at all), change their party size, and camp out all night, all of which prevented that precious second seating.

I used to get so upset when guests bailed on a reservation that I would call them up and ask what they did for a living. Oh, you're a dentist? How would you feel if I made an appointment and didn't come? It happened so often at Tribeca Grill that I needed to devise a new system for holding people accountable.

I thought we should request a credit card deposit for large parties—you put a deposit down for other large purchases, I figured, so why not dinner? But I was terrified to implement such a policy. No one had ever asked for a deposit on a reservation before, and I thought guests would balk. It took me weeks of hand-wringing to pull the trigger. And when I finally did, guess what? It worked! People gave their credit card and started showing up for their table. It was a win-win for everyone.

I paid attention to everything, for better or worse. I eked twenty-five hours out of every day, watching over Tribeca Grill like a hawk, all while paying attention to Montrachet, too. I needed to prove—to the guests, to the press, to Bob De Niro, and most importantly, to myself—that I could handle it all. I was determined to keep the quality high, even in a restaurant that trafficked in quantity. Seeing all two hundred of our seats at Tribeca filled and turned over twice a day was the ultimate validation. I felt like I had achieved some level of control, and therefore success, but running two restaurants wouldn't keep me content for long.

Chapter 9

Going West

My goal was always to open many restaurants, but I wasn't confident I could do it. I idolized Joe Baum and the Restaurant Associates group in the sixties, but unlike Baum, I was risk averse and had no corporate entity backing me. Still, between Montrachet's critical clout and Tribeca Grill's celebrity buzz, word about me was spreading like wildfire.

In 1992, Florence Fabricant declared I was "following close on the heels of Sirio Maccioni of Le Cirque," and she called me a "diplomat and rising star." A few years later, *The New York Times* Sunday magazine sent a writer, Arthur Lubow, to follow me around Tribeca for a few days. In his profile, he described me as "the most dynamic restaurateur in the country." I developed a reputation as *the* guy you call when you want to open a restaurant.

It was a funny moment in time. Of course I loved the attention—I was doing exactly what I'd set out to do as a kid, and succeeding at a high level. When I was growing up, restaurant owners were the stars of the show. Guys like Sirio Maccioni, Joe Baum, and Vincent Sardi ruled my world. Chefs were not yet a commodity, or even really thought about by the dining public unless they were also the owners of the place. I saw myself as continuing in a grand tradition of front-of-house showmen who built legendary restaurants.

Around the time when Tribeca Grill opened, public interest in food and restaurants skyrocketed. Just as I was starting to blow up, so were chefs. Most people couldn't tell the difference between a chef and a restaurateur, including the executives of the newly launched Food Network, which debuted in 1993. They approached me about doing a slew of shows—one was called *Grilling with Drew*, which they filmed in my suburban backyard; another was called *Chef du Jour*; and at one point they wanted me to take over *Taste* from David Rosengarten.

I filmed a few episodes—I loved having the spotlight—but ultimately felt that television was not my path. Food Network was in its infancy, and there was no guarantee of its success. I was freaked out that filming would keep me away from my restaurants for too long. Plus, they kept wanting me to do these cooking shows, but I was a restaurateur, not a TV chef. (This did not stop Wolfgang Puck from referring me to the producers of *Good Morning America*, who invited me to carve a turkey live on the air one Thanksgiving, an opportunity I happily accepted.)

On the real estate side, I was fielding all kinds of offers. Rich guys always think it would be fun to have a restaurant. Every developer in town was calling me to discuss their ideas—I called their pitches "the deal of the day." I was torn. I wanted to open more restaurants but didn't know if I could stay hands-on the more I extended myself. And when I'm not hands-on, I get agitated because I might miss things. Systems might start to fall apart. Figuring out how to scale is the fundamental issue for any small business owner, and I was working hard to stay on top of everything.

I said no to the majority of opportunities. Robert De Niro once said that the power is in your choice. When you choose to say yes to a certain role, you're probably saying no to several others. With that in my head, I weighed every offer carefully.

The thing that tipped me was seeing people who were nowhere near as capable take on new projects. It's a little petty, I know, but I knew I could do better than them. Once again, I was driven by the desire to prove myself.

I realized, however, that I couldn't do it all myself. So, shortly after Tribeca Grill opened, I formed the Myriad Restaurant Group as a vehicle for two things. One was to analyze potential new deals, and the other was to build a network of people around me to support those deals. It wasn't the most organized corporate entity—it was me and a handful of people I was already working with taking on some extra projects and hoping to share the wealth.

There was Marty Shapiro, my extremely competent general manager at Tribeca Grill; Agnes Chiao, an accounting whiz whose husband sold me one of my first POS computers; Michael Bonadies, a writer working at Montrachet I'd known since my Tavern days; Daniel Johnnes; and my brother, Tracy, who had been working in advertising. No one quit their day jobs, and one or two people came on board later, but at least we had an official-sounding name. In a nod to my time at Maxwell's Plum, I had business cards printed up that said "Restaurant Director."

Myriad would come in and do a bit of everything. If you were a billionaire developer who owned a hotel in Midtown with a restaurant you didn't know what to do with, you'd call us. In fact, this is how Myriad's first project started: I was on a plane coming back from a charity event in Florida when I met Harry Macklowe, who asked me if I would consider working with him on a restaurant called Charlotte in the Macklowe Hotel.

For better or worse, I approached each opportunity like it was a completely unique undertaking. I wouldn't give you our brands, Montrachet or Tribeca Grill, but would conceive of a totally distinct idea that fit your space and your clientele, then find you the perfect chef, hire the staff, train them, and hope for great results. In exchange, we were usually paid a fee or a percentage of gross sales. I don't like to use the word *consultant* because what we did was much more hands-on, but if it helps you visualize what I'm talking about, sure, go ahead.

In 1992, Jerry Della Femina approached me with an idea for a new restaurant in the Hamptons. Della Femina is a legendary ad man (he's said to have inspired *Mad Men*) and a totally over-the-top personality—Brooklyn-born, brash, loud, opinionated. He loved good food almost as much as he loved attention. We hit it off right away.

Jerry had partnered with Ben Krupinski, the "builder to the stars" in the Hamptons, who had built houses for Billy Joel and Martha Stewart. Krupinski was a real cowboy, so I had my reservations as I went out to visit the construction site.

First glance at the floor plans and I sensed something was off. I asked, "Where are you being greeted by the host?" They showed me the plan—it involved entering the restaurant, walking down a long corridor, and meeting the host right in front of the bathrooms. I told them that wasn't a good idea. "Why don't you do it like this?" I asked and showed them a revised plan where you would enter and immediately turn left into the dining room. Sure, you had to go up three steps, but that was better than navigating a labyrinth to the toilet before checking in. Plus, my plan fit at least five more tables, which was probably an additional $50,000 in revenue over the course of a year.

Krupinski wasn't pleased. He whined about how much money it would cost to redo his layout. I stuck to my guns—an extra $50,000 a year would more than make up for the change in plans. Once again, I felt I was dealing with people who had no idea how to build a restaurant. I didn't suggest these things to be difficult—I suggested them because I knew they worked, and that's why they hired me to begin with. They relented, and Della Femina opened to much fanfare. I promoted Pat Trama, one of my best opening sous chefs from Tribeca Grill, who was itching for a new opportunity and ready to take the reins on his own.

The restaurant was an immediate hit with the Hamptons crowd and quickly cemented its reputation as the place to see and be seen within its first summer. The food and service were better than any of the tourist traps in town, on par with serious destinations in the city. Business was so good that the next year, we decided to open another restaurant together called East Hampton Point. There, I promoted Gerry Hayden, another one of my most capable sous chefs at Tribeca Grill. As Myriad expanded, there was plenty of opportunity for my people to move around and up within the group, and that was very much by design.

Chefs, waiters, managers—they can all get bored of doing the same thing over and over again, and I was happy to move my best people around if it kept them invested.

East Hampton Point was also a hit—a beautiful room, with waterfront views, and an elite clientele to match. I thought I was pretty seasoned at appeasing egos when working the door and seating the room, but the Hamptons crowd was on another level of entitlement.

One night, as I was working the door, a well-dressed gentleman got in my face. "I don't like what you did tonight," he said.

I was confused. What did I do?

"I don't like the table you gave us," he said.

I said, "Sir, you make the table. The table doesn't make you."

I walked away, thinking that was the end of it. A few seconds later, I felt a tap on my shoulder. I turned around, and before I had time to realize what was about to happen, this guy's boyfriend sucker punched me right between the eyes. He hit my glasses, which shielded me from the worst of the impact—they must have been made of steel.

I almost went down but stayed upright and wobbly. I could overhear the tables nearby shouting, "Get his keys! Don't let him leave!"

"Did you just hit me?" I asked, trying to regain my composure.

"You motherfucker!" he screamed as he ran out the door.

The valet wouldn't give him his car, and the police showed up pretty fast. I was fine, more in shock than anything, but it just goes to show how far people will go for a "good" table.

Going West

Shortly after East Hampton Point opened, my old Montrachet builder and friend John Gaul reached out about a space in San Francisco. It was a townhouse-esque building in the Financial District, very different in style from the big-box restaurants like Stars that were popular in the city at the time. I was riding high off the success of Montrachet and Tribeca Grill, and though Silverado Trail hadn't come to pass, I was still smitten with California cuisine and wine country. Plus, this was an opportunity to buy the building, which had worked out very well for us at Tribeca Grill. I jumped at the chance.

I've always felt that the space dictates the idea of the restaurant, not the other way around. The size and layout in this building, which was tall and skinny and stretched across two floors with a separate basement for prep, reminded me of Montrachet. And once De Niro convinced his buddy Francis Ford Coppola to come on board, the idea quickly coalesced; Francis owned the Niebaum-Coppola Winery in Napa Valley, where they produced the prestigious red wine Rubicon. Naming a restaurant after a great wine had worked before, why not try it again?

Robin Williams, who lived in San Francisco, came on board as an investor, too. He followed all the great European chefs fanatically; he had great taste. His wife, Marsha, would call me and ask for restaurant recommendations when they traveled to Paris. This connection, too, was De Niro's handiwork; he had starred with Robin in the film *Awakenings* a few years earlier, and the two remained friendly.

I dislike the word *concept* because I prefer a restaurant to evolve organically. I never say, "I want this to be a New Wave

French restaurant" or "a red-sauce Italian place." I had the basics sketched out: Rubicon was going to be a West Coast restaurant inspired by the Napa Valley—but I wanted to give it room to take on a life of its own.

I was also sensitive about entering this new city properly. I didn't want to be perceived as a carpetbagger, so I got an apartment nearby, much to Ann's chagrin. Back home, we had just welcomed a second child, a daughter, Gabrielle, but I felt I needed to be in San Francisco more often. As always, I knew of the much-feared local critic, Michael Bauer, and his personal tastes; I'd been religiously reading his reviews for years. My goal was to open another stellar restaurant on the West Coast, a spiritual sibling to Montrachet.

Talent-wise, I had my people dialed in, and I was careful not to import them from New York. The kitchen would be overseen by Traci Des Jardins, who had cooked under Debra Ponzek at Montrachet before returning to her home state and racking up accolades at restaurants like Patina in Los Angeles and Elka in San Francisco. I had kept my eye on her from afar, and I knew she had both a great palate and a great deal of confidence in the kitchen. Her cooking was lean and powerful, with real finesse— I've to this day never tasted a better pan-roasted chicken. She got the skin so crisp, I can still feel it shattering. Her menu was straightforward, French-inflected California fare, and I let her do her thing, though I did request we include a Petrale sole, a nod to my old inspiration and local hero, the Tadich Grill.

The wine component was crucial. I had Daniel Johnnes in New York, but I needed someone homegrown at the helm here, in a restaurant so close to wine country. A few years earlier, the sommelier Larry Stone had called me to ask whether he should take the suitcase full of money that Tavern on the Green was offering him. Larry was a wine savant, one of the first Master Sommeliers in the United States (he eventually won the title of World's Best), and had worked at Charlie Trotter's, The Ritz, and the Four Seasons. I told him to avoid the Tavern, which had long since passed its prime, and we'd loosely kept in touch. He was born and raised on the West Coast and understood the local terroir better than anyone I knew. He agreed to come on board and set about crafting what would become a legendary 1,500-plus bottle list that drew wine lovers from all around the world.

To round it out, I hired Klaus Puck, Wolfgang's brother and a fellow Cornell grad, to work the floor, hoping that the apple wouldn't fall far from the tree. (It didn't.) I was, however, in for an awakening about the more liberal style that San Franciscans adopted even at a nicer restaurant. When it came time to interview potential waiters, I was warned: The guys are going to have ponytails and facial piercings. It wasn't my favorite aesthetic, but that was San Francisco in the nineties.

When it comes to hiring, especially for front-of-house positions and managers, I keep a close watch over every candidate. This was even more the case at Rubicon, knowing that I wouldn't be there every night forever. I value loyalty as much as, if not more than, raw talent. I wanted a team who would stay true to me and my vision for the restaurant, but being at the top—and having been burned before—I was sensitive to any sign of betrayal.

There is no magic technique to keep employees honest and straight. You just gotta lay down the law, and even that is not always enough. I told people when I hired them that I took everything very personally. Even little slights or rude comments affected me on an almost primal level. That scared the smart ones straight, and the ones who didn't believe me at first found out the hard way. Later in Rubicon's existence, we'd deal with staff that had drug habits and sticky fingers—the usual crap— but the first crew was tight-knit, good workers with good character.

One hire I wasn't worried about was Larry Bogdanow, the architect behind Union Square Café and the Cub Room in New York, who designed a handsome, flowing two-story dining room with exposed brick, a semiexposed kitchen, and earthquake beams crisscrossing the windows. It was sophisticated without feeling stuffy—a restaurant for grown-ups with good taste and an eye for value.

I hoped that San Franciscans would appreciate the effort, but I was nervous that my particular style of dining would be lost in translation on the West Coast. In 1994, California was still crawling out of a recession, and the dot-com bubble was in its infancy. San Francisco was decidedly *not* used to flashy celebrity-backed restaurants, and I knew our reputation preceded us. I was determined to win over local diners with the quality of our offerings, not the boldfaced names attached.

When we opened in spring 1994, diners came flooding in, followed shortly by the critics. Some, I knew, wanted to see us fail. But that's fuel to me, and I made damn sure we were ready from the get-go. I think people were surprised at how frankly unglitzy the restaurant was. That was intentional; I wanted the focus to be, first and foremost, on the food and wine. The fact that it was all affordable and served by a polished, professional staff who genuinely enjoyed working there? Well, that was just another way of proving the doubters wrong.

As usual, I worked the door most nights in the early weeks of Rubicon. I immediately noticed that diners there were easier to please than New Yorkers. They dressed more casually and were generally friendlier. If you tried to bring a guest upstairs in New York, they'd look at you like you were fucking their mother. In San Francisco, people were more concerned with the food than the mood, and they'd happily sit wherever you wanted. The food was serious, but the environment was relaxed, and the crowd followed suit.

Michael Bauer, the fearsome *San Francisco Chronicle* critic, quickly gave us three stars and praised Traci's cooking as having "the gutsiness appreciated by Bay Area diners, with a refined presentation." It was the praise I so craved, delivered against all odds. And it was just the tip of the iceberg.

That year, 1994, was a big one for me, in every conceivable way. Because barely five months after Rubicon opened, in a stunning one-two punch, I unveiled my follow-up, the single most successful restaurant of my career, in partnership with a man who needs only one name:

Nobu.

Chapter 10

Nobu
The Beginning

B ob was a fan of Matsuhisa, a sushi restaurant in Beverly
Hills run by a Japanese chef named Nobuyuki Matsuhisa.
Matsuhisa, who went by Nobu, had worked in Peru and Alaska
before landing in California, and the no-frills little storefront
where he combined traditional Japanese techniques with flavors he'd gleaned from his travels was earning serious critical
acclaim on the West Coast. Bob had become a regular, introduced to Nobu by the agent Roland Joffé.

I was familiar with Nobu because in 1989 he'd been named
one of Food & Wine's Best New Chefs, along with Debra
Ponzek, who was then my chef at Montrachet. (Also honored
that year was David Bouley.) We all descended on Snowmass,
Colorado, over Fourth of July for the party, where the honorees
had to cook a dish.

Debra was tasked with making financiers for dessert, and we were struggling with the altitude, butter bleeding out of the pastry on every tray she pulled from the oven. The day of the party, a Nobu assistant named Mrs. Q, a tiny Japanese lady, approached one of the magazine's editors, Peter Prescott. He must have stood a full two feet over her. She peered up at him: "All the fish you sent us is no good," she said. "Nobu needs new fish." Peter looked at her like she was out of her goddamn mind. Where was he supposed to find new fish in the middle of an isolated mountain town on a holiday weekend?

The event was insanely busy. Huge lines and hungry people everywhere. These events are always difficult, and the food stations struggled to keep up, sometimes running out of food. Maybe half an hour in, I see Nobu leaving his station. As he passed us, I asked him, "What's up?" He looked at me and said, "We served two hundred people, and we're finished."

Straightforward as that. He wasn't bitching, he wasn't saying they ran out of food; it was just like, *We did it, we're done, we're out*. I'm pretty certain he never got that new fish.

I had loosely kept tabs on Nobu ever since and had visited Matsuhisa in LA. The space was very basic, small and spare, with just a few tables and a sushi bar. It also had an enormous menu bound in a leather book that was difficult for guests to navigate. Most regulars knew to just put themselves in Nobu's hands and let him send out whatever he pleased.

Nobu turned out exquisite stuff. The simplicity of the room melted away as soon as Nobu's food hit your mouth. He fused flavors from Japan and South America, mixing ingredients that had never seen the inside of a sushi bar: chiles, olive oil, garlic, truffles. He was creative, playful. One of his best-known dishes was tender, barely cooked squid, sliced to resemble pasta, served with warm garlic and asparagus. He put jalapeños on top of yellowtail sashimi and twisted deep-fried eel spines into festive bow tie garnishes.

This was radical stuff, especially compared to the rest of the Japanese food in the country in the late eighties and early nineties. Japanese restaurants at that time catered almost exclusively to a Japanese clientele. They served traditional food, bound by the customs and history of the cuisine, to people who were already familiar with them. The entire time my father worked for the State Liquor Authority, not one of the restaurants he helped get a liquor license was Japanese. Most Americans didn't know anything about eating raw fish.

Nobu blew the lid off all that. He was open and communicative in a way that virtually no other Japanese chef had been with the American dining public. He was dedicated to his craft, but friendly about it, approachable. He was quiet, but he also played the game—already used to catering to celebrities and Hollywood hotshots.

For me, Nobu was a change of pace. At my previous restaurants, I'd had the vision and then handpicked the talent, usually from relative obscurity. Nobu was well established by the time we got involved with one another, but with his humble and hardworking nature, I was sure we could do great things together.

Bob wanted Nobu to come to New York. In fact, when we were opening Tribeca Grill, he thought Nobu could be the chef. That was a moment of bad casting. There was no way that Nobu was leaving his little sushi bar, where he personally served each VIP seared monkfish liver and miso-lacquered black cod, to run our juggernaut grill in New York. And to his credit, Nobu, after seeing the size of Tribeca Grill, demurred and said, "Maybe one day I do a small sushi bar with you."

I could see the kinship between the two of them—the actor and the chef, both artists—and in seeing myself as the director of the whole production, I made it my business to make this work. In the restaurant business you have to be willing to play the long game, and I had plenty keeping me busy in the meantime. We kept in touch with Nobu, and his star continued to rise. I knew Bob saw him when he was in LA, but I also knew that in order to open a restaurant, you need to do more than just talk. You need an idea, the talent, the space, and then, of course, the money.

So it felt like the stars aligned in 1993 when a little Italian restaurant frequented by low-level mobsters just up the block from Tribeca Grill at 105 Hudson Street went up for sale at a bankruptcy proceeding. It was about 2,500 square feet—nothing compared to the behemoth that was Tribeca Grill. It couldn't be more conveniently located. My gut told me this was the opportunity we'd been waiting for to bring Nobu to New York, and I bought the space for $100,000. It was risky on my part to buy the lease in advance, but I was convinced that this was the moment it would all come together. Overjoyed at my find, I called Nobu to share the good news. "I found the space!" I exclaimed.

Silence. "Oh. I didn't tell you. I made another deal."

What? Another deal? "Nobu, what are you talking about?"

"I'll be in New York tomorrow and I'll come speak to you," he said.

The next day, he came to Tribeca Grill, where we sat outside on the loading dock. He told me, politely and somewhat apologetically, that he had signed a deal to open a sushi restaurant called Shin in the Parker Meridien hotel in Midtown. I was dumbfounded. Robert De Niro and I had been courting Nobu for three years. I just dropped $100K on a space for him, and he made another deal?

I called Bob to come downstairs and speak with Nobu. "I don't understand. I thought we were friends," he said.

"Nobu," I said. "Pretend we never even talked about going into business together and we were just buddies. You call me up one day and ask about what the Parker Meridien is like. I would tell you, honestly, about all the reasons it's a bad idea to go into business there."

Both Bob and I really laid into him. Nobu's expression darkened and I could see he was getting upset. As we finished and he stood up to leave, he looked at us and said, "Maybe I never open restaurant in New York City." He bowed and took off.

I thought the deal was dead. But, to Nobu's credit and my pleasant surprise, he called me the next day. "I thought about it, and I'm going to stick with you," he said. That was the beginning of one of the greatest, and most complicated, partnerships of my career.

We had one successful restaurant in New York City under our belt already with Tribeca Grill, but this time, Bob didn't want to bring on a whole roster of other partners. The space was smaller, and Nobu already had a name, so he wanted to keep things tight. Nobu and I would represent the sweat equity, while Bob and one other partner, an Israeli named Meir Teper, put up the cash. Meir was an aspiring producer who had worked his way into Bob's inner circle before Bob became famous. Like many close to Bob, he questioned my every move. But Bob trusted him, and they had each other's back.

In the early stages of planning, Bob wanted me to work with Bert Padell again. I handed him some initial projections for the first year, which showed a $50 average check and gross sales of $2.5 million. He eyed me warily: "Who the hell is gonna pay fifty dollars for raw fish?" he said. "Just trust me," I replied. Suffice it to say, that first year, we did closer to $9 million. Remember: Underpromise and overdeliver.

So now we had the space, the talent, and the funding. Next we needed a name. For me, it was always "Nobu." But Meir insisted "Matsuhisa" was the brand. I told him Matsuhisa sounded like an electronics company. "Nobu" was easy to pronounce. He had Matsuhisa on the West Coast, Nobu on the East. It's lyrical, it's correct. It just flows. Nobu agreed with me—thank God—and we moved forward.

We needed an architect who could design a space as ambitious as Nobu's food. The original Matsuhisa, obviously, wasn't going to provide that inspiration. A young architect named David Rockwell had been constantly hounding me to do something together. He called me every other week about some new idea. He had designed one sushi bar—not a particularly attractive one—but I liked him a lot, and this was a big opportunity.

David's mother was also in showbiz—she was a vaudeville dancer and choreographer—so he, like me, had an almost subliminally imprinted understanding of a restaurant as theater. He had a flair for the dramatic in his taste for materials and lighting and a knack for creating a heightened sense of reality. Nobu himself was pretty subdued, but he had a playful side, and mostly let David do his thing. David tried to capture Nobu's story in material form, which translated to lots of terrazzo and bamboo surfaces, walls decorated with birch trees and river stones, and the sushi bar chair legs carved to resemble chopsticks. It was fun, flashy, and unlike any other Japanese restaurant in New York.

David and I shared a love of live experience, and I immediately liked his design. There was really only one big conflict during the buildout. Nobu didn't want any steps in the restaurant. In David's design, there was one area near the booths where he'd drawn up a little platform, where diners would have to step up into the seating area. Nobu saw this and balked.

"This is no good. No platform," he said. I asked him why. He said, "Japanese people drink, and when they leave the table, they're going to fall down." Okay, fair enough. I went back to David and told him Nobu ixnayed the platform. It wasn't a battle I was invested in fighting.

But a few days later, David called and started begging for the platform, saying he needed it, he's gotta have it, on and on and on. The way he described it, the platform was integral to the design, imperative to the success of the whole restaurant—it was enough to convince me. I said, "You know what? Nobu's not going to notice this one step, just put the platform in."

Dead wrong. Nobu came in a few days later and went ballistic. This quiet Japanese man, yelling, steam coming out his ears. He had said no and we did it anyway, so he was within his rights to be pissed. We took the step out. To Nobu's credit, he has certain ways he wants things to be done. And I respect that.

The most important decision was where to put the sushi bar. To me, the sushi bar was the heartbeat of the restaurant, the place where all the energy coalesced and radiated out. I wanted the high-impact choreography of the sushi chefs to be the first thing you saw when you walked in. It would set the mood and announce that we were a serious destination for a new and exciting way of eating.

David loved to create rooms within rooms (even though I preferred the flexibility, and earning potential, of open seating), so his initial design had the sushi bar situated all the way in the back, with a liquor bar in the front. I told him that wasn't going to fly.

"If you move the sushi bar up," he said, "where are you going to put the regular bar?"

I said, "You know what? Let's not even have a bar."

David was shocked. "What do you mean? You have to have a bar!"

I had my reasons, though. A sushi bar would allow us to seat more people for a full meal, as opposed to just drinks. I didn't yet know how popular Nobu would become, but I had a hunch that with Nobu's and De Niro's names attached, more people were going to want to come in than we had room for. It didn't hurt that we'd make more revenue this way, either.

Plus, I was a little nervous about the neighborhood wiseguys who'd hung out at the previous space. No disrespect intended, but they weren't really the clientele I was hoping to attract. Lo and behold, on our very first night, Joey Scar and Charlie Pots and Pans showed up at their old haunt. The first thing out of their mouths: "Where's the bar?" I looked at them and said,

"I'm very sorry, gentlemen. We don't have a bar here." They looked me up and down, looked at each other, and snorted. "No bar? We're outta here." And they never, ever came back.

———

Nobu was very much the master of his domain. He already had decades of sushi-making experience under his belt, and my knowledge of Japanese food was limited.

The dishes that are today considered his signatures, the classics that haven't left the menu in thirty years, the ones that have been ripped off by every corner-joint sushi menu from here to Timbuktu? They were all completely dialed in by the time Nobu opened.

I'm talking about the ethereal miso-marinated black cod, sweet and savory all at once, with umami sneaking in before people even knew what umami was. I mean the yellowtail sashimi, fanned out over a moat of yuzu-infused soy sauce and topped with thinly sliced jalapeño and cilantro. The wholly addictive rock shrimp tempura, with a spicy-creamy or ponzu dipping sauce—those dishes were already well-established pillars of Nobu's repertoire by the time he came to New York. And Nobu had zero interest in altering his dishes to appeal to the guests' tastes—there would be no substitutions or sauces on the side here.

But Nobu was twice the size of Matsuhisa, with a hundred seats and a lot more star power behind it. I respected Nobu's vision as a chef, but as a hospitality person, I knew we had to make some tweaks to the operations. My biggest gripe was that the menu was just too big. It probably had a hundred different items and was confusing for diners. It was going to be hard to source ingredients for everything he wanted to make, keep it all fresh, and cook it all perfectly. When the menu is that big, not every single dish is going to be a home run. Sometimes you have to simplify, to edit things down.

Note that I say *edit* things down, not *dumb* them down. I saw my role as a producer—someone who would capture Nobu's uniqueness and help it appeal to the masses. I had a very strategic vision for how to do so, informed by my years of experience.

I didn't want to change the integrity of Nobu's food itself. He was already freely combining ingredients and techniques from across different cultures. But there were little things that I knew we could tweak to make the experience more accessible. It could be presented in a way that wasn't pretentious or intimidating, but rather, fun and exciting. The icing would be the stylish environment and a finely honed team that took care of your every need. Taking the fear factor out of this new way of eating was the key to success.

We set the tables simply, with just chopsticks and a napkin—no tablecloths, no cascade of silverware. It was a move thematically aligned with the Japanese style of dining, so Nobu approved. It also saved us a ton of money. No laundry, no extra dishes to wash, no wasted food. The setup was brilliant.

There were, however, some hiccups in the beginning as we learned how to present Nobu's food. The hot kitchen was next to the sushi bar, so even though the food was prepared in separate areas, it was designed to be picked up from the same location. My thinking was the expediter was going to coordinate everything to come out together—there's a hot chicken teriyaki going out with a cold plate of sushi, delivered simultaneously. Americans were used to ordering individual plates and having them served at the same time so everyone at the table could eat "together." But in the Nobu system, when the food was ready, it went out. In the early days, guests were not aware of the Nobu system and complained to me—*Why did my husband get his chicken first, and I had to wait twenty minutes for my sushi?*

I realized we had to rework the style of service. Instead of listing items as individual entrées, we explained that dishes were meant to be shared. That way, you could drop a dish in the middle of the table for everyone, while other dishes were being prepared. Nowadays we call this "family style," and everybody in America knows what it is. In the beginning, though, there was a real learning curve; we had to teach people to order for the table. Once they finally grasped this idea—helped along by our endlessly patient servers—people finally stopped complaining.

It was a learning curve for me, too. I hadn't encountered these issues at my other restaurants. At Nobu, more education for the guest was required about the flow of the meal and about the flavors—most diners had never tasted things like yuzu soy sauce, let alone pearlescent raw yellowtail on top of it. We comped some dishes in the first few weeks to encourage skeptical guests to give the uni or raw lobster a try. But it didn't take long for Nobu's mastery of exciting flavors and ingredients to win people over.

This was also the beginning of a new phenomenon of people writing about their food experiences online. We were still a few years away from websites like eGullet and Chowhound being founded, but diners were already posting things on personal websites with headlines like "How to Order at Nobu." Guests would come in with printouts of the list, with step-by-step tips to make the most of the meal. To be honest, I loved it—I always wanted people to be really into the food, and now I had proof that they were. The validation was thrilling.

Although I was used to an invisible divide between front of house and back, I was unprepared for the dynamic between the sushi chefs and the rest of the cooks—the former being a particularly insular group and in the beginning almost entirely Japanese. The sushi bar operated as its own little island, with a tight-knit crew who did not seem keen to fraternize with the rough-and-tumble cooks in the back. The exception here was Masaharu Morimoto, one of our opening sushi chefs, who was always personable and friendly with everyone—which might explain why he got chosen as an *Iron Chef* soon after.

———

Other issues, I knew all too well. People wanted reservations. Would do anything for a table. Begged, borrowed, and stole for one. I was always on the lookout for phonies trying to scam their way in. One of my favorite tricks went like this: The guy (it was always a guy) would swagger up and announce himself as "Johnson, party of four."

I'd look at my book and go, "Hmm, I don't see you in here. When did you book the table?"

"I called last week." Johnson would glare. "It should be in there."

I'd make a whole show of reading the list again. "Last week, you say? And you talked to a man who took your name?"

"Yes," he'd huff, impatiently.

"Well, Mr. Johnson," I'd say, "we only have female reservationists here, so I'm afraid you may be at the wrong place."

We only took reservations from 10:00 a.m. to 5:00 p.m. and had all four of our full-time reservationists stationed at the first booth in the restaurant during lunch. The idea was that when guests walked in, the first thing they noticed was that our phones were ringing off the hook. Not that we really needed to play up how tough it was to land a spot.

We had neighbors coming in, tourists coming in, Japanese people coming in, celebrities coming in, and at various points we had to turn all of them away, supermodels included. It was stressful working the door, and after a few months of madness, I enacted a policy of always holding back two or three tables for friends of the house who would inevitably drop by unannounced. (JFK Jr., who lived around the corner, was a frequent impromptu visitor, and we often seated him in what was frankly a not-so-great table near the back—but he never seemed to mind.)

One night not long after we opened, I got a call. *Muhammad Ali is in.* Immediately, I was transported back to my parents' bedroom, huddling with my father and brother around the radio that cold winter night. Out of all the celebrities I'd crossed paths with, Ali meant more to me than anyone else. I made sure to be there when Ali, visibly suffering from Parkinson's, arrived with a friend. "Champ," said the friend Ali was dining with. "This is Drew Nieporent, he owns the restaurant." Ali put out his hand, shaking, and said nothing. I stood there, feeling a bit shaky myself, in awe of my childhood hero.

Ali sat down, unfurled a napkin at the table, and started doodling. For a full five minutes, I stood there in uncomfortable silence while my idol scribbled on a napkin. He unfolded another section and kept going. After what felt like half an hour, he handed me the finished drawing: two mountain ranges, a ship with a plume of smoke, and clouds. It was so detailed it was almost like a painting, and he signed it before handing it to me with a smile. It's one of my most prized possessions.

A few months later, Sirio Maccioni, the legendary owner of Le Cirque, was hosting a dinner for the greatest French chefs in the world—Paul Bocuse, Alain Ducasse, Roger Vergé, Michel Guerard, Daniel Boulud, and others. He called me for a favor: "Can you take a table of six at Nobu on Saturday night?" Of course! I was flattered. I revered these chefs.

Saturday night rolls around and of course the chefs are late. Remember, Nobu has no bar for people to wait at, so it's important that parties show up on time and complete, because there isn't much room for error. I called Sirio: "Are they still coming?" *Yes, yes, they're on their way.* "Still six people?" *Yes, six, they'll be there soon.* Great. We had spent all week putting together a special menu for these exceptional chefs, and we were comping the bill.

When they finally showed up, there were more than six people. In fact, thirteen of them showed up at the hottest restaurant in New York City on an already-packed Saturday night. I had no idea where to seat them, but I had to figure it out, and fast. I prayed my idols wouldn't see me break a sweat. I told them to follow me, and as we walked past the sushi bar, Morimoto gave me a panicked look. I knew what he was thinking. "I know," I said when I passed back his way. "We just have to make it work. For the six, do the menu we discussed. For the others, do whatever the fuck you want."

All night, I snuck glances at their table. These legendary chefs—many of the men whose restaurants I had visited in 1980—had an absolute ball. They drank, they smoked, they marveled over the way Morimoto sliced the raw fish into beautifully artistic shapes.

By coincidence, Robin Williams also happened to be at Nobu that night. He was almost as obsessive about French chefs as me, and he eagerly ran after them as they stepped outside to smoke between courses, all manic energy and sparkling eyes. Ron Perelman was also there, seated at a booth right behind the host stand, and as I came back to my perch, he said, "Hey, man, I've been watching you tonight, and what you did is unbelievable." I took that compliment to heart. I had kept my cool and worked it out—as usual.

———

We had some bumps in the early days, behind-the-scenes stuff that customers never saw. Not long after we opened, after service one night, a group of armed robbers snuck in through an unlocked side door. They went to the office—I wasn't there, but Nobu was—and put a gun to his back, demanding that he open the safe. But Nobu didn't have the combination. A few of the other sushi chefs and employees were there, too, and they fought back. A gun went off, and one of the sushi chefs, Shin Tsujimura, got shot in the leg, along with a waitress and a dishwasher, though fortunately none of them was critically injured. The assailants fled the scene without getting much money, and the cops later arrested one of them, though he refused to give up his partners.

We had issues with our superintendent, too, apparently an aspiring arsonist who enjoyed lighting fires in the basement of the building. Many nights I could smell smoke, and more than once wondered if he'd one day burn the whole place down.

By 1995, I was, professionally speaking, on top of the world. I had three successful restaurants within blocks of each other in Tribeca, another going gangbusters in San Francisco, celebrity partners, and some lucrative consulting-style gigs on the side. The critical acclaim was piling up. In addition to the good marks for the food, Montrachet had just earned a Grand Award from *Wine Spectator*, arguably the highest wine honor in the biz, and Daniel Johnnes and I were hosting a series of well-received winemaker dinners that would snowball into his wildly successful La Paulée wine parties. I was traveling between coasts overseeing my growing empire. I had always dreamed of having restaurants in New York and California, and now they were here, garnering rave reviews and booking out weeks ahead of time. I felt unstoppable.

On the personal front, however, my quality time with my wife and young kids, who had moved to the New Jersey suburbs, was limited. Andrew, my son, was displaying behavioral issues that would later be diagnosed as autism spectrum disorder. He was, among other things, a picky eater, and I remember begging him, bribing him with every gift conceivable, to eat one single pea. He refused, and I felt a flash of the anger my father had sometimes directed at me. But family issues were Ann's domain—she devoted countless hours to taking Andrew to and from appointments, while I pulled long days and nights in the city, shuttled to and from by a limousine service—I had still never gotten my license. At the time I didn't feel like I had a choice—work came first, always.

The 1995 James Beard Awards were a night to remember. The televised reception was held at the Marriott Marquis in Times Square, a fittingly cinematic location for the so-called Oscars of the Food World. Robin Leach, the inimitable host of *Lifestyles of the Rich and Famous*, emceed, along with Donna Hanover Guiliani, who had a show on Food Network. I arrived with quite a posse because of the sheer volume of nominations my restaurants had received. I had been diligent about my promotional efforts to the writers and industry professionals who served as judges for the awards; exposure was key to success. I always said yes to participating in dinners and charity events and made sure my chefs shook hands with anyone who could impact their future.

Montrachet had been nominated for Outstanding Service for the previous two years and finally took it home that night, along with Outstanding Wine Service for Daniel's exceptional work. I would have been happy with even one award, but that same night, Traci Des Jardins, my chef at Rubicon, was named the Rising Star Chef of the Year, and Nobu, which had been nominated alongside Rubicon, was crowned Best New Restaurant in America. They were all major victories, but the win for Nobu was huge—the industry had been dominated by European chefs for so long, and this was the beginning of a new era of mainstream acceptance of Japanese cuisine in the States. I was proud to play a role in ushering it in.

That night, I felt invincible. Just a few blocks from where I stood as I accepted awards for my restaurants, my Cornell professors had tried to throw me off a bus. I laughed to myself thinking about all the people who didn't believe in me. I was finally being recognized for what I had built, and nothing could touch me now. Or so I thought.

Chapter 11

Nobu
Continued

About a year after Nobu opened, we got a call from London. Ong Beng Seng and Christina Ong, billionaire Singaporean hotel and retail tycoons, were taking over the Londonderry Hotel and rebranding it as the Metropolitan. They wanted it to have a Nobu. I took the meeting. B. S. Ong, despite his immense wealth, was very approachable, and Christina, a formidable businesswoman, was elegant and composed. She may have been the first to see the potential of Nobu as a global brand.

Their offer was intriguing. I had never opened a second location of one of my restaurants, and I wasn't interested in doing a cookie-cutter repeat of the first. But this would be an opportunity to introduce Nobu to a whole new audience in Europe, where there was nothing like it. I felt that if we could personalize this Nobu to its new city, and really make it distinct, it would be a slam dunk.

But we had no infrastructure in London—we didn't know the cost of a napkin across the pond, let alone how to build a new Nobu. We had no talent pool to pull from to guarantee this thing would be run up to the correct standards. And it was in their hotel, meaning we'd have less control over everything. Given our limitations, I thought we should enact a management deal—essentially, the hotel would kick us a percentage of the earnings in exchange for permission to use Nobu's name and food, but they would provide the infrastructure for payroll, accounting, and back-of-house systems.

I thought this deal made the most sense for Nobu and me. At this point, there was no operating agreement, no Nobu corporate, no restaurant group guiding an expansion plan. De Niro had a personal accountant named Ira Yohalem who would frequently admonish me: "Drew, Bob's in the movie business, not the restaurant business." So when the London opportunity came around, I was trying to keep it simple.

I met with Nobu to pitch him on the Ongs' idea. "Have you ever been to London?" I asked. *No.* "Do you want to go?" *No.* "Why not? It's a great opportunity for us."

"I don't want to go," he said.

Nobu was conservative in this way, and frankly, I was frustrated. When I spoke to De Niro about it, he said, "No means no. Why are you pushing him?"

But B. S. Ong wanted Nobu in the worst way, and he was a persuasive guy. A few weeks later, he arranged for Nobu to fly to London on the Concorde. I worked every day, so I took a redeye that arrived the next morning. Bleary-eyed as my cab pulled up to the hotel, I saw Nobu outside with a huge grin. I stepped out and said, "I guess we're doing London." He nodded. We went around the corner to a Chinese restaurant and then returned home on the Concorde. I was in London for less than three hours.

When Nobu agreed, Bob and Meir switched gears. They wanted in on London. And they wanted to take a bigger role—instead of doing a management deal, they wanted to partner directly with the hotel, which would complicate things. But that was how they wanted to proceed, and I felt it was best that we stick together. I figured we'd do it the same way we had in New York, with me overseeing all the logistics, Nobu on the food, and Bob and Meir as investors.

A few months before the London location was set to open, I was in Paris. It was the end of a trip to Champagne that I'd taken with my Rubicon chef Traci Des Jardins, along with Francis Ford Coppola and his family, Larry Stone, and David Rosengarten, among others. I was lying in bed before going out to dinner when I received a call. It was Meir, Bob, and Nobu. I have no idea where they all were, just that they were together. Meir started to talk. "You're going to have a reduced role in London," he said.

"A what?" I asked.

"A reduced role."

"What the hell are you talking about?" I said, sitting upright. "B. S. Ong wants a *Nobu* in London, not a Matsuhisa, and I had something to do with that," I said, incensed. The way I saw it, Nobu was an incredible chef, but it was our collaboration that made us the Best New Restaurant in America. I felt my participation was vital, and I wasn't about to take a "reduced role" in London, whatever that meant.

The next thing I heard was Robert De Niro, at the top of his voice, laying into me with every nasty insult imaginable. When he was done with his tirade, I was, for once in my life, at a loss for words. My partners were trying to cut me out. "Well, I guess that about sums it up," I said, and hung up the phone.

A few weeks later, we were all back in New York and a meeting was scheduled. The call in Paris had struck a nerve, and everyone wanted to smooth things over. *Sorry, sorry, lost my temper.* I could roll with it. All was forgiven. The restaurant industry is full of big egos and hot tempers, mine included, but luckily, my partners changed their minds, and my role in London was no longer "reduced." I had stood up for myself yet again, and I was still a part of the deal. With my position secured, I set about doing my job—opening another great restaurant.

Partnering with a hotel had challenges that our stand-alone Nobu did not. I wanted to hire David Rockwell again because I believed his design was an integral part of the restaurant's success. But Christina Ong wouldn't have it—B. S. was an investor in Planet Hollywood, which David had also designed—and she didn't want his signature razzle-dazzle in her elegant hotel. We instead hired Keith Hobbs, whose vision for Nobu was sleek and minimalist, emphasis on white and beige. Unfortunately, unlike in New York, the only place to put the sushi bar in the long room was all the way in the back. This was a battle I couldn't win, so I let it go, though I did successfully lobby to lay out a row of round tables in the dining room, which gave us flexibility and a sense of drama.

The hotel inserted themselves into nearly every decision we made, which resulted in us hiring a few people for the front of house we weren't completely satisfied with. Most hotel general managers know very little about food and beverage. It was like my Cornell days all over again, when they had all of us aspiring hoteliers learn how to reheat canned soup. But once again, I devised new layers to the system and compiled a detailed training manual for all employees, trying to raise the standards.

Being a hotel, they were obligated to serve three meals a day. Nobu was only open for dinner, but the hotel wanted to use our dining room to seat people throughout the morning and afternoon. Nobu would not have it—breakfast service in *his* restaurant? That was a dealbreaker. After many meetings, we worked out that breakfast would be served in a room adjacent to the main dining room so that Nobu could remain a sovereign entity at all times.

Like the New York location, London was an immediate hit. The crowd there was very posh, sophisticated, and international. Women showed up in Chanel and men in bespoke suits from Savile Row. Actors and pop stars came by, sure, but also banking bigwigs, politicians, and members of the royal family. Compared to the New York location, London felt even more exclusive.

Londoners were also more conservative in their approach to service. In New York, we instructed waiters to bend down on one knee to make level eye contact with the guest while taking the order. That didn't fly in London, where the gesture could be misinterpreted as too casual; nor did discussing the price of a custom omakase meal. "You cannot seriously be in here trying to openly discuss money in the dining room," one of my managers explained, so we made tweaks accordingly. And eventually, as we racked up more and more press, London diners began to relax a bit—though we did still have to remind them that the little bowls on the table were for soy sauce, not cigarette butts.

At this point, my days were a blur of cross-Atlantic flights, while I tried to keep eyes on everyone and everything. My favorite tool during this era was the fax machine, which I'd fire up at all hours to send intel (press clippings, photos of critics, reservation sheets with my handwritten notations about guests) to my staff stationed around the world. I'm sure this annoyed some of them, but if it did, I didn't want them working for me anyway.

There was one VIP I made sure to handle personally. A few months after we opened, Christina Ong came to me and said she was going to have lunch with Princess Diana. We weren't open for lunch, but for that day, we were sure as hell going to make it happen. I was surprised at how low-key the princess's entrance was, even with security—they were very inconspicuous—and she was dressed casually. We seated them away from the entrance, where it was quiet. I handpicked their waiter, Kurt Zdesar, who later became a manager with us (and has since gone on to open several successful restaurants in London, notably Chotto Matte).

Christina Ong had preordered the menu, and the two sat opposite one another. There was a lot of chatter in the press those days about Diana's eating disorder, and we weren't sure if she would even want to eat. Kurt and I had discussed several possible scenarios, ranging from "what if she doesn't touch her food?" to "what if Christina eats more than her?" Our goal, as in any situation, was to make the meal flow as smoothly as possible.

Once Kurt delivered the plates, I was delighted that Diana seemed eager to try the food. But from what I could witness from my little perch behind the service station, Christina wasn't touching hers. I couldn't hear what they were talking about, but I could see the platters of fish sitting idle on the table. Diana was clearly self-conscious about digging in on her own, and was trying to be polite by holding back. Throughout this awkward lunch, she managed to maintain her signature expression— that sort of shy sideways glance that endeared her to millions. It made me sad for her, this facade. Still, it was the thrill of a lifetime to serve Lady Diana, even if I'll never know what she thought of the miso cod.

There was a lot going on in London in the late nineties. The city was just becoming a global culinary capital. I hung out with the chefs who were changing the scene—the bad-boy genius Marco Pierre White, who looked me dead in the eye and said, "David Bouley, he thinks very highly of himself, doesn't he?" which endeared him to me immediately, and Sir Terence Conran, the tremendously impactful designer and restaurateur who helped make British style an influence around the world.

I also spent time with Raymond Blanc, the chef of the renowned Le Manoir aux Quat' Saisons. Raymond was a big thinker, and he hosted a two-day event, a conference of sorts, at Le Manoir to discuss the fact that the French were losing control of gastronomy to the Spanish. He invited Thomas Keller, Larry Stone, Charlie Palmer, and many more to participate in talks and dinners. His hypothesis about the Spaniards was controversial at the time, but in the end, he was right. The guy predicted the future, and in the decades that followed, the French did indeed loosen their stranglehold on the world of fine dining. Chefs in London, Spain, and America were shaking things up, Nobu among them.

Spending time in London opened my eyes to the world. I had spent so many of my formative years idolizing French cuisine, but in England, I tasted flavors from North Africa, Peru, India, and more. Every trip was an opportunity for me to try something new. I felt like a kid again. I was proud, too, to be a part of a restaurant that was so original and had such impact on the scene as it shifted in Europe.

———

Meanwhile, back in New York, the first Nobu was going gangbusters. So much so that it was becoming clear we needed to expand, somehow, to accommodate all the people who were trying to come in. One day, Chuck Low approached me outside Tribeca Grill. Chuck was Robert De Niro's landlord, and a real character. De Niro had cast him in several of his movies—a bit part as Morrie in *Goodfellas*, the wig guy who gets killed with a screwdriver. I liked him a lot, and he was always tapped into the local real estate scene. He told me to follow him because he wanted to give me a tour of a former art gallery right next door to Nobu.

It was a terrific space, but, unfortunately, there was no way to connect the gallery and the restaurant without knocking down a foundational wall. The only way to go between the spaces was through the basement. In my mind, it wouldn't work as a Nobu expansion, but the connected basements definitely piqued my interest.

I brainstormed for something more akin to a Nobu spinoff—an idea that capitalized on the Nobu name but that wouldn't compete with the original. I came up with something called Nobu's Noodles, which I envisioned as a more casual ramen and raw seafood bar. Ramen was becoming very popular, but there were few restaurants serving it in New York. And because of its proximity to Nobu, it seemed like a no-brainer that we should take the space.

So convinced was I that this was a slam dunk that I signed the lease for the next-door space in my own name, for a cool $100,000. I was putting myself on the line here again, but I felt confident that Nobu and my partners would get on board.

I was wrong. As it turned out, Nobu was not keen to make ramen. Plus, someone had told him that *noodle* was slang for brains in America, and he didn't like the sound of Nobu's Noodles at all. I had hit a brick wall. Fine, I relented. Just call it Next Door Nobu, and do whatever you want.

The menu at Next Door wound up being very similar to Nobu's, though it did ultimately have some noodles and a raw bar. Unlike the original, it didn't take reservations, wasn't open for lunch, and felt slightly more casual. My concern was that we already had three stars for Nobu, and what if its spinoff only got two? Who would want to eat at a lesser Nobu?

Fortunately, my fears were assuaged by Ruth Reichl, then the critic at *The New York Times*. I had been following her work for years even before she landed at the *Times*—I used to pay a guy at one of those international newsstands to clip all the food articles from magazines and newspapers around the world, just so I knew who was writing about what. She had written for some obscure magazine in California before becoming the critic at the *Los Angeles Times*, and I always enjoyed her writing from the West Coast. When she moved to New York, my California friends, guys like Wolfgang Puck and Piero Selvaggio, told me I was screwed. She had written a review of Le Cirque that made waves, calling out the discrepancy in treatment she got when she went incognito versus when she was recognized. She's very tough, they warned, she's going to hate New York restaurants.

Nothing could have been further from the truth. In 1995, Ruth had given the original Nobu three stars, writing that it was "a restaurant that cannot be compared to anything else." She was delighted by the creativity at work in the kitchen, once it was "liberated from [the] tradition" of classic Japanese fare. I found her smart and fair, always accurate in her assessment. All you can hope for with a critic is that they get it right, and they don't hurt you. And in my opinion, she got it right every time.

So I was relieved when, a few months after we opened Next Door in 1998, Ruth graced us with another three-star review. She praised the subtle differences between the two Nobus and seemed to get that Next Door had its own identity. Now I had three three-star restaurants within blocks of each other downtown, plus Nobu London, plus Rubicon in San Francisco, plus Tribeca Grill. I was riding high.

––––––––––

Meanwhile, Myriad started getting involved in more deals in New York and beyond. In Martha's Vineyard, we opened a New England–style restaurant called the Coach House, with Ryan Hardy, who had cooked at Rubicon. (Ryan now owns Charlie Bird and Pasquale Jones in New York. Actually, a lot of great

cooks passed through the Coach House—so did Chris Cosentino, of *Top Chef* fame, who I stay in touch with to this day.) We
opened an Italian restaurant called Lucca for the chichi Boca
Raton Resort and Club in Florida, and the upscale Steelhead
Grill for the Marriott City Center in Pittsburgh. And closer to
home, in Tribeca, we opened Layla, a fantastic and fantastically
over-the-top Middle Eastern restaurant complete with Arabic
mosaics, belly dancers, and a young chef Joey Fortunato at the
helm, who turned out beautifully blistered pita and charred
squab in grape leaves.

Each new restaurant idea completely consumed me, and
I started every one from scratch. In retrospect, I would have
made it much easier on myself—and better for Myriad's bottom
line—if I had developed a consistent system for executing all
new projects. But, true to form, I took them all very personally,
even when I was just an advisor. I was too caught up with micromanaging each restaurant to strategically scale Myriad into the
restaurant group I had dreamed of running, though I couldn't
see it at the time.

Around this time, David Rockwell referred us to the W
Hotel in Midtown Manhattan, and they brought us on to
develop the restaurant. In 1998, W Hotels were brand-new and
promising to be the hottest thing in New York. Rande Gerber,
aka Cindy Crawford's husband, was opening a Whiskey Blue
bar there, and I was excited to be involved.

I had watched an episode of *Charlie Rose* where Rose interviewed Disney CEO Michael Eisner, who had just had quadru-
ple bypass surgery. They spent a ton of time talking about the
importance of eating heart-healthy foods. I myself was pushing
three hundred pounds, but I had a feeling that a heart-healthy

restaurant would do well in the W. My idea was basically a spin on spa food—healthy food that tasted good.

I had this wonderful hippie chef at Tribeca Grill, Michel Nischan. He had a ponytail and a laid-back vibe, and was very into organic produce and fresh food. I thought he was tailor-made for this restaurant, which I had dubbed Heartbeat. The idea was low-fat and low-salt. No hiding flavors under piles of butter or cream. Lots of vegetables. This may not sound all that radical now, but at the time, there was nothing like it in Midtown Manhattan.

Michel went to work like a mad scientist developing a beautiful and unique menu with all kinds of colorful juices and vegetable stocks. It wasn't vegetarian—sure, there was tofu, but also lots of seafood and rack of lamb. We had wine, but also a tea sommelier. I think it came as a pleasant surprise to people, and Heartbeat did very well, leading to Myriad opening restaurants in other W Hotels. (Michel went on to become Paul Newman's partner at the Dressing Room in Connecticut, to win the Humanitarian of the Year James Beard Award, and to start his own healthy food nonprofit, Wholesome Wave, so I guess my instincts about him were correct.)

I was constantly meeting chefs during this time because I had so many new projects in development or coming to fruition. Even if I didn't necessarily have a job for someone, I always took the meeting—you never know who you'll talk to. I remember interviewing an up-and-coming Spanish chef named José Andrés at one of my other W Hotel restaurants, Icon. He was referred to me by someone at Nobu, and I took a liking to him right away. I didn't end up working with him, but we stayed in touch and developed a friendship over the years. I'm proud to have José in my life, especially because he has gone on to establish himself not just as an incredible chef but also as a world-changing humanitarian force for good.

But not everyone I met became a friend. In 1997, I got a message about a new project coming together on the West Side of Manhattan. The team had apparently been talking to David Bouley about coming in, but he wasn't turning up for meetings. Frustrated, they wanted to talk to me instead.

So I took a meeting with Philip Johnson, the esteemed architect who had done the Four Seasons Restaurant and the AT&T Building on Madison Avenue. We met at an office with windows overlooking Central Park West. Johnson, with snow-white hair and his signature thick-rimmed eyeglasses, was pushing ninety at the time. He was sharp as a tack and eager to discuss his latest design. He proceeded to show me his early draft, which resembled a cave-like structure, complete with tiny little porthole windows.

"What do you think?" Johnson asked.

I took a deep breath. "Well, I'd imagine that since you have Central Park right outside the windows, you'd want to create an outdoor-indoor feel, not something so dark," I replied carefully.

He peered at me from behind his bottle-cap glasses, and I was certain I'd ruined my chance to work with the legendary architect. But Philip just shrugged. "Maybe you're right," he said. "Let's work on it together." I was astonished, but tried to play it cool.

The next day I got a call saying "Philip Johnson loved you. There's just one thing: You're going to have to meet our other partner." I said, "Okay, who's that?" "Donald Trump. Now, he only owns 5 percent of the deal, but when you meet him, he's going to talk to you like he owns everything. Just keep in mind, we own 95 percent. He's a minority partner, 5 percent, so just let it go in one ear and out the other. This meeting is just a formality."

I figured I could handle that. Philip Johnson loved me, and I clearly thought the deal was mine. So I headed up to Trump's offices at the Trump Tower, with a gorgeous view of Central Park. He welcomed me in and shook my hand, his hair already levitating several inches above his forehead in his now-signature bouffant.

"Hey, Drew," he said, launching right into it. No small talk, no let-me-get-to-know-you kind of stuff. "Drew, everybody wants this space, you gotta give me your best deal. If you're serious about putting a restaurant here, I'm just telling you right now, you have to give me your best deal, because a lot of people want it." I tried not to roll my eyes, to just let him talk. He only owned 5 percent, his partners had assured me.

I could barely get a word in edgewise, but I told Trump I'd think about some numbers and get back to him. At the end of the meeting, Trump turns to his bodyguard, Matt Calamari, and says, "Matt, please take Drew back downtown. Drew's a downtown type of guy. This restaurant is uptown, I don't think it's right for him." I didn't feel the need to argue because I figured that Philip Johnson and the other partners had my back.

A couple weeks later, I was doing a charitable event in Hawaii when my mother called and said, "I'm reading in *New York* magazine that Donald Trump chose Jean-Georges Vongerichten to do a restaurant on the West Side. I thought that was the restaurant project you were telling me about?"

I immediately called Phil Suarez, who was Jean-Georges's business partner, and I said, "Phil, what's going on?"

"Drew," he replied, "it was Donald Trump. I just offered him $100,000 more rent, and we made the deal."

A hundred thousand dollars? That's nothing in this business! But I hadn't negotiated with Trump because I thought the deal was mine. Well, I was wrong. Trump had somehow wedged his little stake into a big one and bulldozed right over his partners to get what he wanted. (When Trump ran for president, I immediately recognized all the things he pulled on me in that meeting: talking over everyone, projecting all this macho swagger, bragging about his own abilities. It proved to me that the leopard does not change its spots.)

Other ones got away too. Todd English backed out of a deal with me for W Union Square. His restaurant, when it eventually opened, turned out to be a one-star dud, which I felt was poetic justice. But then there was Rick Bayless, an enormously talented chef I had approached about doing something together in New York but eventually backed off of because I got the sense he'd be difficult to work with. When he won the James Beard Award for Outstanding Chef, I thought to myself, *Man, was I wrong about him.*

Those projects never came to be, but one that very much did was Berkeley Bar & Grill. I was drawn to the project because of the history of the space—the former site of the Quilted Giraffe in the Sony Building in Midtown Manhattan. It was a terrific opportunity, and the rent was extremely attractive, but the space itself was awkward. It was situated in the glass-enclosed atrium, where there wasn't a ton of foot traffic. Still, I figured

I could build something with good enough food that people would find us.

New York has many French restaurants and many Italian restaurants, and I thought to myself, *Never mind their popularity—let's do something different.* I decided the theme would revolve around sixties-era Berkeley, California. We designed a hippie-themed space complete with tie-dye curtains and colorful painted glass art. We played The Doors and Grateful Dead and took menu inspiration from Alice Waters's Chez Panisse. I even hired a chef who had worked there, a young Jonathan Waxman, but our partnership was difficult. I replaced him with Patricia Williams, who had been our chef at City Wine & Cigar, another short-lived project we did in Tribeca, but she didn't last either. Our third chef, Richard Farnabe, had worked in Paris and at the Mercer Kitchen with Jean-Georges. He was unbelievably talented and had a deft touch with bistro-meets-Cali-style food.

I stand by Richard's cooking to this day, but the menu was confusing to people. Berkeley did not represent a clear food idea, and the "hash brownie" with Cherry Garcia ice cream that I thought was a whimsical dessert (the hash was oregano) was roundly mocked. The fact that we'd burned through three chefs in our first year and were situated in a weird glass box in Midtown didn't help matters. We got a few solid reviews, but then the Grim Reaper appeared in the form of William Grimes.

Grimes, succeeding Ruth Reichl, was the new restaurant critic at *The New York Times*. Reichl understood food and hospitality in a way that Grimes did not. During his brief tenure, he knocked a lot of iconic places down a star or gave no star at all. I knew he was coming in, so as I had done at Montrachet, I placed friends to the left and right of his table to eavesdrop. I, of course, was in the house. I know for a fact that the food he ate during his visits was nothing short of fantastic. I even said to my friends, "If he gives us anything less than two, I'll kill him."

Lo and behold, a few weeks later, the review dropped. One star. He called Berkeley "peculiar" and "addled," though he praised the cooking. I was on a red-eye flying back from Las Vegas when I found out. It was my first one-star review, which is pretty much the death knell. I went straight to the restaurant from the airport. I was pacing around the empty dining room early that morning, stewing in my own anger, when the phone rang. I picked up only to hear the unmistakable voice of Mimi Sheraton, the sharp-tongued former *Times* critic. "Listen," she said. "I know you're upset. Don't be. You'll never win a battle with a food critic. Let it go."

Wise words, Mimi, but I did the exact opposite. She was right, but I was righteous, and in my anger, I fired off a letter to the *Times*'s executive editor, laying into Grimes. He had come in for lunch *after* calling to fact-check his own review, and that struck me as devious. Was he making last-minute changes without verifying them? I never heard back from the paper, but it felt important to stick up for myself and my chef.

A few weeks later, I bumped into Florence Fabricant, another food writer at the *Times*. "What did you do to Bill Grimes?" she demanded.

"What are you talking about?" I said. "I didn't do anything."

"Well," she said, "I saw some of the higher-ups at the paper pull Grimes into their office and give him a talking-to."

I did take some satisfaction in hearing that, whether it was true or not. But it couldn't save the restaurant: I sold Berkeley Bar & Grill not long afterward.

In 1995, the day after I won the James Beard Awards, I got on
a plane to Vegas at the behest of casino impresario Steve Wynn.
I was skeptical of Las Vegas, but Robert De Niro had just finished filming *Casino*, and he was convinced that Vegas was the
future. A classmate from Cornell, Dan Lee, was working for
Wynn, and he picked me up at the airport. As Dan drove me
down the Strip, he pointed out a hole in the ground, albeit a
very expensive hole in the ground. "We just bought that lot," he
said. "We're building a new hotel there called the Bellagio."

We got to the meeting with Steve and I was immediately
nervous. One of Wynn's family members had recently been kid-
napped and a million-dollar-plus ransom payment demanded.
Because of that, Wynn had recently purchased a purebred guard
dog that probably cost a fortune. I had heard stories about the dog
going after guests. As the impresario opened the door, I wasn't
sure whether to shake his hand, pat the dog, or completely ignore
everyone so as not to alarm the beast. After a tense moment, the
dog approached me, sniffed, and allowed me to enter.

I began chatting with one of the most powerful men in
Vegas. He was friendly, charismatic, larger than life—Vegas
in a nutshell. Everything in his office was plush, his desk was
enormous. Wynn was building out the Bellagio, and he showed
me a virtual-reality video of the hotel that did not yet exist. He
wanted only a few restaurants, and Nobu was at the top of his
list, along with Le Cirque. He was close with Sirio Maccioni,
and now he was making his pitch to me.

"I have a sushi bar at the Mirage," he said. "But you have
to give me something we don't have." He offered me a deal:
5 percent of gross and 10 percent of net. This sounded like a

great opportunity and a fair deal. I told him I'd talk to Robert De Niro and get back to him. Suddenly, Wynn was flustered. "Whaddya need Robert De Niro for? You're the star. Nobu is the star. Fuck Robert De Niro. When I have stars, I have to buy their food, buy their room, everything. Fuck De Niro," he reiterated for good measure.

I thought to myself, *Well, that's one deal that will never happen. He's trying to hose Robert De Niro!* Frankly, I thought it was off-putting that he was so forthright about trying to drive a wedge between me and my partner. But I took it in, thanked him for his time, and returned to New York.

Upon my return, I met with Bob, who started grilling me about the meeting. *What did Steve Wynn say?* I deflected. "Bob, Vegas really isn't for us, I don't think it's such a good idea." Confused, Bob started pressing me about what Steve had said. So I took a deep breath and recounted the conversation, expletives included. The next thing I knew, De Niro blew past me, called Wynn in Vegas, and was screaming bloody murder at him. I thought I was doing a mitzvah by being honest and loyal. But somehow, what transpired in Vegas turned out to be bad news for me.

In fact, Wynn totally changed the way he did business after that. He started bypassing the restaurateur and negotiating straight with the chefs instead, offering them a huge salary and their name on the door. Why should he bother with the chef's partners when he can have the chef directly?

After the Wynn incident, we were approached by Peter Morton, the founder of the Hard Rock Cafe, which had recently opened a hotel in Vegas. He, too, wanted a Nobu. The hotel was far off the Strip, but he offered us a rent-free deal. Although Vegas was still uncharted waters, De Niro had an instinct that there would be terrific opportunities.

We were hesitant about opening too many spinoffs, but for the right location, at the right price, with the right people, we could talk. The deal Morton was offering was almost too good to be true. It was impossible to say no. Bob and Meir wanted to do it. It would be a little challenging, but we were up to the task.

As we left the meeting with Morton, I got in the car with Meir. We drove a few blocks and stopped at a red light. To my right, in the driver's seat of a convertible smoking a cigar was Arnold Schwarzenegger. I thought to myself, *That's Vegas, baby.*

I was flying high: By the late nineties, Myriad owned and oversaw more than twenty restaurants across the country. I was on the road constantly, visiting properties and negotiating new deals, emceeing charity events and scoping out new chef talent everywhere I went. Money was flowing and I had ceased worrying about spreading myself too thin. I was working nonstop, but I was also enjoying perks like hobnobbing with the rock stars I'd grown up idolizing. I was living large, in more ways than one.

But the more you take on, the higher the risk. And Nobu Vegas was problematic. The Hard Rock location, opened in 1999, wasn't a smash right out of the gate like New York and London. The food was excellent as always, but our location was difficult, and at the beginning, the restaurant just wasn't that profitable.

Around the same time, we were pursuing another potential deal in Vegas. We didn't have an expansion plan; we were taking opportunities as they came. Hammering out this new deal entailed many meetings and lots of paperwork. I, as ever, was concerned about the operations and logistics on the ground. The four of us—Bob, Meir, Nobu, and I—were rarely in the same place. We'd never had an equal partnership to begin with, but with every new Nobu, we tweaked the formula a little bit and parceled out equity percentage point by percentage point, with final figures a bit of a moving target.

On all the previous deals, I negotiated for myself and for Nobu because we were the sweat equity. Obviously, there would be no Nobu without Nobu, so I always negotiated to get more on his behalf, even if I took less. I also felt I was an essential part of the DNA of Nobu, so I fought to get us both good deals.

But all that pushing over the years had consequences. I found out the hard way.

It all came to a head in early 2000. At this point, I'd been business partners with Robert De Niro for almost a decade. We'd had our fair share of arguments, but there hadn't been any major blowups in a while. I felt that everything was status quo—barring the headache with Nobu Vegas, our joint restaurants were on solid footing.

Which is why I was unconcerned when, in the midst of negotiating for the second Nobu in Vegas, Bob's accountant Ira Yohalem (the one who was always telling me Bob made movies, not restaurants) called me in New York. "It's about the new deal," he said. "Nobu wants more." "How much more?" I asked. "Five percent." I felt reassured. "Five percent is nothing," I said. "We'll give it to him. Me, Bob, and Meir will split it."

"No, no, no," Ira said. "It has to come from you. Bob and Meir aren't giving anything up."

I thought this was completely unfair, and I called Bob to ask what was going on. The conversation was short. "Listen," he said. "This is the way it's going to be. And if you don't like it, we're going to go ahead and do stuff without you."

Click. It was a gut punch.

It took until that call for me to realize that my partners had been trying to marginalize me for years. Maybe they were still upset about my initial proposal in London. I had a flashback to that phone call I had received in Paris. Or maybe they just didn't like me—a big personality with big opinions, who won't back down and who feels the need to be in charge. The fact that I had gotten so much press, I'm sure, rubbed them the wrong way. I hadn't been able to recognize it, but this was how they could bully me, even if it had taken years to come to the forefront.

In retrospect, I probably should have seen it coming. I'd had to fight for every single thing, starting with putting the bar from Maxwell's Plum in the middle of Tribeca Grill. I poured my heart and soul into these restaurants, but it turned out I was merely playing a part in Bob's world. I had given him the goods, in the form of several highly successful restaurants.

My lawyer got involved. He came back to me and basically said they wanted a divorce. Have you ever been through a divorce? There's not much you can do when one side says it's really over. The way I interpreted it was, if somebody doesn't want to be with you, you can't force them, no matter how badly you might want to work it out. Every relationship has a break-ing point, and this was ours.

I was exhausted from the on-again, off-again fighting, con-stantly being questioned, and continually being made to feel like my input didn't matter. That sort of stuff chips away at you over time, even if I didn't realize it in the moment. I was never fighting about the money—for me, it was always about the rec-ognition, and all the bravado in the world couldn't mask the fact that my contributions were minimized at every turn.

Plus, I'm not psychic. I didn't realize what a cash cow Nobu would become. There were only four locations, and Vegas was struggling. I didn't understand the magnitude of what they wanted me to give up, so I didn't fight that hard to keep it.

I told my attorney to shore up my arrangements in New York and London, make sure I stayed invested in the locations I'd built. But if they wanted my piece of the action in Vegas, fine—it wasn't doing so hot, anyway, and in exchange, they agreed to pay off all the debts on a long-stalled Nobu San Francisco that had never gotten off the ground. Once that was settled, I signed an omnibus agreement that enabled them—meaning Bob, Nobu, and Meir—to do things without me, and me to do things without them.

That was that. I was officially out of what would become a global franchise that rakes in millions every year. But in exchange, I had something no amount of money could buy: my freedom.

At the time, I felt relieved. I had long struggled with the idea of simply taking a cookie-cutter approach to replicating past successes. I wanted every one of my restaurants to have its own unique identity. I never wanted to run a chain where I can't check on everything. I'm way too much of a control freak—about the quality, yes, but also about the soul of a restaurant. I take it all very personally. As any parent who's watched a kid go off to college can tell you, it's hard to let go.

Over the twenty-something years that have passed since we signed that agreement, dozens more Nobus have opened. There are moments when I feel bitter, seeing how successful an entity Nobu has become. Other days, I'm much more at peace with the way everything shook out. It's just money, after all, and I have plenty, enough to take care of the people I care about.

I think the only thing I really wish for is more recognition, that what I did back in 1994 helped turn Nobu into the juggernaut it is today. Nobu describes me as "his partner in New York," which is fine. But I know my contributions exceed just that, and I still feel a loyalty to the partnership.

I try not to let those thoughts consume me. When I start to get down, I remind myself to look at the success of my other restaurants and the health and happiness of my family, and that's all the proof I need—all of my hard work has paid off.

Chapter 12

Heavy Days

While everything was going down with the Nobu partnership, my personal life began falling apart, too.

After my father died in 1986, my mom, Sybil, continued living in the same apartment in Peter Cooper Village where Tracy and I had grown up. And she had lost none of her lust for life. After retiring from radio and stage work, she had found success as a voiceover actor and casting director for the ad agency Young & Rubicam. She also, in her spare time, answered the phones at Montrachet, a job she delighted in and one for which she was particularly well suited: When Ruth Reichl rereviewed us in 1994, she wrote, "The woman on the phone has the most delicious voice: low, slightly husky, completely inviting. Just calling for a reservation makes you eager to eat at Montrachet."

Suffice it to say, we were still very close when she was diagnosed with lymphoma in 1999. Sybil wasn't all that old at the time—seventy-two—but her mother had died of cancer very young, and she herself had already survived a brush with breast cancer nearly twenty years prior. The prognosis wasn't great, but Sybil was as proud and vain as ever. She made me take her to a voiceover audition as her body was falling apart. She was weeks away from dying, yet she covered her balding head in a stylish scarf and went all in, making me promise not to tell the casting director she was sick.

But by the following summer, Sybil had decided she was ready to go. She stopped all treatment and insisted on going home, back to the apartment, where she could die in peace. There, she was pretty much in a coma, and Tracy and I took turns visiting, though it's debatable whether she was aware of our presence.

My birthday is on June 4, and the date was approaching. "She's going to die on your birthday," Tracy said a few days beforehand. I hoped he was wrong, but I had to admit there was a distinct possibility.

I spent my birthday that year at a coworker's wedding, and afterward I stopped at my mom's apartment with Tracy. Sybil had one of those hospital-style daybeds set up in the living room and a nurse who fiddled with the tubes and machines sticking out of her. "Hey, Mom," I said, as I eased onto the same couch I'd played on as a child. I weighed nearly 335 pounds, a fact which devastated my bird-boned mother, who regularly pleaded with me to take better care of myself. The couch groaned as I settled in.

That night was the Tony Awards, which were being broadcast live on TV. My mother was devoted to the theater and tracked the Tonys religiously. So despite the fact that her eyes were closed, she couldn't speak, and her corporeal form was essentially being kept alive by sugar water, we decided to turn on the show for her. During commercial breaks, I'd switch to the NBA finals a few channels over. But I swear to God, every time I touched the remote, I could feel the daggers shooting out of my comatose mother's eyes, hear her saying, "Don't you dare" every time I changed the channel.

The awards wrapped up and Tracy and I decided to call it a night. "Guess she's not gonna die on my birthday," I said to him, and we parted ways. I was living about an hour outside of the city, in suburban New Jersey. It was late when I got home, and the quiet of my sleeping house was broken by a phone call. "Mr. Nieporent?" It was my mother's nurse. "I'm sorry to have to tell you that your mother has just passed away." I looked at the clock. Just after midnight. She had waited until after the Tonys—and after my birthday—to finally let go.

I knew my mother's death was coming, and for that I am grateful. I think I was grieving a little bit in advance without even realizing it, watching her steadily lose her fight with cancer. She didn't wallow in self-pity for even a second, and accordingly, neither did I. It's not the Nieporent nature to dwell on tough times—remember, Sybil became famous for a show called *Let's Pretend*. So although the pain of no longer having either parent was deep, it was also dulled by my insistence on getting back to work. I put on my best professional face and pretended to be fine. After all, my mother lived, and died, by the mantra *The show must go on*.

Maybe watching my mother die of lymphoma while simultaneously ballooning to my highest weight ever contributed to me saying "fuck it" to the Nobu deal—though while it was happening I was too wrapped up in my own drama to parse that out. One thing I did know was that if I didn't lose some weight, I'd be seeing my parents again sooner than I should.

How had I gotten to be 335 pounds by the time my mother died? The struggle is, simply put, that I love food more than arguably anything else on this earth. My entire life has revolved around food. My father loved to eat, loved to take us to restaurants, loved to bring home takeout and prepared foods. Every family event centered around food, and my appetite never went away.

My weight yo-yoed up and down between high school and my mid-forties. I was never really *thin*, but in the early eighties, I was fit enough to run the New York Marathon. But I used to joke that every time I opened a restaurant, I gained thirty pounds. And between 1985 and 2000, I opened *a lot* of restaurants. I was also traveling constantly, expanding my empire, doing several charities, and hitting the event circuit coast to coast. Whether I registered it or not, the stress was enormous.

Things at home weren't exactly great at this point either. Ann had her hands full with Andrew's unique needs, while she tried not to let Gabrielle slip through the cracks, and I wasn't around to offer much help. Ann and I briefly separated during this period, and I moved into the city, alone with my reckless habits.

Sometimes I feel like a bottomless pit, like there can never be enough: food, of course, but also praise. In this business, you're only as good as your last project, and that weighed on me, no pun intended. Publicly, I projected a lot of bluster and a big ego, but internally, I was afraid of screwing it all up.

Food was the only thing that I could always rely on to be there for me.

So it's not like the weight happened all of a sudden. I'd been steadily working my way there, losing a little, gaining a lot, repeat ad nauseam, for close to twenty years. Of course I knew I was fat. My skin was all stretched out, my belts were enormous. My mother had been delicate in her suggestion that I try to lose some weight; my wife, less so. "You're killing yourself with food," she'd say. I thought I knew about nutrition and had even opened a heart-healthy restaurant, for Chrissake. But it was like none of that applied to me. Not that I thought I was above it, just that I couldn't control my eating—it was my source of comfort, joy, and social currency.

But it was getting hard to ignore the consequences, and it wasn't just my family that was worried. My friends were, too, and although some were too polite to say anything, George Lang, the elegant Hungarian owner of Café des Artistes, wasn't. In his thick accent, he told me it was time to visit a doctor. Better yet, he knew one at the Mayo Clinic in Rochester, Minnesota. It wasn't like some big dramatic intervention, but I needed help, and his forthrightness basically saved my life.

I flew out there for a few days of assessment, subjecting myself to head-to-toe tests for pretty much any ailment you could think of. I never spent a lot of time at the doctor; I figured they'd just tell me what I already knew. The results, when they were revealed in a thick report a few days later, went beyond what I could have imagined: morbid obesity, which I already knew; "significant coronary arterial calcification," and something called hypertrophic cardiomyopathy, a disorder resulting in abnormally thick heart muscles that cause the heart to become enlarged. This can make it hard for the heart to pump blood, leading, in some cases, to sudden death.

That last one was the real kicker for me: sudden death? That's not how I want to go out. Even though hypertrophic cardiomyopathy is a genetic issue, I knew my XXXL frame wasn't doing my heart any favors. It was a wake-up call. One of the doctors at Mayo suggested I get bariatric surgery, but between my appetite and my stubbornness, I decided to do things the old-fashioned way: by dieting. The diet was simple: low everything. Calories, carbs, fat, sugar, alcohol, dairy; really, anything that makes food taste good was out or consumed in very limited quantities.

It was an extreme test of willpower, but I consider this period my version of finding religion. And you know what? It worked. Between 2000 and 2001, I really started shedding the weight, sometimes even a pound a day. I lost over a hundred pounds in about a year after my mother's death. I went from a size 56 to a 44 and started throwing out my fat pants. *48 Hours* did a segment on me; I told them the secret was to just smell the food instead of actually tasting it. It pained me to visit my chef friends—most of whom wanted to send out the whole menu— and politely decline their largesse, but I tried to remind myself that this temporary denial would enable many more meals in the future.

By the fall of 2001, I looked good, and I was finally starting to feel good, too. Ann and I were on the mend; I was back home in New Jersey where I belonged. I was starting to look ahead and consider what the next project would be—maybe something Mexican? And then, one fine day in September, everything changed.

I was at home pedaling away on my stationary bike—another post–Mayo Clinic habit—watching the news when it happened. My wife was in the shower, and I remember calling to her, "They hit the Trade Towers!" The news anchors all looked panicked, casting their eyes frantically at the teleprompter for more information. It was a beautiful sunny day, skies glassy and clear; this didn't make any sense.

We lived in Ridgewood, New Jersey, about an hour from downtown Manhattan. I took the train in daily. Tribeca Grill is a ten-minute walk from the World Trade Center stop. I'd spent fifteen years walking those streets, ping-ponging from Montrachet to Tribeca Grill to Nobu to Layla to my newly opened café, Tribakery. I'd watched as Tribeca transformed from a wobbly collection of dead-end blocks that flummoxed cabbies into a real neighborhood, and a thriving one, at that. Hell, I'd been the one to chase after lost cabs, guiding them to Montrachet throughout the eighties. When I saw what had happened— even though I couldn't comprehend it—my immediate instinct was to get there as fast as I could.

Ann agreed to take me to the train station. I hopped on a train to Hoboken, where I'd transfer to another train to the World Trade Center. A few minutes into the ride, a murmur rippled through the passengers: Another plane hit the Pentagon. *What the fuck?* The conductor's voice, staticky and garbled, announced they were stopping all trains into Manhattan. All passengers poured out into the street in Rutherford, New Jersey.

We blinked in the midmorning sun. The day had only gotten more beautiful. Nobody quite knew what to do, where to go, what was happening. You could actually see a vista of the

World Trade Center from where we were standing, and though the towers had not yet collapsed, plumes of smoke were rising into the sky. A current of panic spread through the crowd.

I switched gears, from wanting to get to my restaurants to wanting to get home to my family. A few taxis waited at the train stop, and people were piling in, six at a time, desperate to get away. I stopped one car as it was pulling out and crammed myself into the front seat, promising to pay for everyone's ride if they could just, please, take me back to Ridgewood.

When I finally made it home, my kids were okay, my wife was shaken, but thank goodness everyone was safe. There was this one street in town where we'd often walk the dog, with sweeping views of Lower Manhattan. I marched over there—along with seemingly half the rest of the town—and we could see, clear as day, the smoke billowing, the chaos unfolding across the river. I spent the rest of the day holed up at home, watching the news until I went numb and finally fell asleep.

———

The next day, I knew for real this time that I needed to get downtown to check on my restaurants. I had hundreds of employees to take care of, not to mention thousands of pounds of fresh food. There was just one problem: The police weren't letting anyone below 14th Street. Lower Manhattan was completely barricaded, closed to all traffic unless you lived there. Well, I didn't technically live there, but my livelihood was there, and there was no way they were going to keep me out. I managed to wrangle credentials through the assistance of an NYPD captain named Ed Mamet and headed downtown.

Because I never learned to drive, I often used a limo service to get home late at night after work. One driver—a particularly bright young man named Tony Torres—often took me home. I liked Tony's respectful demeanor and his soft-spoken nature. I proposed he leave the limo company and work for me directly, which turned out to be one of the best hires I ever made. Tony drove me to and from the city on most days, and on September 12, he expertly navigated us downtown while we took in the whole awful scene.

When we got there, Greenwich Street, the major thorough-fare where Tribeca Grill is situated, was like a war zone. In my wildest nightmares I couldn't have imagined anything like it. There were military-style tanks in the street. Dust everywhere so deep you had to shuffle your feet through it to walk down the street. There were mounds of warped, mangled objects fro-zen in place beneath a sheath of dust, like a macabre sculpture garden.

And the smell—burning metal, hot and sharp. It was still burning on September 12 and would continue for weeks, filling the air with acrid smoke. They'd eventually give us gas masks to protect our lungs, but not until days later. There were papers everywhere, too, countless documents from all the offices in the towers. I bent down to pick up a sheet so neatly singed around the edges that I could still make out the company name. It was on letterhead from Carr Futures, the brokerage firm where one of my neighbors, who coached my daughter's softball team, worked during the week. I soon found out he never came home.

For the first time in my professional life, I had no idea how to proceed. My restaurants were closed. Hell, all downtown

Manhattan was closed. Financially, it was dangerous; a few days of missed profits can mean the difference between making payroll and not. In a business where the margins are 10 percent, generously, you can't really afford to keep the doors shut.

Still, I had people who relied on me. After a few hours debating my options, I made the decision to continue paying salaried employees. I'd be bleeding money, but it was the right thing to do.

The other immediate concern was what to do with all our food. Although they weren't letting any pedestrians downtown, Ground Zero was filled with rescue workers. They were searching around the clock for survivors, sifting through the still-smoldering ruins, draining every last drop of their physical and emotional reserves. And they were being fed with canned food.

I was disgusted. Did someone actually expect these heroes to eat cold food from a can while they worked tirelessly at the site of the worst terrorist attack in American history? These people deserved hot food, a real meal, one tiny moment of respite.

There was one thing we could do. We could feed them. Real food from a real chef.

My chef at Tribeca Grill, Don Pintabona, and my partner, Marty Shapiro, sprang into action. We transformed Tribeca Grill into a commissary kitchen overnight. Every restaurant and distributor in the city had food they wanted to donate, but the logistics of getting the food downtown past all the blockades and security checkpoints proved challenging.

We cobbled together a rough system to transport donated food to Tribeca Grill, where our team and dozens of volunteers cooked and assembled meals around the clock. We packed them up and ferried them, by golf cart, ten blocks south to Ground Zero and other sites where rescue workers were stationed. When the exhausted workers tucked into a cup of hot soup made by a real chef, their eyes lit up. I have never served guests who mattered more.

We weren't the only ones helping to dole out food at Ground Zero. Another prominent downtown chef-turned-owner was also preparing and delivering food for the rescue workers: David Bouley.

David and I hadn't spoken much since his unceremonious exit from Montrachet. In the sixteen years that had passed, he'd gone on to establish his own growing empire in the neighborhood and was rightly considered one of the greatest chefs in the city. We'd seen each other a handful of times at food events, and scrupulously avoided one another. But one year to the day before 9/11, on September 11, 2000, we were at an awards ceremony together given by *Bon Appétit* magazine, where I was honored with Restaurateur of the Year.

That same night, David was also being honored. The dinner was a real who's who—Julia Child and Alice Waters were there—and David and I wound up talking to one another for the first time in years. It wasn't some grand reunion; we didn't rehash the past or air all our grievances. We were just nice to each other, and that little bit went a long way. A photographer from *Nation's Restaurant News* snapped a picture of us embracing, captioning it something like, "Drew and David get together again." A bit of a stretch, but the sentiment was kind.

When I found out that David was also doing his part to feed the rescue workers, I was happy to be there alongside him, to work together toward something bigger. It's impossible to put a silver lining on 9/11, but for this one small thing, I am grateful.

A few days later, Don managed to get a hold of Spirit Cruises, which ran dinner cruises along the Hudson. It was such a nightmare to get food downtown by land, why not by sea? His idea was brilliant. Almost immediately, Spirit donated an entire ship to transport food downtown, docking just a few short blocks from Ground Zero.

Don commandeered the boat, working day and night to feed thousands of emergency workers. Soon, other chef friends started chipping in—Daniel Boulud, Gray Kunz, and Charlie Palmer all volunteered to cook (Boulud made meatloaf with prime sirloin one day)—as well as hundreds of other cooks and culinary students. Waldy Malouf, the chef at the nearby Hudson River Club, along with countless others, donated a ton of food.

The cruise ship became a popular place for rescue workers to come on their breaks for a hot meal or just to rest their eyes for a few minutes. It was heartbreaking to see; they were just so spent after hours of searching through the rubble. But the food seemed to cheer them, and this meant everything. These guys were the real heroes; we were just there to serve them.

I was proud of Don and Marty for taking charge and organizing the logistics. Because all my spots in Tribeca were still closed, I dispatched cooks from the other restaurants to help out. That meant Nobu chefs and Tribakery bakers were all pitching in on the hot line. All told, the crew on the boat served close to a half million in just a few weeks, and Don's reputation as a local hero was cemented in a glowing profile in *Newsweek*.

Heavy Days

Three days after the attacks, it was announced that President George W. Bush would come to visit Ground Zero for the first time. The area was still shut down, but with my credentials, I went to see what all the hubbub was about. I tried to keep a low profile while I looked for a place to stand. I could see Hillary Clinton, Chuck Schumer, and Rudy Giuliani talking among themselves.

I hoisted myself onto a half-constructed lamppost to get a better look. Behind me a bunch of construction workers sat on the hood of a truck, waiting for a chance to see the president. Moments later, Bush appeared, bullhorn in one hand, his other arm wrapped around a firefighter atop a demolished fire truck. I was maybe twenty yards away, with an unobstructed view.

Amid the wreckage, it was tough to make out what he was saying. The workers behind me start yelling: *We can't hear you!* Bush whipped around and spoke clearly into the bullhorn, "Well, I can hear you! I can hear you! The rest of the world hears you. And the people who knocked these buildings down will hear all of us soon!" The crowd erupted, cheering and chanting "USA! USA!"

When I returned to the office that day and turned on the TV, the newscasters were talking about the speech, already describing it as one of the greatest moments of Bush's presidency—which was ridiculous because the whole speech was almost an accident. Yet it galvanized the country and set the stage for us to invade Iraq. But in that moment, it was really just one man responding to the shouts of another at the scene of a horrific event. And I saw it all, perched atop my little post, not knowing I was witnessing history.

We wound up being closed for more than two weeks, during which time we lost almost a million dollars in sales and I paid out something like $300,000 to staff, and I have zero regrets about that.

Once people were allowed back into the neighborhood, they really showed up. Longtime regulars were calling me for tables, eager to return. They wanted to have a night out, feel something normal and good again. I thought of my mother, and how proud she'd be to see the whole city getting on with the show.

Most of my restaurants came roaring back to life. Don parted ways with Tribeca Grill and his sous chef Steve Lewandowski stepped up admirably, ensuring a smooth transition. (Steve wound up running the show for a decade-plus and remains one of my favorite collaborators.) But there was one tricky situation. Layla was my Middle Eastern restaurant, which literally looked out on the World Trade Center. It was an important restaurant to me and had been well reviewed and quite popular when it opened in 1995. Carrie Bradshaw even had her birthday party there in an episode of *Sex and the City*.

But following the attacks, there was so much animosity toward the Middle East—valid or not—that I struggled with how to proceed. Somebody had written in lipstick on the front window, "Drew, please reopen." But still, I was worried about how it would be perceived.

I decided to tweak the menu to reflect a more Mediterranean theme. It never quite took off, and I decided years later to convert the space into a Mexican restaurant called Centrico, which did well for a few years before ultimately closing.

In the year or two following 9/11, I slowed down a bit, relatively speaking. I had my newfound health to take care of and a renewed commitment to spending time with my family. I wasn't really in the market to open something new—I felt that this was the time to nurture what I already had, get all the businesses on solid footing, recoup some of our losses. And that's just what I did, until Nobu came calling again in 2005.

In the five years since signing the agreement that we'd do things separately, the Nobu brand had been busy. After a disastrous attempt to expand to Paris (which made me feel a little vindicated), the team had figured out a formula that worked. They'd opened several new Nobus around the world, from Dallas to Milan to the Bahamas. I tried not to obsess over the new openings, knowing I still had a stake in New York and London. But, eventually, things came full circle, and I found myself back in the center of it all.

A decade after the original Nobu opened on Hudson Street, Nobu decided to play it again in New York, in a new location in Midtown. Per our agreement, I was back in, though our partnership this time was a little different: My share was shaved down a few more percentage points, but I went along with it so as not to rock the boat. I had learned my lesson the hard way, and I didn't have it in me to pick this fight again. I was excited to have a new Nobu project, was proud to have built it up, and I knew that this was all but guaranteed to be a hit. I felt like, finally, my partners recognized that in New York, I played an integral role.

That's not to say it was all smooth sailing. I didn't love the location, in a former Scandinavian ski shop on 57th Street. I had built my entire reputation on being the downtown guy; all my other restaurants were south of 14th Street, and I liked being able to check in on them all in one swoop. But we brought back David Rockwell for the design and hired Matt Hoyle, a level-headed Brit who had worked for Nobu in London, as the chef.

Newly launched around the same time was a food blog called *Eater*. Run by two young guys named Ben Leventhal and Lockhart Steele, *Eater* obsessively tracked New York restaurant world news in short, opinionated posts. Unlike the more established, old-school publications, *Eater* published hearsay and gossip, and a lot of it.

They made pets out of certain chefs and restaurants, and Nobu 57 quickly became one of their favorites. They breathlessly tracked our every move in the months leading up to the opening, excitedly announcing when reservations finally went live. I cared far less about *Eater*'s opinion than I did about the critics, but I wasn't mad that this little website was directing so much attention to us. It was all a part of building the hype.

Nobu 57 opened in August 2005, traditionally a slow month because many of the city's movers and shakers are on vacation. Not for us, though—57 was slammed the second we flipped the lights on. VIPs were calling and requesting tables ahead of time, downtown regulars were trying to pull rank at the door, Midtown bigwigs with their expense accounts were demanding a better table.

It felt fantastic to once again work the room, greeting faces familiar and new. I was proud to see how smoothly the

managers ran the place, knowing I'd helped invent and implement many of the systems they were using. And I didn't have
to worry about the food: Nobu's menu hadn't changed much
since the beginning, because it didn't need to. Sure, he'd added a
few new dishes and tweaked some existing ones, but the classics
remained unimpeachable.

Still, there would be no resting on our laurels here. I knew
that the critics wouldn't give us much of a grace period to
smooth things out. Nobu was becoming a global brand, and
the expectation was that we'd be firing on all cylinders from
day one.

Frank Bruni was now the critic at *The New York Times*,
and I kept a close watch over his reviews and trained the staff
to watch for any signs of his arrival. Bruni was a savvy one—he
played the cat-and-mouse game better than anyone, constantly
switching the names on the reservations to avoid detection.
At one point, I had something like twelve pages' worth of his
aliases in my files. But there's always a photo out there, somewhere, even if it's a bad one, and that photo gets circulated to
every restaurant in town. It was no different for Bruni.

About a month after we opened, sure enough, it happened.
Bruni in the house. I was at a Jets game when I got a call; I'm a
die-hard Jets fan, but it could have been the Super Bowl and I
wouldn't have cared. I left the game and shot back to Midtown
in record time.

It doesn't matter how many times your restaurants get
reviewed: When the critic who controls your future is in the
house, it's always a shot of pure adrenaline. The whole staff is
on a knife's edge, but trying to play it cool; your heart is jack-
hammering away while you pretend like nothing unusual is

happening. I looked at Bruni's order and saw one of Nobu's newer inventions, a king crab tempura with a sweet-and-sour amazu ponzu sauce. The plating instructions called for the hot tempura to be placed on top of a little pool of sauce before it was delivered to the table.

I knew that if Bruni waited for longer than five seconds to dig into that particular dish, the tempura might go soggy and lose its luster. So I made a split-second decision that I'm sure would have infuriated Nobu had he been there: I told the waiter to pour the sauce tableside. That way, the ethereal crispy texture of the tempura would be preserved for a little longer, and Bruni would likely take notice of this presentation and decide to try a bite right away. The waiter hesitated—this was not how they were trained to do things. "Just do it," I said, and sent him out with the plate in one hand and a little carafe of sauce in the other. All I could do from that point was watch and smile as my idea played out as I had hoped. I left that night feeling good about our chances.

But before Bruni had a chance to file, we were blindsided by a different critic. Adam Platt of *New York* magazine had come in around the same time as Bruni and dropped his review first. It wasn't pretty: He dissed Nobu for expanding, called our primary goal "entertainment," and compared us to a Chili's. It was like he had tapped directly into all my deepest fears about opening multiple Nobus and had exposed them for the world to see.

But my outrage was short-lived. Just a few days later, Bruni's review came out. His verdict? Three stars. He spoke to the impact Nobu had had on American diners' perception of Japanese food over the past decade, compared 57 to the original downtown location, then praised our largely unchanged menu for its consistency and discipline. The food at 57, he said, was "terrific," the sushi "exemplary," the lobster "gorgeous and sweet."

One thing got a special mention: the king crab tempura and its dipping sauce.

Drew as Ivory Snow baby. *Photo courtesy of the author*

Baby Drew.
*Photo courtesy of
the author*

Drew with older brother Tracy. *Photo courtesy
of the author*

The Nieporent family:
Drew, Sybil, Tracy, and
Andrew. *Photo courtesy
of the author*

Drew serving in the on-campus
restaurant at Cornell.
Photo courtesy of the author

With Colonel Sanders and Ray Lund.
Photo courtesy of the author

Cornell college
graduation.
Photo courtesy of the author

MS *Sagafjord* team of cruise ship servers.
Photo courtesy of the author

Drew in his server uniform
on MS *Vistafjord*.
Photo courtesy of the author

Young man Drew.
Photo courtesy of the author

Tony Zazula and
The Tavern on
the Green team.
*Photo courtesy
of the author*

With Sybil and
Andrew Nieporent.
*Photo courtesy of the
author*

Meeting Frédy Girardet in Crissier,
Switzerland, at his restaurant.
Photo courtesy of the author

Working the front desk at 24 Fifth Avenue.
Photo courtesy of the author

With Sybil and Andrew Nieporent.
Photo courtesy of the author

Finishing the
New York Marathon in
1983. Not a bad time!
*Photo courtesy of
the author*

Left: Montrachet while being built.
Photo courtesy of the author

Below: Young Drew and David Bouley while Montrachet was being built.
Photo courtesy of the author

Bill Yosses, Dale Balsamo, Gus Cholakis, Drew, and David Bouley in the Montrachet kitchen.
Photo courtesy of the author

Ciro Santoro, Bill Yosses, David Bouley, Andrea Soorikian, Sybil Nieporent, Dale Balsamo, Gus Cholakis, Jennifer Schiff Berg, Raul Acosta, Drew, and Nate Oderkirk. *Photo courtesy of the author*

Wedding to Ann LiPuma on April 27, 1986. *Photo courtesy of the author*

With Daniel Johnnes, director of the wine program at Montrachet. *Photo courtesy of the author*

Robert De Niro and Toukie Smith at Montrachet celebrating De Niro's birthday. Cake shaped like a cell phone, Martin Scorsese, Robert De Niro Sr. in background. *Photo courtesy of the author*

Right: Debra Ponzek and Daniel Johnnes in the Montrachet dining room. *Photo courtesy of the author*

Below: (Left to right) Maxime Ribera, Jacques Pépin, Jean-Georges Vongerichten, Paul Bocuse, David Blom, Debra Ponzek, Chris Gesualdi, Drew, Jean Banchet, Pierre Franey, Charles van Over, and Anne de Revel (four unnamed). *Photo courtesy of the author*

Left: Drew and Robert De Niro opening Tribeca Grill. *Photo courtesy of James Hamilton*

Below: Tribeca Grill opening team: Peter Klein, Gerry Hayden, Victor Tiffany, Drew, Michael Trenk, Robert De Niro, Don Pintabona, and Marty Shapiro. *Photo courtesy of the author*

Rubicon team: Larry Stone, Michael Trenk, Klaus Puck, Tom Sudinsky, Francis Ford Coppola, Robert, Drew, Traci Des Jardins, and Robin Williams. *Photo courtesy of the author*

Left: Drew with the greats: Gerard Boye[r], Paul Bocuse, and Paul Prudhomme. *Photo courtesy of the author*

Below: Drew was honored at the Cornell Hotelier of the Year, and all h[is] chefs at the time joined. *Photo courtes[y] of the author*

Foreground: Robin Leach, Cornell Dean David Dittman, and Jonathan Tisch

Background: Masaharu Morimoto, Jo[e] Fortunato, Luis Branez, Chet Abramso[n], Rob Larcom, Chris Gesualdi, Don Pintabona, Nobu Matsuhisa, Drew, Patrick Clark, Frank Falcinelli, Marc Murphy, and Patricia Williams

From a party in the Hamptons. *Phot[o] courtesy of Jowdy Photography*

Front row: Toshio Tomita, Robert De Niro, Bill Clinton, Nobu Matsuhisa, Drew, and Aiko Fujii

Crouching: Hillary Clinton and Meir Teper

Party celebrating Nobu: Ricky Estrellado, Brian Wieler, Steve Lewandowski, Tony Torres, Drew, Edwin Ferrari, Nobu Matsuhisa, June Fujise, Joan Takayama, Risa Yamada, and Anne Yamamoto. *Photo courtesy of the author*

Layla team with De Niro: (Left to right) Tracy Nieporent, Michael Carlucci, James Gersten, Frank Soto, Joey Fortunato, Mina Newman, Drew, and Robert De Niro. *Photo courtesy of the author*

Drew meeting JFK Jr. *Photo coutesy of Bettina Cirone*

Chefs: (Back row) Daniel Johnnes, Drew,
Eric Ripert, Laurent Manrique, Gray Kunz,
and Michel Richard. *Photo courtesy of the
author*

(Front row) Daniel Boulud, Jean-Louis
Palladin, Kirk Avondoglio, and Michael
Ginor

Drew as Forrest Gump. *Photo
courtesy of the* New York Post

Drew and Tracy Nieporent at
Ground Zero. *Photo courtesy of
the author*

NYPD Captain Ed Mamet at Ground Zero with Drew, Robert Wuhl, and Tony Torres. *Photo courtesy of Line & Grade South Contractors*

Right: Tribeca Grill team Marty Shapiro and Don Pintabona with Bill Clinton. *Photo courtesy of the author*

Below: Nieporent family with Bruce Springsteeen in 2006. *Photo courtesy of the author*

Meeting Barack Obama (a senator at the time).
Photo courtesy of the author

Drew and Tony Torres meeting Muhammed Ali at Nobu. *Photo courtesy of the autho*

At Bette Midler's Hulaween Party. *Photo courtesy of the author*

Background: David Chang, Kurt Gutenbrunner, Fergus Henderson, and Jonathan Waxman

Foreground: Bette Midler and Drew

Drew, Markus Glocker, and John Winterman, winning the James Beard Award for Best New Restaurant in 2015 for Bâtard. *Photo courtesy of the author*

David Bouley and Drew on a rooftop overlooking the old Montrachet space. *Photo courtesy of the author*

Drew in his office on the
Tribeca Grill loading
dock. *Photo courtesy of
the author*

Drew with his wife, Ann
son, Andrew; anc
daughter, Gabrielle. *Photc
courtesy of Julie Staper*

Drew, Ann, and Andrew at
Gabrielle and Devin's wedding
in 2011. *Photo courtesy of
Christopher Duggan*

Chapter 13

The Corton Years

For twenty years, there was one constant in my life: Montrachet. I'd held the lease at 239 West Broadway since 1985 and had started leasing an office space down the block. West Broadway became my spiritual and physical headquarters, and I often found myself retreating there at the end of a long day, crashing on the couch I'd set up for this very purpose. I put a TV in there to watch basketball or football while I unwound with my favorite late-night snack, a pickle.

Your first restaurant is special. All of them are, sure, but number one is personal. Montrachet still felt like my baby, and even though my attention was sometimes diverted elsewhere, I made sure it was always in good hands. Tony Zazula, my original partner, was still there, and so was sommelier Daniel Johnnes. Following Bouley's swift, dramatic tenure, we'd cycled through just a handful of chefs in twenty years. We'd been rereviewed five times over, each time retaining the incredible three stars that had announced our arrival seven weeks after opening. I was immensely attached to Montrachet and guarded its three-star reputation fiercely.

We still did a solid business, especially post-9/11, when downtown diners came rushing back to support their neighborhood favorites. But we weren't attracting new fans. It is an undeniable fact of New York dining that people will seek out that which is new and hip. I have a theory that every time some hot new restaurant opens, they take two deuces from you. Four fewer customers per day. It's not enough to really notice, until you step back and realize that a hundred new restaurants have opened, and you only have ninety-something seats. Still, I was never concerned about the numbers at Montrachet. We had a well-established customer base, and the people who loved us *really* loved us.

Unfortunately, the one person whose opinion mattered most did not. In 2004, *The New York Times* had an interim food critic named Amanda Hesser in between when William Grimes stepped down and Frank Bruni took the job. Hesser's tenure was a blip—she filed just a handful of reviews—but the consequences of her takedown of Montrachet in 2004 were deadly.

Chris Gesualdi, who had been promoted from under Debra Ponzek, was leading the kitchen. Chris had a steady hand and a good team. There was really no reason for the restaurant to be reviewed again, but we were coming up on our twentieth anniversary, which may have been impetus enough. I'll never know why, but in March 2004, Amanda Hesser destroyed Montrachet.

I mean it: This has to be one of the worst two-star reviews in the history of two-star reviews. "I hadn't been to Montrachet in years, and I suddenly felt the disappointment of returning to a childhood home and finding that the backyard is not so big as you remembered, that the curtains are kind of shabby. Montrachet even smells old," she wrote. I mean, this was cruel. Hesser was an interim critic, and her journalistic ethics were later publicly called into question when it came out that the chef of another restaurant she lavished praise upon had blurbed one of her books.

But it didn't matter. The damage was done. In one fell swoop, Montrachet was demoted from three stars to two, and that changed everything. Tribeca was always a pain in the ass to get to, but it used to be worth the schlep for three-star food. Now, with hotter and newer restaurants stealing our covers, there was no reason to come down to our stretch of West Broadway. I remember watching Hesser's blurred-out face teasing the review on the local news the night before it came out, talking about how a restaurant would be "disappointed" to go down a star. Disappointed? More like devastated. It felt like a hot knife to the chest.

Some of her points—namely, that the room felt dated—contained a kernel of truth. I had been commissioning new renderings from a few designers, considering ways to revamp the space. We could have used a fresh coat of paint, maybe some new art on the walls. I wasn't happy with the first two proposals I'd received, but commissioning a third was taking longer than I anticipated. Her digs on the food, though? I thought they were way off base—we knew what we were doing in that department.

When you get knocked down a star, it's not like you close the next day. I tried to rally, boost the staff's morale. Chris was gutted, and I didn't want to make him feel worse than he already did. But it's a slow drip of losing customers after a review like that. It didn't help that Daniel Johnnes, a few months later, announced his departure to go work with Daniel Boulud. I couldn't blame him; he'd spent twenty years building this thing with me, and I'm sure the review stung just as much for him.

On top of all that, things with Tony Zazula were falling apart. A few years after we opened Montrachet, with my blessing, he had taken another job with Joe Baum at the Rainbow Room. We worked separately, but Montrachet was our common ground. As I got busier with other restaurants, he assumed more of the day-to-day operations at Montrachet—until one day he didn't. It seemed like he just stopped caring. I couldn't stand to watch him totally check out while the business suffered, so I felt the need to remove him.

The proceedings were protracted, with arguments about money and who owned what, which I was by now unfortunately accustomed to. Tony and I may not have been best friends, but we shared a lot of history and had accomplished incredible things together. I felt anger over the dissolution of our partnership, but also sadness.

The way Montrachet closed was not with a bang but with a whimper. In the summer of 2006, about two years after Hesser's review came out, and a year after Daniel Johnnes left and Tony and I started falling out, I closed the door to 239 West Broadway. I didn't make an announcement about it. I wanted to hang on to the name and the space (we still had a great deal on rent), so I simply said the restaurant was closing for renovations and would be back soon.

I believed it to be true. I thought Montrachet still had some life in it, especially if I could spruce up the room. I wasn't ready to let it go—not out of nostalgia but because I really thought we could take another swing. I committed myself to updating the space and finding a new chef. The difference was, at this point, I had over a dozen restaurants to my name. That meant I had more resources to pour into the project, but also less time.

Rubicon, in San Francisco, for example, was becoming more and more of a problem. Not from a food, wine, or operations perspective; after Traci left to open her own acclaimed restaurant, Jardinière, Rubicon cycled through several incredible chefs in the late nineties and early 2000s: Scott Newman, then Dennis Leary, and, finally, Stuart Brioza and Nicole Krasinski, who now run State Bird Provisions and The Progress in San Francisco. They were all very capable chefs who had kept the restaurant running as I'd originally envisioned.

But around the same time that Montrachet went on hiatus, it became clear that the numbers in San Francisco just weren't working. We never hurt for business, but I made some missteps along the way, starting with selling the building I had once been so excited to own and promptly getting crushed by a massive rent hike as soon as I became the tenant. That was a bad call— we should have held on to the real estate, which is now home to a Tyler Florence restaurant, Wayfare Tavern.

The cost of doing business in New York is high, but in San Francisco it was untenable. Our rent was something like $30,000 a month. The labor laws in California were challenging— minimum wage was much higher, and the tip pool was distributed differently—and my payroll at Rubicon was $100,000 more in the front of the house than at any of my places in New York. The health insurance requirements alone were killing us. There was a bizarre class-action lawsuit involving gift certificates. All that, combined with the astronomical rent? We simply couldn't make enough money, no matter how many tables we turned.

I'm guilty of hanging on to things for too long, in both life and business. Rubicon was painful to close because we were still busy, Stuart's food was phenomenal, and the wine program under Larry Stone had never been anything less than best in class. We maintained our critical standing for almost fifteen years, and I used to think that if you could hang on to your stars and your reputation, you were unsinkable. I was wrong.

In retrospect, I probably should have closed Rubicon earlier, if for no other reason than to stem the financial bleeding. But my restaurants are my children. I had put so much effort into making Rubicon a serious destination. I had a lot to prove when it opened, and I had a lot to uphold when it hit big right out of the gate. So, how could I take it out back and shoot it when it still had life left to live? I couldn't, I didn't, and so it bled me dry for longer than it should have, until I finally decided to close in 2008.

The pain, however, was tempered by the excitement of a new project: The space formerly known as Montrachet came roaring back to life, with a new chef and a new name.

———

Paul Liebrandt was a British chef in New York who, despite his young age, had already made quite an impression in the city's fine-dining circles. He was kind of a prodigy. Soft-spoken and socially awkward, he'd trained under Pierre Gagnaire in Paris and was capable of producing exquisite, borderline avant-garde French food. He had also, in the five years since arriving in New York, developed a reputation as an enfant terrible, after burning through several high-profile restaurants that didn't appreciate his genius.

As a prodigious consumer of food media, I had of course read about Paul, though I had never tried his food. In 2000, he was the youngest chef ever to receive three stars from *The New York Times* at Atlas, for making things like eel with watermelon and edible violets and green-apple-and-wasabi sorbet. I thought it sounded insane. A few months later, following 9/11, word spread that the owners wanted to simplify their menu, and Paul quit in protest.

He surfaced a few years later at a flashy new restaurant called Gilt, in the former Le Cirque 2000 space in the Palace Hotel. By this time, 2006, Frank Bruni was the critic at the *Times,* and he was not a fan of Liebrandt's fussy, intricate food. Everything about Gilt screamed "gunning for three stars," but Bruni slapped it with a harsh two-star assessment that read like an obituary.

I had never met Paul—he didn't participate in many events or social functions—but I felt that we had something in common. Both of us had three-star ambitions that had been thwarted by the critics. I wasn't into the avant-garde stuff myself, but I am into working with the best chefs, and Liebrandt was stellar. I knew that Paul had been fired from Gilt shortly after his disappointing review, and I was busy sitting on the grave of Montrachet.

I saw an opportunity for both of us to redeem ourselves. If Liebrandt's food was as good as its reputation, I would be able to present it, price it, and pair it with a wine list in such a way that three stars were all but guaranteed. But I was practicing what Professor Christian preached, with twenty years of owning three-star restaurants under my belt, and all the confidence in this guy's talent.

So I pitched Paul on taking over Montrachet. In person, he was shy, with this sad-eyed baby face that looked totally out of place with his oversized frame. I'd done some recon with friends in the industry, who assured me that, although Paul could be a bit volatile (like most chefs), he didn't have any major red flags. Plus, we bonded over our shared experiences with David Bouley, whom Paul had previously worked under.

Paul played hard to get at first. He was doing some consulting work, making gourmet marshmallows or some bullshit. But I knew he still wanted three stars, and I was pitching him the platform to do it. We could redo the whole thing, I told Paul. I already wanted to give the whole dining room a makeover, and he could build the kitchen of his dreams. He could choose the designer. I gave him a stake in the ownership, an unusual move for me, but I thought it would make him more committed. Finally, he agreed. But this wasn't going to be Paul taking over Montrachet. This was he and I opening a whole new restaurant, one that deserved its own identity. And so we settled on a new name, inspired by another iconic Burgundy wine: Corton.

I recruited new investors and, with my own contributions, raised something like $2 million for the rehab. I settled the outstanding debts left over from Montrachet and we got to work. Paul and I hired a designer, Stephanie Goto, to redo the space. The shift was dramatic: Montrachet had a tiny kitchen in the front and about ninety seats across three rooms. At Corton, we moved the kitchen to the larger back room, where we previously served private parties, and Paul built a state-of-the-art facility full of electric equipment.

I was flipping the script: less volume and higher price. It was a risky formula. The Great Recession was in full swing, but I had faith: We opened with a three-course prix fixe menu at seventy-six dollars, still a relative bargain, and I knew we'd give people their money's worth.

Paul had total freedom over the menu, but he was concerned that he'd been burned by Bruni for his more esoteric creations. This time, he crafted more restrained dishes like foie gras encased in an eye-catching beet-and-hibiscus gelée, and a gorgeous salad from the garden, painstakingly prepared with a dozen different vegetables, all cooked in different ways. I felt the food was still artistic and intricate, but no longer incomprehensible. It was fantastic and I told him as much.

Stephanie made major changes to the aesthetic, too. The walls were painted a cool, austere white, with gold accent leaves and little trees stenciled in, and slender tubular light fixtures hung from the ceiling. The new kitchen had a long, narrow window peering out to the dining room, which gave guests a glimpse of the chef and his minions from the waist up. It was sleek, it was modern, it was dramatic: a true upgrade from Montrachet.

Still, I was concerned about our new opening. Not only was I nostalgic for the address itself, but also anticipation was building in the media. Montrachet had been sitting dormant, and there was a lot of speculation about what I was going to do with the space. The bloggers over at *Eater* threw all kinds of rumors into the wind. Even Florence Fabricant at the *Times*, when I announced the project a few months earlier, wrote in her intro, "It hasn't been the best kept secret, but it has kept the New York restaurant world wondering for two years: What is

Drew Nieporent going to do with Montrachet, the restaurant that helped recast dining in the city?"

We took such pains to eliminate any association with the dark, "musty" old Montrachet room that we went slightly overboard. In the weeks leading up to the official opening, we had a "friends and family" tasting and invited industry professionals to come eat as our guests, in the hopes that they'd be honest about any improvements we could make.

We didn't have much time; I knew all eyes would be on us the second we opened, and most new restaurants get reviewed within their first two to three months. I invited Joe Bastianich, a native New Yorker and fellow restaurateur who owned Babbo, Becco, and Del Posto. The first thing he said to me after I seated him was, "Why is it so goddamn bright in here?"

He was right. We'd built the restaurant during the day, when the sun streamed in through the one window near the entrance. But at night, absent of natural light, the room, with its eggshell walls and cold, clean-lined fixtures, took on a hospital-like hue. Dimming the lights didn't work—there was no way to adjust the harsh tone.

The next day, I called Stephanie Goto's office to ask for her help. "Oh, Stephanie is in Russia," her assistant told me. "She'll be back next week." Next week? I'm opening a restaurant next week, and I had a problem that needed fixing immediately. Not sure how to proceed, I called my friend Glen Coben, another architect who had done beautiful work for many restaurants I admired, and asked him for advice.

Glen took one look at the room and diagnosed the problem: "I would paint the whole place," he said. I was flabbergasted. We'd just spent a ridiculous amount of money on Stephanie's precious gold-accented design, and he's telling me to make everything darker? Just a shade, he clarified. I was dubious but decided to trust his judgment. Less than a week out, we repainted the whole room a creamy off-white with green-gold tones. Glen was right: That subtle change improved the lighting and feel of the room at night.

Upon Stephanie's return from Russia, she visited us at Corton. "You ruined my restaurant!" she gasped as she walked in. "No, Stephanie," I said to her. "It's not your restaurant. It's *my* restaurant."

The opening of Corton brought some new problems. Montrachet had a lot of staff that had been there for years. The front of house–back of house tensions that often plague a restaurant had been largely smoothed over simply by virtue of so many people working together for so long. But opening Corton necessitated hiring all new people, and some of those tensions inevitably resumed.

It only took a few days to realize that Paul had a temper. He would raise his voice and threaten to put people's heads through the wall if they didn't plate something perfectly. He was demanding and exacting, worked long hours, and expected the same from his team. His outbursts could be unpredictable, and his staff was often on edge, waiting to be berated within an inch of their life for minor infractions. He'd dump entire sheet trays of nearly finished canapés in the trash if one was set slightly off. I tried to keep an eye on his behavior—I didn't want to get sued because of this guy.

Paul came as a sort of package deal with his girlfriend, Arleene Oconitrillo, a manager in the front of the house. They'd met working together at Gilt, and I hired her to be our general manager at Corton, where she ran a tight ship. But any hopes I had that their personal partnership would smooth front-and-back relationships were squashed. They were the masters of their respective domains, so Arleene wouldn't dare to cross him in the kitchen.

Paul didn't do much to inspire camaraderie among his crew; he used to sulk around, and I never saw him share a family meal with the staff. It made for a tense environment. On our very first night of service, a waiter pulled me aside: "I just want you to know that Paul called me a motherfucker."

"Okay," I said. "I'll handle this." I went back into the kitchen and said to Paul: "It's unacceptable to call anyone a motherfucker, okay?"

"I didn't, I didn't," he mumbled.

"Okay. Just don't do it," I said. He rolled his eyes but nodded he understood.

The next night, I went back into the kitchen. I could see Paul, face red, about to blow. I caught his eye and shot him a stern look. *Don't do it*, I mouthed. *Let it go*. Third night, the same thing happened. Eventually, it seemed to me he had gotten the urge to excoriate people out of his system, and I felt quite proud that calmed him down. Unfortunately, in the years since, several former kitchen staffers have shared horror stories with me about being berated by Paul.

Despite his temper—or, perhaps, because of it—Paul had attracted the attention of a documentary filmmaker named Sally Rowe. She had been following him around for years prior to Corton, documenting his time at Atlas and Gilt, even filming him and Arleene at home in their apartment. When Sally first approached me about filming Paul at the new restaurant,

I thought she was out of her mind. I remember telling her that she'd be filming us disagreeing over a bunch of stuff. But she was lovely and persistent, and eventually I was disarmed.

Sally was very good at her job. She blended into the kitchen and dining room without causing a fuss. She didn't push any agenda; she was there to observe. I'm not quite sure how Paul felt about being the focus of so much attention—he was tough to read in that way—but I loved it. For a kid who grew up with an actress mother, being filmed was an enjoyable novelty. The film that Sally put together, *A Matter of Taste*, follows the buildout and opening of Corton and its subsequent review by Frank Bruni. In fact, when the film came out, it was so well received that it won a James Beard journalism award.

Corton was a hit with most critics from the start. Food media was online now, and there seemed to be more pressure to publish reviews quickly. Adam Platt at *New York* magazine gave an over-the-top favorable review barely a month after we opened. But Bruni took his time to come in. I knew he would, though, and it made for a juicy storyline: a scorned chef teaming up with a veteran restaurateur and taking another swing in a legendary space that had held on to three stars for decades.

The night of Bruni's visit, it was late, and there was only one party left to arrive. When they showed up, I barely even clocked the guests as I led them to their table. But the moment I pulled out their chairs, suddenly, not one inch away, was Bruni. "It's his birthday," he said to me, gesturing to another man in the party. Startled, I looked at my staff, trying to urgently convey that *this was the guy*. But they already knew. A small nod was all it took: *Don't worry, we got this.*

My protocol for critics in the house has remained largely unchanged since Montrachet first opened: Just do your job, and do it well.

Bruni came in a few more times. Paul's food on that opening menu was really brilliant, much better than the tortured plates he'd twisted himself into knots over amid the uptown pretension and ridiculous ceremony of Gilt. For as much as Corton was different from Montrachet, we upheld the same unassuming attitude that had brought diners to Tribeca two decades earlier. Paul's cooking was, accordingly, more relaxed, which suited the space to a T.

Bruni reached out to fact-check, but did not want to talk to Paul. He wanted all responses to be written. We anticipated that the review was about to drop. The previous week, however, he had awarded three stars to Momofuku Ssäm Bar, David Chang's casual, rowdy late-night spot. I was surprised by the rating: If Bruni was handing out three stars to Momofuku, would we, I dared to wonder, be primed for four?

The afternoon before the print edition with our review came out, the online version was published. This was unusual, and Sally Rowe was filming in the restaurant that day. I called her over and said, "Why don't you film me reading the review to the staff for the first time?" None of us had seen it, so the reactions would be genuine. She grabbed her camera and I assembled the team for a meeting.

The entire staff sat with me in an empty dining room as I began reading the review aloud. As I started the first paragraph, I knew right away it was three stars. Words like *wonderful*, *beautiful*, and *master class* were present, followed by descriptions of a "sublimely prepared" foie gras and a "triumphant glory of a beef." Bruni correctly noticed that Paul had "calm[ed] down and wise[d] up," and praised his newfound restraint. "Imagination, Say Hello to Discipline" was the headline.

As I was reading, Paul was pacing furiously in the back. By the end, when Bruni declared that "Corton is for the most part superb, and joins the constantly improving Eleven Madison Park as a restaurant hovering just below the very summit of fine dining in New York," I knew we weren't going to land four stars, but this was a very solid three.

For some reason, no stars were attached to the online review. It wasn't until the printed copy appeared, three stars intact, that Paul was willing to believe it was true. That night, the whole team celebrated at Tribeca Grill, and Paul cracked a smile for possibly the first time ever. Ah, the sweet taste of redemption!

I was thrilled that Corton earned its three stars, but Paul didn't seem content. Shortly after we were reviewed, Eleven Madison Park, then owned by Danny Meyer, with Will Guidara and chef Daniel Humm operating, attained four stars in the *Times*. It was a beautiful review, heaping praise on Humm's tasting menu and the professionalism of the dining room. I could almost see the steam pouring out of Liebrandt's ears.

Corton's original menu was set up as a prix fixe, a choice of five appetizers, entrées, and desserts for a set price. A tasting menu, however, gives guests no choice: You eat what the chef prepares. For a chef, a tasting menu is the ultimate stage on which to show off—no more bowing to customers' whims. It puts the chef fully in control, and the format tends to attract diners and critics—who consider themselves serious gourmets. Following EMP's review, Paul suggested we switch to a tasting menu format.

Although I had never run a tasting menu–only restaurant, I was open to the idea. From a business perspective, tasting menus can make a lot of sense. And, of course, Paul told me something that every restaurateur wants to hear: *I'll save you money on food, I'll save you money on payroll.* It had worked for Eleven Madison, catapulting them onto the rarefied four-star stage, and Paul felt strongly that it would work for us, too. I figured we'd give it a shot.

Once we made the switch, shades of the Gilt-era Paul began creeping onto the menu. I've always strived to make the food easy for the guest. But my chef couldn't help himself—he abandoned the simpler pleasures of our opening menu in favor of ever more elaborate dishes. The food went from artful-but-accessible to artful-and-challenging. It no longer required enjoying; it required submission.

The new menu was controversial and attracted a lot of attention when we first announced it. But it became apparent after several weeks, when our covers started shrinking, that no one really wanted it. I'm not obsessed with making money, but a restaurant has to at least break even. I'd learned that the hard way with Rubicon. At Corton, the tasting menu was well received, but it certainly wasn't *saving* us money.

Lower food costs? Ha. I saw an article in the paper that lobsters were the lowest price they'd been in years. I mentioned it to Paul, who thanked me, said he'd been thinking about putting lobster on the menu. I walked away from that conversation feeling good, like I'd fed him a useful idea. A day or two later, during the preservice meeting, I heard Paul address the waiters:

"Tonight, our special is lobster." I nodded, pleased with myself. But then he continued: "Blue lobster from Nova Scotia," he said. The meat, he went on to explain in a hushed, almost reverent tone, is sweeter and more succulent than Maine lobster, it's a true delicacy, and so on.

In all my years in restaurants, I had never heard of blue lobsters. I called my purchaser at Tribeca Grill and asked him if he'd ever heard of blue lobsters and how much they cost. "Oh yeah, they're like nineteen dollars a pound," he said. That was twice as much as Maine lobsters, which were already an indulgence. But that's Paul for you—he couldn't help but find a way to take what should be a bargain and make it as expensive as possible.

Labor-wise, it was the same story. Paul had nineteen cooks under him, necessary, he claimed, to produce his tiny modernist masterpieces. But within a few months of switching menus, we were serving fewer than a hundred covers a night—the tasting menu was three hours long, meaning we couldn't turn tables— so we should not have more than a dozen people in the kitchen. That's the math, and payroll is one of the highest expenses we endure.

I've always had the same objectives in any of my restaurants: Open the doors, honor reservations, give the people great food and wine, and get them the hell out. That just wasn't happening at Corton.

Beyond all that, Paul insisted that diners be forbidden from photographing his food. He was worried his genius would be ripped off. One night a writer from StarChefs came in and tried to take pictures. This set him off. He could never confront a guest to their face, but he seethed and skulked around the kitchen like a petulant child. It was stupid—this was in 2011, around the time that Instagram was becoming popular, and I felt that Paul was shooting himself in the foot by refusing the free publicity that would come with sharing photos.

I say all this now with the benefit of hindsight, but at the time, I wasn't as tuned in to our drop in covers. The reviews were still strong, which made it seem like the tasting menu format was working. We even got two Michelin stars, which made me immensely proud, thinking back to the Michelin-starred restaurants I'd eaten at with Tony Zazula on that trip to Europe back in 1980. I was dividing my days among Corton, Tribeca Grill, multiple Nobus, and some management deals. And our tasting menu was still considerably more affordable than those on offer at Daniel, Jean-Georges, or Le Bernardin, so I wasn't overly concerned that we were driving people away with the price. But sure enough, by the time I looked at the numbers, it was too late.

We were losing something like $1,000 a day. How did I let that happen? I suppose I let the problem linger without correcting it immediately, like I should have.

Fortunately, I had a few other things going on. In early 2012, I had been approached by the executives at Madison Square Garden about doing one of the new concessions they were planning as part of the arena's billion-dollar "reimagining." I had so many memories at the Garden, attending Knicks and Rangers games, and even seeing my first concert ever there (The Doors). For a music-and-sports-loving kid who'd grown up within walking distance of the Garden, this was a dream come true.

I wanted to do a chicken parm sandwich. They called me the next day and told me I got the hamburger. The Garden had had a mediocre burger for years. Absolutely not, I said. "Well, it's the only item left," they replied. "Either do the hamburger or do nothing."

So I thought about it, and I decided to take on the challenge. Because of my experience at McDonald's, I felt I had the knowledge to produce a superior burger. Working with my chef Steve Lewandowski, we decided to break down all the ingredients to determine the best possible way to construct it.

The meat was easy. Pat LaFrieda was the butcher to the stars, so I called him. We chose a unique bun, a Portuguese bread made in Massachusetts that looks like an English muffin but that tastes sweeter and is softer, all the better for catching burger juices. I didn't want to cook burgers on a flattop grill. We'd used those at McDonald's and everything wound up overcooked and greasy. As I was doing my research, I came across this miraculous conveyor belt unit from Japan that broils the meat both top and bottom. You season the hamburgers, feed the machine, and in four minutes it produces eighteen perfect hamburgers. It also toasts the bottoms of the buns while it's at it. The only problem with the conveyor belt was that you couldn't slap a piece of cheese on the meat. The solution? Make my own sauces and condiments, namely, a cheese and ale sauce, a jalapeño relish, and a bacon-onion jam.

I call the result the Daily Burger. It took off like crazy. We went from one concession to four, and we're now served, by popular demand, in the suites and club-level rooms. We sell a thousand burgers a game. As proud as I am of this delicious creation, it's not my only sports-related concession venture. I was also asked to do the food for the VIP suite at the MetLife Stadium in New Jersey. As a lifelong Jets fan, this was a major honor.

But business was not the only thing that kept me from keeping a close eye on Corton. Around the time Corton switched to a tasting menu, for once, work took a temporary back seat to my health. I was at a friend's daughter's wedding in New Jersey in the spring of 2012 when I started feeling sick. My stomach was bothering me, but my chest felt funny, too. I told Ann we had to leave early, which is out of character for me—I love a good wedding reception. On the way home, Ann begged to take me to the ER, but I refused. I figured I had eaten something weird, and that this would pass. Plus, I had a reservation for lunch at the opening of Hakkasan, a new upscale Chinese restaurant, the next day.

I could barely sleep that night. My breath was coming in fits and starts, and Ann was freaking out. In the morning, she called my cardiologist, who was about to board a plane. But he took the call, and after listening to Ann describe my symptoms, he referred us right away to a colleague of his at Mount Sinai Hospital. "When you get there, you're going to see her straight away, no waiting," he said. "There's no time for the ER."

Upon arrival, I was whisked in for a series of tests, including a CAT scan. The whole time, I figured, *Hey, this is great, I got right in—I can still make my lunch.* Ann was in the corner of this tiny cubicle of a waiting room, beside herself with worry. After a few minutes, the doctor came back, looking serious. "Drew," she said. "I'm sorry to report that you have pulmonary embolisms, also known as blood clots."

"Oh, okay," I said. "That's not so serious, you scared me for a second there. You're going to give me some meds and I'm going to head down to lunch, right?"

The doctor stood up, walked across the cubicle, and gave Ann a hug. The two of them glared at me. "It is quite serious," she said. "You're being admitted right now, and you won't even be allowed to get up to go to the bathroom. One false move, and the embolism could go straight to your heart."

"Oh," I said. "Guess I'm not making it to Hakkasan today."

At this point, I had gained back a considerable amount of the weight I'd lost after 9/11, and though I wasn't at my heaviest, it's hard to isolate other health issues from my obesity. I ate when I was happy, when I was sad, when I was stressed, when I was celebrating. But now, after years of yo-yoing up and down in weight, my body was beginning to sputter out.

They kept me at the hospital on a new floor for about a week. The food was better than expected, but I hated the monotony of being there, unable to escape. This was the longest I'd ever been away from my restaurants.

At first, I forbade Ann from telling anyone why I was gone. I was in a vulnerable place, essentially tied to a hospital bed, and I didn't want people to know. But within a few days, I couldn't help myself. I had two cell phones, and even if I couldn't physically be there, I could be on one (or both) of them constantly, calling my people and checking in from afar.

When my doctor finally let me go, on a new regimen of blood thinners, she told me to take it easy, give my body time to heal. She wanted me to avoid certain foods, and Ann took detailed notes in an attempt to keep me on track. But that's not how I roll, and I was eager to get back to work.

That fall, a few months later, a cook at Corton asked me, "When are we going to Brooklyn?"

I stared at him blankly. "What are you talking about?" I asked. The poor kid looked confused.

"Paul told us all we're going to Brooklyn," he replied, and shrugged.

What in the hell was this? Paul hadn't discussed anything with me about Brooklyn. However, this was not the time to confront him about whatever new plan he was cooking up—it was right before the holidays, our busiest time of the year. So, deciding to wait until after the holiday season, I didn't rock the boat.

But I did a little digging and found out what Liebrandt was up to. Apparently, he'd been approached by the developers of a hotel in newly gentrified Williamsburg, Brooklyn, about opening a new restaurant there. Something more casual, less expensive than Corton. There would definitely *not* be a tasting menu. I visited the site and was incredulous that Paul had not brought any of this to my attention—remember, he wasn't just my chef but also my partner.

In January, Paul and I sat down face-to-face. He looked nervous. "So, what's going on?" I asked, casually.

He didn't even pretend to be surprised. "You know everything," he replied.

I continued playing dumb. "You haven't told me anything."

"But you know," he insisted.

Of course I knew. I knew everything.

"But don't worry," he continued. "I'm going to keep both places."

I nearly burst out laughing. There was no way in hell that I was keeping this guy as a partner, bleeding me dry while he made glorified hotel food across the river. "I do *not* want people going to Brooklyn and getting your food for half the price,"

I said. "You and I are finished." He may have been surprised, but to me the equation was simple: My partner cannot be my competitor.

It took a few months to unwind everything at Corton. We briefly discussed the idea of Paul buying me out and taking full ownership of the space, but it never came together. In the middle of hashing things out, Paul's new project, dubbed The Elm, was announced. "Fine-dining chef goes to Brooklyn" was an enticing storyline for a journalist, and Paul became the subject of a great deal of press. Every article, amid breathless coverage of his upcoming project, claimed he would remain a partner at Corton. It annoyed me to no end, but I wasn't yet ready to go public with the news of our breakup. Much like I had with the closure of Montrachet, I considered whether I could keep Corton running and what my other options were. One thing was for sure: We needed to start making money in the space.

In June 2013, before our split was public, Jeff Gordinier at *The New York Times* wrote a profile of Paul and interviewed me about our relationship. "It's complicated," I mustered.

Barely a month later, news of Paul leaving went public. I told the press, quite honestly, that I was not yet sure what I'd do with the space, but I wished Paul well. And it's true. Paul is a visionary in the kitchen, and we achieved a great deal together. We just couldn't make it work at Corton.

I was hurt. Even after decades in this business, I still took things too personally. Here was another chef, I felt, who had to prove he could do it without me. But I couldn't dwell on Corton's failure for long. I had no intention of giving up the lease at 239 West Broadway. I still had some fight left—I just had to figure out how to pivot yet again.

Chapter 14

Bâtard Rises.
Health Falls.

I couldn't keep the name Corton. That had been Paul's restaurant, and, after his unceremonious departure, I was ready to reclaim the space. I was open to all kinds of chefs and all kinds of ideas, but I had learned from Montrachet's transformation that changing the name of a restaurant is a rebirth of sorts, a fresh start.

Although the fundamental business of making and serving food hasn't changed much in the last one hundred years, the dining landscape shifted in that first decade or so of the new millennium. Although I had been around for the birth of Food Network, food blogs, and social media, the chefs I once shared the spotlight with had now eclipsed me in both fame and recognition.

It was becoming a chef's world, and guys like me? The restaurateurs who tried to bridge the gap between the front of house and back? The ones who were in the house night after night, making sure everything ran as it should? We were getting phased out. Now it was all about how the chef thought you should experience a restaurant, your comfort and preferences be damned. You want vegetables instead of french fries? Fuck you! No substitutions. You're packed in like sardines in a tiny dining room? Deal with it. The highly codified rules of the Le's and La's of years past might have been gone, but in their place— whether they realized it or not—a new generation of so-called chef-forward restaurants were just repackaging pretension in a more casual atmosphere.

As a restaurateur, the only way to really make your mark was to expand your empire by opening more and more of the same kind of spot that got you attention to begin with. I don't like to repeat myself, and I don't like to let others run my show. I hated the idea of any of my highly personalized restaurants, the ones I'd poured all of myself into, simply becoming part of a "brand" rather than being their own living, breathing entities.

It didn't happen all at once, but things started to change for me. I had already slowed down a little post-9/11. The idea of opening new places was no longer my end-all—I had my health to take care of and a roster of stable businesses that kept me busy.

But the opportunities that came to me started changing, too. Despite my ego, I've never aggressively chased after new deals. I prefer to let people come to me. If you want what I have to offer, you know where to find me. But people stopped coming to me largely, I suspect, because of how I like to do business. I don't open cookie-cutter repeats, and I don't have the name-brand recognition of a TV star, nor the sex appeal of a tattooed bad-boy chef. Somehow, I graduated to a sort of elder-statesman figure in the business: respected for my experience, but passed over for new projects.

I wasn't happy about this: I considered myself still fully in the game. To prove it, I set out to score an unprecedented triple-header in the space where I'd made my first win.

I took my time planning my next move in the former Montrachet space. It was important to find a chef I was compatible with, especially because Corton was short-lived. I was prepared to search far and wide for a good fit and reviewed my extensive notes from meals out and events. I hold on to everything for this very occasion. I also kept all my original investors from Corton—I didn't have to, but I respected them and felt it was important to return their investment.

Corton closed quietly in fall 2013. There was no farewell party; we closed for a planned summer vacation and didn't come back. Paul had already announced he was leaving, so I don't think it came as a surprise to anyone. While the space was shuttered, I spent a few months testing the waters to see who might be interested in teaming up. This phase is always fun and a little frustrating. Lots of chefs in New York play their cards close to their chests, and you never know who's just using you to get a better counteroffer somewhere else. I met with a lot of people, some of whom had really interesting ideas, but nothing was quite sticking.

A few months before Corton closed, we had participated in an autism fundraiser at Cipriani. There were several food stations, lots of well-heeled guests, and Champagne in abundance.

The organizing chef had already called me, annoyed with Paul for spending a ridiculous amount of money for his rental needs, but other than that, it turned out to be a smooth evening.

At events like that, I'm always in varying degrees of talent-scouting mode. You can learn a lot about a chef from what they choose to put out and how they behave in these gala-type settings, not to mention get a sense of how well they can actually cook. I wandered over to the Gordon Ramsay station not expecting much. I respect Ramsay as a chef, but his New York outpost was in a hotel, and he wasn't personally cooking there. I was shocked at the quality of the food. *Wow*, I thought. *Whoever is making this can really cook.*

I introduced myself to the chef, a tall, square-jawed Austrian named Markus Glocker. I made a mental note to keep an eye on him.

Fast-forward to me seeking a new chef. Markus's food popped back into mind. I decided to reach out. When I'm interested in working with somebody, I don't dance around it. To me, it's simple: You either want to work together or you don't. Markus was very polite, demure even, but he told me he had another project in the works. Disappointed, I said, "Good luck to you. I'm looking forward to visiting when it's open." I didn't think much about it and kept considering the other chefs on my list.

A few weeks later, Markus called. I was pleasantly surprised to hear from him. "I have another idea," he said. "I'd like to discuss it with you." He had teamed up with John Winterman, a handsome, charismatic front-of-house guy who had put in stints running the rooms at Gary Danko in San Francisco and Daniel in New York. They had both worked for Charlie Trotter in Chicago (though not at the same time) and had apparently talked about opening a place together.

It was very unusual for a chef and a maître d' to come to me together as a packaged deal. I was surprised that Markus was so willing to vouch for John, but I took it as a good omen. This could be the start of something really great.

I read their business plan, and it encapsulated almost everything I wanted in a restaurant. They were pitching a modest concept with good food, great wine, and fair prices. There were no bells and whistles, but there was plenty of attention to detail and a simpatico mentality to how I like to do things. Cuisine-wise, Markus was schooled in classic French cooking, with an added dash of Austrian flavor from his upbringing. In keeping with Montrachet and Corton's French heritage, I thought it was the perfect fit.

I like a name that has more than one meaning, so we started brainstorming possible titles for the restaurant. Within the Montrachet vineyard in France, there are several small villages, including one called Bâtard-Montrachet, which makes a wine of the same name. Bâtard-Montrachet wine is delicious, though one step below Montrachet in terms of price and quality. I thought that made for a fitting follow-up, and I loved that *bâtard* also means "bastard" in French, a cheeky little nod to the younger, more rambunctious sibling of the original tenant.

For the second time in six years, we gave the space a facelift, courtesy of Glen Coben, the designer who recommended I repaint the walls at Corton. Gone were the modernist light fixtures and the stark white walls, replaced with warm amber hues. We nixed the tablecloths and bought new chairs. Took out the carpet and redid the floors in a fine hardwood herringbone, converted the kitchen back to gas. I paid out of my own pocket for some of these changes, but it was worth the investment to bring the room back to its comfort-first baseline.

Markus brought good people into the kitchen and dialed in dishes like an eye-catching pastrami-spiced octopus terrine and an insanely delicious caramelized milk bread for dessert. I loved the fact that Markus was Austrian and encouraged him to play that up on the menu—not an Austrian restaurant, per se, but something influenced by Middle Europa.

Markus was resistant, perhaps eager to show off his French repertoire. We discussed adding a schnitzel to the menu, which I harped on for weeks. He finally relented, allowing it as an off-menu special, and added a beautifully cooked, golden-brown chicken schnitzel with God's most perfect potato salad. People loved it. On our first night, half the orders were for the schnitzel.

We went back to a prix fixe format and I set prices at seventy-six dollars to start, same as Corton when it first opened. Most things in New York, including food cost and labor, had increased since then, but I wanted people to feel like they were getting a good value for their money. For the wine, we had leftover inventory from Corton and put together another Burgundy-focused list with both usual and not-so-usual suspects.

Bâtard felt, to me, like a return to form. In truth, the way I run my restaurants has changed very little in forty years. By the time it opened in the spring of 2014, so many trends had come and gone: Fine dining had died, been reborn, and died again; small plates were in until they were out; *fusion* had become a dirty word. I no longer felt the need to stay ahead of them. I had a time-tested formula that I knew worked, so why mess with it now?

When Bâtard opened, no one really knew Markus's name. He had a stellar résumé, but this was his first time in the spotlight as the co-owner of a restaurant that had been made over in his image. Markus was a true talent, and I was excited to give him a platform. His partnership with Winterman had several benefits, too, such as John's connections with important food writers who helped spread the word. Not that we were hurting for attention: The press and diners alike were curious about what I would do in the space formerly known as Montrachet and Corton; it had to be significant. I devoted 100 percent of my energy to opening Bâtard with a bang.

Our first year was phenomenal. Absolutely fantastic. Sometimes a restaurant just comes together right away, and that's what happened with Bâtard. I felt the weight of living up to my own reputation in the space, but I didn't need to worry. Everyone there was professional, sharp, experienced. Winterman worked the door with finesse, and I was overjoyed to have a team that knew what they were doing. Of course, there were minor hiccups in those first few weeks of figuring out the flow of service and tweaking the dishes, but Bâtard, more than almost any of my other restaurants, came to life easily and naturally.

The reviews were almost uniformly positive. Diners and critics alike seemed relieved that Liebrandt's challenging reign was over. The mood was fun but professional, and it felt like the good old days at Montrachet.

With Markus and John running the show, I was able to step back from day-to-day operations. I still spent a lot of time on reservations because I have always insisted on knowing every-thing I can about guests. That part of the job is hardwired into my DNA, and I couldn't stop even if I tried. Tribeca is still, despite becoming more expensive, a tight-knit community, and a lot of longtime customers were coming out of the woodwork now that Bâtard had replaced Corton. I wanted to take care of everyone, but I no longer felt compelled to work the floor every single night. The restaurant was in good hands, and I began to think that Markus and John might eventually be good stewards of the lease.

I'd been in the game for so long that I'd become friends with the critics I once feared; one night I invited Mimi Sheraton, in her eighties at that point but still sharp as a tack, to dine with me at Bâtard. Mimi had written a German cookbook and I knew she'd pull no punches about Markus's food. She arrived in a fetching coral-red shirt with a beaded necklace; her approval of Markus's schnitzel gave me all the confidence I needed that we were doing things right.

In the spring of 2015, the James Beard Awards moved from their longtime home in New York City to Chicago. I thought it was an odd choice, but Markus, John, and I were happy to travel because we were nominated for Best New Restaurant. After my sweep in 1995, I had been to the awards almost every year, as either a committee member or a nominee, but I hadn't been up to the podium since 2009, when I was named Outstand-ing Restaurateur. Six years later, Bâtard received the recogni-tion it deserved, and I found myself back onstage once more, surrounded by flashbulbs and Champagne.

Best New Restaurant is a particularly validating award. It's one thing to drum up excitement for a new opening, but it's an altogether different challenge to actually deliver at a professional level right from the start. I was so proud of Markus and John for nailing it. An award like that pretty much solidifies your business for the next few years, and unlike a *New York Times* review—the paper might dispatch the food critic to rereview a restaurant if it's been open long enough—a James Beard Award is permanent.

Bâtard never hurt for business. It was a genuine crowd-pleaser, well priced and consistently full. *The New York Times* food critic Pete Wells bestowed a glowing three-star review upon us—my third consecutive three-star review at 239 West Broadway. Having three three-star restaurants in the same space over the course of thirty-plus years is no small feat. I actually don't know whether anyone else has ever pulled it off. I was enjoying Bâtard's success, but things were not destined to run smoothly for long.

Ann had noticed a weird mole on my nose. I hadn't paid much attention to it, but she kept poking at my face, saying she didn't like the look of it. In the spring of 2018, I agreed to go to the dermatologist for a biopsy. Ann was right—the skin around my right nostril was deemed cancerous.

Fortunately, because of its size and location, they told me I was a good candidate for Mohs surgery: basically, the surgeon would slice off thin layers of skin like salami until all the cancerous cells are gone. It's an incredible thing, an outpatient procedure where you're awake the whole time, with a minimal recovery period. Given that, the cancer diagnosis didn't feel like a big deal.

Perhaps I had waited too long, because the cancerous cells on my nose went a lot deeper than we first thought. The Mohs surgeon was going to have to shave off a big chunk of my nostril. He recommended that I go straight from the surgery to a reconstructive plastic surgeon to reform my nose. I wasn't thrilled, but what choice did I have? I didn't want half a schnozz hanging off my face.

A few days before the surgery, I was instructed to stop taking the blood thinners I'd been on since my pulmonary embolism in 2012. This was nerve-wracking, but Mohs surgery can be messy, and they didn't want me losing too much blood during the procedure.

The operation went off without a hitch. They sent me out in a pleasantly drug-induced haze with my face all bandaged up beneath several layers of gauze.

Afterward, my driver, Tony Torres, took me to the plastic surgeon for part two of the operation. I was sitting in the examination room when the surgeon, Dr. Copeland, came in. She lifted my bandages, and I'll never forget her face—just pure, unadulterated horror. She collected herself, then called my wife into her office.

I wasn't in the room, but apparently Dr. Copeland showed Ann images of what was left of my nose. She was upset that the Mohs surgeon had left her "nothing to work with" skin-wise. There was no easy path for her to rebuild my face. She wound up taking a piece of skin from in between my nose and lip and grafting it into a new nostril. That procedure, too, went as well as it could have, considering the circumstances.

At home, I had to sleep sitting up in a chair, and poor Ann had to play nurse for me, cleaning the hole in my face with a

Q-tip at all hours. I had to have a follow-up procedure about a week after the first to separate the skin from the blood supply once the graft took. I needed to get back on blood thinners as soon as possible, but Dr. Copeland was worried about how my bleeding might complicate the second procedure. After some debate, she decided it was better to put me back on thinners before the surgery, even if it meant her job would be a little messier.

Within seventy-two hours, all hell broke loose.

According to my handwritten calendar, on April 26, 2018, I spent the day in the city, ate Chinese food for dinner, and attended a screening of *Sweetbitter*, a show based on a dishy book written by a former waitress at Union Square Cafe. Tony dropped me off at home in Rockland County at about nine that night. Ann was already upstairs in the bedroom, and I called up to her that I'd be there in a minute.

I was standing in front of the refrigerator putting away my Chinese leftovers one minute and the next grabbing reflexively at the aluminum chair by the butcher-block island as I crashed down to the floor, bringing the chair down with me. Later, Ann said the noise of the metal against the tile is the only reason she came downstairs. I was on the floor, on my side, and couldn't move one half of my body. I tried to call out to Ann but couldn't speak. I could only make vague garbled noises with my throat. I strangely felt no pain, and I began to drift off into unconsciousness. I remember seeing lemons spilled across the tile.

Then I heard Ann screaming that she was calling 911. I flopped around on the floor, waving my one working hand, trying to calm her down, gurgling "No." I must have looked insane: My face was still bandaged from the nostril surgery, and

I was severely overweight. Ann saw me spasming on the tile and making weird noises, and yelled, "Fuck you, I'm calling 911!"

Within seconds, the entire fire department and EMS team in my little town was in our driveway. They struggled to get me onto the gurney and down the stairs to our front door—I was too big. I was only dimly aware of what was happening, but even in that moment, I felt acutely aware—and ashamed—of my size.

In the ambulance, I felt every bump in the road, but I was in a dream state—I couldn't say anything. It was like I was looking at myself from a distance. I could see my body, but I couldn't do anything about it. They first brought me to the local hospital near my house, but they didn't have a stroke unit there. They proceeded to put me back in the ambulance, with full sirens blaring, and we raced across the Tappan Zee Bridge to the Bronx to Montefiore Einstein Hospital. It was three in the morning. My brother Tracy and his wife were there. Ann must have called them. My daughter, Gabrielle, and her boyfriend Devin were there, too, along with Tony. I still had no idea what had happened to me. I just wanted to go home.

Soon, I found out: I had had a stroke—a catastrophic stroke, the kind that can leave you in a coma indefinitely. The only reason I'm not a vegetable right now is because almost immediately following the stroke, my body somehow began supplying blood to my brain through alternate routes. It was nothing short of a miracle, or so they told me. My memory of that night and the next few days is hazy, but I know I was poked and prodded and evaluated. I was eventually transferred to Mount Sinai, where all my doctors are, and where the whole blood clot debacle had begun years earlier.

My care at Mount Sinai was excellent, and once I had stabilized, I went through rehab. Even though my stroke was bad, it could have been worse. I quickly regained my ability to speak, and with few issues. But I had to relearn how to walk, and my memory was shot. They used to play these memory games with me, show me flashcards, and I couldn't identify the word on the picture. "Say three words that rhyme with *glass*," my occupational therapists would gently prod, and I couldn't do it. It was mortifying. My mind—always reliable, indispensable in my career—was blank.

I'm told that people came to visit me in the hospital, but I have little recollection of it. My memory of almost everything poststroke is nowhere near as crisp as my long-term memory, and apparently that's a common outcome. I was inpatient for three weeks and felt weak the whole time. I had no control over anything. One day, they asked me if I wanted to go outside for a short walk. It was a beautiful morning, and Central Park was right across the street. It felt like winning the lottery. It was my first taste of fresh air in weeks, and that walk was one of the most sensational feelings of my life.

My stroke was humbling. For the first time, I truly considered my own mortality. I wasn't actively thinking about my restaurants. I had hired well, so they were all in good shape and could run without me.

I was a shell of my former self, quieter and more subdued than I'd ever been, and I didn't want many people to see me like that. Ann kept telling me I wasn't myself, and my kids treated me like a baby, tiptoeing around and speaking slowly. I had to focus to understand even simple conversations, and it was even harder to respond. My speech therapist said I was lucky just to be able to talk again.

When they let me go home, I continued physical and cognitive therapy there, transforming the basement into a little rehab cave. Ann moved a daybed down there, we put in a treadmill, and I basically lived there, slowly walking on the machine while I watched the news on TV and tried to make sense of it all.

Incredibly, within a few weeks, and against my family's wishes, I was back in action—not fully, but my calendar says that I went to a meeting at Bâtard on May 15, attended a Yankees game the next week, and showed my face at Will Guidara's Welcome Conference, an industry event celebrating the front of the house, on June 4.

I had lost some weight from the terrible hospital food and my time on the treadmill, and I actually looked better than I had in a while. Mentally, I wasn't all the way there. I remember taping a podcast interview in mid-May, and one of the host's very simple questions stumped me completely, but I refused to wallow in self-pity. I slowly but surely came out of my shell, and it was good that I did, because not long after, Markus—who had very kindly visited me in the hospital—told me we needed to talk.

"Keith McNally offered me a quarter million dollars," Markus said, brows furrowed. I stared at him. A quarter mill? That was much more than what I could pay him. It was about three months after the stroke, and I didn't know how to respond.

I've known Keith for decades. Our careers have a lot of parallels—two New York restaurateurs with a series of downtown success stories (and later, strokes). We appeared together in an article in the early nineties about restaurateurs; he'd made a name for himself downtown with The Odeon and Balthazar, among others. Keith has always been exceptionally skilled at creating the right mood in a dining room; he's a master of the facade, using golden lighting and bespoke subway tiles as his medium. One time he told me he wished he had my talent for finding chefs; I wished I had his Midas touch for aesthetics. Some restaurants you walk past on the street and, without knowing anything about the chef or the food they're cooking, you're still drawn to them, lured in purely by the look and feel of the room. If you know what kind of restaurant I'm talking about, there's a good chance it's owned by Keith McNally.

Keith had a reputation as an iconoclast. Still, I always considered him a good guy. But in 2017, after I emailed him an article about a colleague's reported sexual misconduct, he stopped speaking to me. Keith was living in London at the time, and he called me from across the pond, demanding to know why I'd sent him the piece. "Well, I know you're friends with him, and I just wanted to make sure you saw it," I said. I wasn't passing judgment, just doing him a favor. "Don't ever do that again," Keith hissed, and hung up. That was the last time we'd spoken.

I do not like to poach talent from other restaurateurs. Everyone talks in this industry, and I don't want a reputation as a chef-stealer. But now Keith was apparently offering Markus a massive salary to cook at Augustine, a new brasserie on the ground floor of the sumptuously redone Beekman hotel in Lower Manhattan.

I couldn't compete with that offer. I appreciated that Markus came to me first, unlike Liebrandt, who'd snuck around behind my back. We had a good kitchen team at Bâtard—Markus's number two, a cook named Kevin McGinley, was ready to step up.

Markus took the job at Augustine but stayed on as a minority partner at Bâtard. I like Markus; we've always treated each other respectfully, and I wanted him to keep a foot in the door. Internally, however, I was hoping this thing with Keith wouldn't work out. My concern was that Markus joining Augustine would create so much fanfare that it would destroy Bâtard's business, just as Paul moving to Brooklyn had destroyed Corton.

That fear turned out to be unfounded. Augustine had already been open for over a year by the time Markus went over, so the hype had died down; and I announced that his role had changed at Bâtard. It was pretty much business as usual, which was exactly what I wanted. McGinley made some tweaks, left his imprint on the menu, but the food was as good as ever.

Bâtard survived this transition successfully, but my health was another story. Just a few months after the stroke that I fought like hell to come back from, I started experiencing severe pains in my abdomen. I staggered up the stairs from my basement lair one morning, gripping my side. Ann insisted I go see the doctor. A CAT scan revealed I had appendicitis. They brought me in for a second scan to confirm the diagnosis, and I saw them studying the screen. Clearly, they'd noticed something else.

"What do you see?" I asked.

"It's a tumor," the doctor said. "On your kidney."

On the ride home, I called Ann to inform her of my diagnosis. I was exhausted, on the brink of tears. This was the year from hell, and I didn't know how much more I could take. Had

Bâtard Rises. Health Falls.

I fucked it all up, was it all my fault for being obese for so long? This must be my punishment, I thought. My body was finally exacting its revenge. I knew I had to take my health seriously after this, if there was an after this.

Feeling utterly defeated, I was scheduled for a six-hour surgery just after Thanksgiving in 2018. Doctors took out my inflamed appendix and one entire kidney. They usually try to preserve a piece of your kidney, but my tumor was too big, so the whole thing had to go. I came home attached to a catheter-like drain. Everything hurt. Sitting hurt. Sleeping hurt. Even talking, my favorite activity, somehow hurt, and for the second time in a year, I was a shell of my former self, feeling raw and scared while I waited for my body to heal. And I was impatient, too—I wanted to get back to work before Christmas and New Year's Eve, the busiest time of the year in restaurant land.

Through sheer force of will, I was back on my feet for the holidays. We were as busy as ever, cranking out hundreds of covers and feeding the masses. Tribeca Grill and Nobu always do a big business at the end of the year, and this was no different. Being back at the restaurants, I was grateful for my health, determined to take care of myself once and for all. But I had no idea that the biggest health risk to my entire career was just around the corner.

Chapter 15

The Beginning
of the End

On March 15, 2020, I was at a food festival in Jackson Hole, Wyoming. I'd been helping the organizers of this particular event choose chefs for years, thanks in part to my obsessive note-keeping about kitchens all over the country.

For weeks beforehand, I'd been seeing stories about this new respiratory virus circulating around China. I'd heard that a few cases were popping up in New York, and I had a vague sense that it wouldn't be good for restaurants. But in that moment in Wyoming, I was busy hanging out with my old Rubicon chef Stuart Brioza, not thinking too much about infectious diseases. That is, until I looked at my phone and saw a notification from the mayor's office in New York demanding that all restaurants cease operations within the next twenty-four hours.

It wasn't entirely unexpected—dozens of restaurants had already shuttered preemptively before the decree came through because officials were warning people away from large gatherings. And there I was, two thousand miles from home, staring at a message on my screen unceremoniously telling me to shut it all down. *I guess this thing is serious*, I realized.

When city authorities shut you down, there's not much you can do about it. I immediately called my managers, but they were already on it, to the extent that anyone could be. No one knew what the hell was going on, information was changing by the hour. I stayed in constant communication, frantically texting with my teams back in New York. A lot of people were saying it would just be for two weeks, to stop the spread of the virus. *Two weeks*, I thought—we'd been closed longer than that for 9/11, and we made it through. We'd survive this too.

I flew home the next day and returned to a city that felt eerily quiet. Everyone looked jumpy and spooked, and it felt like a fight might break out at any moment. For the first time maybe ever, I felt unmoored walking the streets of my hometown.

March 17 was St. Patrick's Day and like any good Jewish boy, I wanted to eat corned beef. Tony drove me over to Katz's deli for a sandwich—Governor Andrew Cuomo had allowed restaurants to still do takeout. It was bizarre to see Katz's iconic dining room, aglow in neon, totally empty, with workers doling out plastic-wrapped takeout containers from behind a glass door. I brought the sandwich back to Tribeca Grill and hungrily dug in. After the first bite, I thought to myself, *Wow, this sandwich sucks. It doesn't have any smell. It doesn't have any flavor. They've really lost their touch.* Little did I know that these were the early symptoms of COVID.

I was laid up for a few days at home, banished once more to my basement lair. My physical symptoms weren't terrible, but what concerned me was the amount of conflicting information going around in those first few days and weeks. We were wearing plastic gloves, but not masks, which we were told were reserved for essential workers. I watched a lot of CNN while I isolated, and people said it would get worse, that it might go on for months. *Is this finally it?* I wondered. *Is it really the end?*

No one wanted to get together in person, so I spent hours on the phone. Everyone wanted to know if they still had a job, if we'd do takeout, if we could sell booze to go. I didn't know what to tell them. I was trying to figure out if we still had to pay rent, if we could get a loan, how we could stay afloat. The Paycheck Protection Program was introduced, and suddenly my days became a maze of navigating government websites, gathering documentation to prove that we needed help.

I soon realized my comparison of COVID to 9/11 was inaccurate because the pandemic didn't seem to have an end. The rules were constantly changing—at one point, we were allowed to reopen at 25 percent capacity, then at 50 percent, then back down when cases started ticking up. Outdoor dining seemed like it might be the solution for a while, but we had to build special structures just so people could sit on the sidewalk, and these were difficult to maintain. The city passed regulations, then changed them with head-spinning speed. We just tried to keep up.

Nobu managed to eke out a decent takeout business, but Tribeca Grill and Bâtard remained closed for the entire spring and much of the summer of 2020. I thought maybe it really would all go up in smoke—not just my career but also my whole industry. I couldn't see how any restaurant would make it out of the mess.

It didn't help that even before COVID, I had begun to think about selling Bâtard. As much as I was attached to the space I'd leased for thirty-five years, the truth was that Bâtard took a lot of effort to maintain. Though popular, it was only breaking even. It was time to pass the torch. The rent was reasonable, and I began to think it would better serve a chef-operator. Markus was top of mind because he was already a partner and had made his name there. We'd been discussing the idea off and on for months, even while he "consulted" at Augustine.

Nothing would have made me happier than seeing Markus fully inhabit Bâtard, but our negotiations went on ice when COVID struck. My concern shifted to saving the restaurant, not selling it. Overnight, I went from stepping back from day-to-day operations to throwing myself into the weeds, trying to keep us afloat. This is the reality of restaurant ownership: Sure, you get to take credit for the wins, but you also have to suffer the losses.

Markus's replacement chef, Kevin McGinley, jumped ship when we first closed, as did several other employees. We weren't open and couldn't pay people, so I couldn't blame them. The people losses stung—I'm always hurt when someone leaves—but this was an unprecedented crisis. Restaurants all around us began closing permanently, announcing their closures with tearful farewells on social media. At the end of June 2020, to my surprise, Keith McNally announced that Augustine, which had also been closed since March, wouldn't reopen. His landlord wouldn't play ball and demanded full rent, which was plainly unfair.

And thus, Markus returned to the kitchen at Bâtard. Although we were still technically closed, I was determined that we would reopen—I would *not* let COVID be the end of my run at 239 West Broadway. Markus's return was a huge relief that enabled me to rally a few more cooks and front-of-house hires. In August 2020, Bâtard reopened with a more streamlined menu for outdoor dining at diminished capacity. Tribeca Grill did the same, and for a brief moment during those warm summer days, it seemed like we might be okay. Much like post-9/11, our regulars, overjoyed, came out to see us.

But the victory was short-lived. Winter was around the corner, and with it another wave of the virus. The city put the kibosh on large indoor gatherings again, and our outdoor set-ups weren't insulated for cold temperatures. Plus, for as much as we tried to create a convivial atmosphere on the sidewalk, the buzz and the warmth of the dining room were gone, and with them, much of the joy of dining out. By November, both restaurants were forced back into hibernation.

That winter was rough. COVID cases surged. I laid low, staying in constant contact with my managers, all of us hoping that with the newly announced vaccine we'd be able to find our footing in the spring. We couldn't rush it, though. Even after the vaccines started rolling out, the city was still mandating limited-capacity dining rooms, and it didn't make sense to open if we couldn't turn a profit.

As winter turned to spring in 2021, I began to feel cautiously optimistic for our recovery. It was a year into the pandemic and we hadn't yet thrown in the towel; the weather was improving; case numbers were dropping. I still thought I'd be able to work out a deal with Markus to buy the restaurant once things stabilized. We had sent a few emails back and forth discussing numbers, but I was holding out for better terms once we reopened. I may have been playing a little hard to get, but that's part of doing business.

I really thought we would work it out. Then in March 2021, I was idly scanning Instagram when something caught me off guard. Nearly a year to the day after we first closed for the pandemic, Markus had posted a picture of himself in front of Bâtard, with the message, "After a great deal of careful thought and consideration, I've decided to move on from my role as Chef/Partner at Bâtard Restaurant."

I stared at my phone, feeling like I'd been kicked in the balls. Markus was giving notice, and this was not how I wanted to find out. I thought the restaurant was worth a certain amount, he thought it was worth another, and we were, as far as I knew, trying to work it out. I wasn't expecting him to walk. The next day, I received a personal note from Markus thanking me for all I'd done for him, but I was still reeling from the shock of his post.

I believe in Markus's talent and I wanted him to be my successor. But once again, a chef I felt I had nurtured wanted to cut the cord, and it stung. I know that chefs want to make their own name. I also know that I have a lot of opinions and can come off as controlling. Those opinions, however, are rooted in decades of experience and a genuine love for this business. I wish that these chefs could see that we're all working toward the same goal (or we should be, anyway). But it didn't matter—Markus had made his decision.

Bâtard was still closed, now down a chef and several staff members. Looking at our payroll, I realized only three people still worked there, a dishwasher, a food runner, and a pastry assistant.

This might have been a good time to wave the white flag and surrender. But I was too proud, and too stubborn, to let a virus end my run on West Broadway. And though I was nearing the traditional age for retirement, I set about rebuilding.

It wasn't easy. An acute labor shortage affected the entire restaurant business. People had left the industry or New York City altogether, or they didn't feel safe working in restaurants, or they were basking in unemployment benefits. The restaurants that had figured out how to reopen were poaching staff left and right, and we were all vying for the same reduced labor pool. Those who were left, and willing to work, might not have been as talented as some of their peers or as reliable. Several chefs I interviewed ghosted me. Waiters whose only experience was at a sandwich shop suddenly seemed like viable candidates. I could "borrow" a few people from Tribeca Grill for a little bit, but that was only a temporary solution; I was getting desperate.

I called every chef I knew to ask if they knew any talented people who were looking for a job. Laurent Tourondel referred me to a chef named Doug Brixton. When I reached out, he had no idea who I was. I told him to take a moment to look up my name and, if he was interested, to call me back. He did. I asked him to cook for me. His food was simple, well presented, and delicious. I took a leap of faith and hired him. In May 2021, after nearly six months dark, Bâtard finally reopened.

I was triumphant. Tribeca Grill had reawaked a few weeks earlier; Nobu had been running for longer. Now the trifecta was complete. I fought tooth and nail to get Bâtard back on its feet, and seeing the books fill up with reservations once again made it all feel worth it. By the summer, we were fully staffed, fully booked, and awarded a Michelin star for the sixth consecutive year.

I felt my work was, if not done exactly, complete. I had rebuilt the restaurant and reclaimed our reputation. And now that the restaurant was in good standing, it was high time to revisit my pre-COVID mission to place it in someone else's capable hands—if not Markus's, then another worthy successor's.

Selling a restaurant is a delicate undertaking. I relied on a network of close friends and confidants to spread the word, and I spoke to some two dozen interested parties. I was picky about candidates; the space still felt like home, so I only met with people I was confident could carry the torch. The timing also wasn't ideal—COVID was in the rearview, but just barely, and many chefs and restaurateurs were playing it safe.

After months of discussions that went nowhere, I reconnected with a couple I'd crossed paths with before. Chip Smith, a chef, and Tina Vaughn, his front-of-house partner in business and life, had run The Simone, a three-star restaurant on the Upper East Side. I admired Chip's cooking—French-inspired and classically informed, it reminded me in some ways of the early offerings at Montrachet. Tina was a wine person, and together they'd run a warm, familiar storefront for years that consistently drew critical acclaim but that largely flew under the radar. The Simone had shuttered permanently during the pandemic, and they were looking for a new space to stage a comeback.

Over the course of many months, we worked out a deal. The idea, at first, was for Chip and Tina to assume ownership, maintain the name Bâtard, and run it as such. I would stay on in a reduced role during the transition to provide professional advice. I liked this setup; it meant that Bâtard would live on under new owners who felt spiritually aligned with my vision. But as the transition drew closer, negotiations grew stickier. Chip and Tina decided to buy the space outright and to retire the name, and my stake in the restaurant, for good.

Bâtard officially closed in May 2023. On its final day, I brought my family in to enjoy one last dinner. The meal was beautiful and bittersweet. Montrachet's birth predated that of my children, who now sat alongside me as adults. So many emotions were running through me, but I was determined to have one final, enjoyable meal at the place where I had invested so much of myself.

Over the course of nearly forty years, I'd poured my heart and soul into 239 West Broadway, and it had rewarded me countless times over. Our achievements there were tremendous. Three restaurants, each maintaining three stars from *The New York Times*, Michelin stars, and an armload of James Beard Awards, and dozens of careers launched. Thousands of meals cooked, countless bottles of wine consumed. I made my name in that space, and it will always have a part of my heart. But it was time. I may have been saying goodbye, but it was no funeral. It was a celebration of life.

Chapter 16

The End

I will be nearly seventy when this book comes out. A man of my age, even in perfect health, moves differently through the world than a young man. I am not in perfect health, and most days, I feel a sense of my own mortality. I know that I'm lucky to be alive.

I am not retiring in the traditional sense of the word. Nobu is celebrating thirty years, and both restaurants are busier than ever. My wine store, Crush Wine & Spirits, turns twenty this year, and in a true full-circle moment from my McDonald's days, we sold 125,000 Daily Burgers at Madison Square Garden last year. In the beginning of 2025, we said goodbye to Tribeca Grill after an incredible thirty-five-year run. Unfortunately, the restaurant never really recovered from the pandemic, but I'm proud of our contributions to the city's dining scene. *The Phantom of the Opera* lasted for a record-setting thirty-five years on Broadway before its final curtain call, as did we. All good things must come to an end.

As I was putting the finishing touches on this manuscript, my old friend and former Montrachet pastry chef Bill Yosses called me. David Bouley, he said, had just died of a massive heart attack. That rocked me. The chef I opened my first restaurant with—barely two years older than me, and an avowed health and nutrition nut—dead, suddenly? Before me? The last time Bouley and I had spoken, I realized with a jolt, was at the memorial service for Alain Sailhac, the former chef of Le Cirque who had died in late 2022. Alain was eighty-six when he passed. David was just seventy.

At Bouley's funeral, there must have been a thousand people, including dozens of the best chefs in the world—Daniel Boulud, Jean-Georges Vongerichten, Eric Ripert, Dan Barber, Gabriel Kreuther, the list goes on. Of course, at a funeral, everybody focuses on the positive. Several people came up to me and said they were sorry for my loss, which was well-intentioned if a bit misguided. Still, even if there was a reality to working with Bouley that wasn't always pleasant, his talent remained undeniable; his impact is apparent on an entire generation of chefs.

Bouley's passing made me think of the family tree of chefs, pastry chefs, and wine professionals who have passed through one of my restaurants in the last forty years. Their collective achievements are overwhelming. Countless critically acclaimed restaurants of their own, James Beard Awards, best-selling cookbooks, extensions around the globe. There's nothing like seeing the people who have worked for you succeed.

I am acutely aware I'm slowing down. This isn't such a bad thing: It has given me time, a luxury I've only recently come to appreciate. It's not my nature to dive headfirst into self-reflective mode, but lately I have had more time than ever to think back on my life, which I've enjoyed immensely. I made a decision when I was still in grade school about what I wanted to do. Then I actually went and did it, despite all obstacles in my way.

So many things in this industry have changed since I tied on my first McDonald's apron. Critics from traditional print publications used to rule the city; now social media influencers do. French cuisine is no longer the be-all and end-all of fine dining. New York restaurants right now have never felt more alive, more unbound by tradition. As one who wholly bucked the codified uptown scene forty years ago with Montrachet, I'm all for it. I applaud anyone who takes a risk.

But also some things have stayed the same. Though the way I do business may feel "old-school" to a younger generation, I still believe that my model—essentially, good food, good service, good value—is the most successful formula you can apply to a restaurant. Sure, innovation is good, and if you don't evolve, you're dead—but the fundamentals remain unchanged.

I am not the first "celebrity restaurateur." Joe Baum, Sirio Maccioni, and Richard Melman, among others, came before me, and Danny Meyer and Stephen Starr (to name just a few) came up alongside me. I am proud to be among a generation of owners who tried to improve the restaurant experience on all sides. I'm not saying I did everything perfectly. My hubris has gotten me into trouble more times than I can count. I still struggle with learning how to let go.

I wish I could care less, but it's just hardwired into me. I am perpetually trying to remind myself that compromise doesn't have to mean compromising my beliefs. If I have inspired anyone to try to make it in this business, I hope they can see that collaboration is the only way to succeed.

I struggle sometimes with the idea of being forgotten. A new generation of younger chefs and restaurateurs are coming into their own, with radically different ideas. This generation will replace me, and many of them have no idea who I am to begin with. I try not to dwell on it. I don't need to prove myself anymore: I know what I've accomplished, and my career speaks for me.

A few years ago, I was asked to give a speech at Will Guidara's Welcome Conference. They wanted me to talk about how to make money in the restaurant business, so I decided to discuss my greatest financial success, Nobu. I kept it short and sweet.

At Nobu, I explained, we use chopsticks, not silverware. We don't offer bread and butter. There are no tablecloths. Boom— you just saved $100,000 a year. In New York, there's a Nobu downtown that does five hundred covers a day at $100 per person. There's a Nobu uptown that does another five hundred covers a day at $100 per person. That's a thousand meals a day, times $100 per person, which comes to $100,000 a day. You do the math. That's how you make money in the restaurant business. And I walked off the stage.

I have even been recognized by my alma mater, despite the bus incident decades ago. In recent years, Cornell's hotel school has been folded into the business school, and the institution has maintained a stellar reputation. In 2022, they established a Cornell Hotel School Hall of Fame, and in that inaugural year, I was inducted at a gala dinner at the Pierre Hotel. Sometimes life has a funny way of coming full circle.

I have been fortunate to meet many of my childhood heroes, which has a way of making my life's work feel complete. I've had moments I barely believed were happening. Serving Bill Graham at Maxwell's Plum and Muhammad Ali at Nobu. Watching Bruce Springsteen, Billy Joel, and Jackson Browne perform at fundraisers at Tribeca Grill. Meeting Sir Paul McCartney at Robert De Niro's eightieth birthday party. For a kid who once dreamed of a career in rock and roll, these moments are monumental.

This postpandemic period has been a transitional period for me, away from fighting to be recognized and into contentment. It's been a time for me to realize, you know what? I'm not all that important anymore. I had my day in the sun, and now is the time to enjoy all my hard work, to spend time with my family, to get all these stories on the page. Take some long walks with my dogs, maybe start campaigning for some grandkids. Untethered by the demands of daily restaurant work, I've enjoyed traveling more and have eaten some of the most spectacular meals of my life just recently, at the next generation of the world's greatest restaurants: Noma, Disfrutar, and Asador Etxebarri, among others.

It's not always easy for me to look back because it means accepting that there's nothing, career-wise, to look forward to. That's tough for me because I still love the game, still think I have some fight in me. I joke that the only restaurants I haven't done are Chinese food and a Jewish deli, but that doesn't mean I should. (Even though I can't help myself from sometimes looking at new spaces...if the perfect opportunity came around, I wouldn't dismiss it out of hand.)

I look at some of my contemporaries, the ones who are still out there cranking out new restaurants and licensing deals and all the rest, and though I get what motivates them, I just don't have that fire anymore. I wanted to make great restaurants, not rule an empire from afar. I needed to be there, to be hands-on, despite the sacrifice that came along with it.

Do I regret it? Maybe a little, but not completely. I'm really trying to be comfortable with what I have. Every time I opened a restaurant, it was to achieve some sort of higher purpose, not just to make money. I have what I need to take care of the people I love, and I'm fortunate that a lot of them love me back.

I sometimes think back to that night sixty years ago, huddling in my parents' bedroom, listening to a young Cassius Clay make history. I rooted for him for his entire career, even when it was clear he was well past his prime. He was an inspiration, but I don't feel the need to keep fighting. Now, I can say with the confidence that has guided my entire career, is the moment to stop—to enjoy all the victories that have led me here and to choose to go out on top.

Acknowledgments

With Gratitude and Appreciation

To Tony Torres, for twenty-five-plus years of loyalty, keeping me safe, and always getting me where I need to be.

To Marty Shapiro, for putting up with all my idiosyncrasies and hanging in there.

To Agnes Chiao, for your honesty, stick-to-itiveness, and always keeping the train on the tracks.

To Frank Franco, for your undying support and financial acumen.

To Jamie Feldmar, for your endless patience and capturing my essence, which is a very difficult thing to do.

To David Black, for encouraging me to tell my story.

To Colin Dickerman and the team at Grand Central, for getting it out into the world.

To my fellow restaurateurs Rich Melman, Danny Meyer, Will Guidara, Stephen Starr, Ken Aretsky, and Shelly Fireman, for setting high standards and sticking to them for many years.

To chefs Daniel Boulud, Jean-Georges Vongerichten, Eric Ripert, Thomas Keller, Traci Des Jardins, Markus Glocker, Stuart

Acknowledgments

Brioza, Gabriel Kreuther, Charlie Palmer, Alice Waters, Bobby Flay, José Andrés, and David Burke, for your endless creativity and perseverance, and always setting a progressive culinary path.

To chefs Stephane Motir, Steve Lewandowski, and Debra Ponzek, for your collaborative spirit and food memories for decades.

To Nobu Matsuhisa, the best chef I know.

To Bob De Niro, for seeing my potential.

To Meir Teper, for thirty-plus years of partnership.

To David Rockwell, for your friendship and genius vision.

To John Gaul, for actualizing and building the dreams.

To Michael Chin and Josh Guberman, two great lifetime partners.

To Richie Elder, Lee Goldstein, Matthew Warshaw, Roger Questel, and Bobby Shagrin, for your lifelong friendships.

To Mitch Modell and Russ Salzberg, for many years of great sports and generosity.

To Robert Wuhl, for your curiosity, brilliance, and good humor.

To Steve Shirripa, for your beautiful spirit and honesty.

To Ted Teng and Bob Grimes, for a lifetime of memorable meals and culinary experiences I will never forget.

To Michael Sirota, Lloyd Friedland, Dr. John Halperin, Dr. Michelle Copeland, and Dr. Mitchell Benson, for your professional help and kindness and keeping me out of trouble.

Acknowledgments

To Jennifer Schiff Berg, Daniel Johnnes, Joe Perret, Kurt Zdesar, and Larry Stone, for your help in jogging my memory and your enduring friendship.

To all my Cornell friends, especially Scott Tremble, Ken Panebianco, Bobby Isaacson, John Lombardo, Ray Lund, Steve Follet, and Giuseppe Pezzotti, for the education of a lifetime.

To anyone who has ever dined at any of my restaurants, thank you.

To my brother, Tracy Nieporent, for your incredible humor and wit and for sharing my life with me.

To Ann, Andrew, and Gabrielle Nieporent, for living an extraordinary life with me and putting up with all the trials and tribulations. To Andrew, for writing the soundtrack to my career. To Gabrielle, for her work on this book, dotting every *i*, crossing every *t*, and helping to put my life in focus. To my loving wife, Ann, for taking care of everything in our life, which made the stories in this book possible.

Appendix

Myriad Restaurant Group

Montrachet—1985

Chefs
David Bouley, Bouley
Brian Whitmer, Hospitality
  Ventures Management Group
Debra Ponzek, Aux Delices
Remi Lauvand, Bacara
Harold Moore, Commerce
Chris Gesualdi, The Penn Club
Richard Farnabe, Forbidden
  Donuts

Pastry Chefs
Bill Yosses, The White House
Claudia Fleming, Gramercy
  Tavern
Vicki Wells, Hunt and Fish Club
David Blom, Hotel del Coronado

Tribeca Grill—1990

Chefs
Don Pintabona, Locale Market
Stephen Lewandowski, The Bridge
Kamal Rose, The Rose Experience
Richard Corbo, RBC Hospitality
  Group
Scott Burnett, Cheeca Lodge &
  Spa
Brenton Lee, Mahi 'ai Table
Stephane Motir

Pastry Chefs
Claudia Fleming, Gramercy
  Tavern

Sherry Yard, Spago
George McKirdy, Meta
Tomas Paulino, Monkey Bar
Stephane Motir
Christiana Younge

Della Femina—1992

Chef
Pat Trama, Trama's Trattoria

East Hampton Point—1993

Chef
Gerry Hayden, North Fork
  Table & Inn

Pine Island Grill—1994

Chefs
Colleen McGurk
Frank Falcinelli, Frankies
  457

Nobu—1994

Chefs
Nobu Matsuhisa, chef, owner
Ricky Estrellado
Shin Tsujimura
Toshio Tomita

Pastry Chefs
Jemal Edwards, CHOCnyc
Sonia El-Nawal, Rooster Boy
  Granola
Jessica Isaacs, Cocoa Bakery
Michele Goldsmith, current

Rubicon—1994

Chefs
Traci Des Jardins, Jardinière
Scott Newman, Chelsea's Kitchen
Dennis Leary, Canteen
Stuart Brioza, State Bird Provisions

Pastry Chefs
Elizabeth Falkner, Citizen Cake
Mutsumi Takehara, The Slanted
    Door
Slade Rushing, Louie London
Nicole Krasinski, State Bird
    Provisions

Tribakery—1995

Chefs
David Norman, Easy Tiger
Felice Ramella
Stephane Motir, Tribeca Grill
Angel Tenesaca, Centrico

Layla—1996

Chefs
Georges Masraff, Gourmet Garage
Joey Fortunato, Extra Virgin
Mina Newman, Sen Sakana
Brian Wieler, Compass Group
Frank Proto, Institute of Culinary
    Education
Carrie Starcher, Reebok

City Wine & Cigar—1996

Chefs
Patricia Williams, 10 Chairs
Bill Snell, Tourterelle

Steelhead Grill—1996

Chefs
John DiLeo, Restaurant
    Associates
Greg Alauzen, Cioppino
    Restaurant & Osteria
Kathleen Blake, The Rusty Spoon

Zeppole—1996

Chefs
Frank Crispo, Crispo
Marc Alvarez, Ember

Freestyle—1997

Chef
Steven Levine, Family Meal

Nobu London—1997

Chefs
Marc Edwards
Thomas Buckley, Nobu Miami
Matt Hoyle, Nobu 57

Coach House—1998

Chefs
Ryan Hardy, Charlie Bird and
    Pasquale Jones
Chris Cosentino, Incanto
Brad Gates, Brad Gates Catering

Heartbeat—1998

Chefs
Michel Nischan,
    Wholesome Wave
John Mooney, Bell Book & Candle

Next Door Nobu—1998

Chef
Shin Tsujimura, Nobu Downtown

Icon—1999

Chefs
Paul Sale, Ace Hotels
Brian Wieler, Compass Group

Pulse—1999

Chefs
James Ackard, Harmon's
    Restaurant
Gary Robins, Prepped LLC
Scott Barton, Notre Dame University
Jake Klein

Appendix: Myriad Restaurant Group

Earth & Ocean—1999

Chefs
Jean-Michel Boulot, TriMark USA
John Sundstrom, Lark
Maria Hines, Tilth

Pastry Chefs
Sue McCown, Taylor Farms

Berkeley Bar & Grill—2000

Chefs
Patricia Williams, 10 Chairs
Richard Farnabe, Forbidden Donuts

Lucca—2000

Chefs
Kevin Garcia, F. Becker Hospitality
Carey Savona, Gulf Stream Bath &
  Tennis Club

15 RIA—2001

Chef
Jamie Leeds, Hank's Oyster Bar

Centrico—2004

Chefs
Aarón Sánchez, *Chopped*,
  MasterChef
Angel Tenesaca

Crush Wine & Spirits—2005

Wine
Bobby Schagrin, partner
Josh Guberman, partner
Ian McFadden, current

Nobu 57—2005

Chefs
Matt Hoyle, current
Joe Ishibashi, head chef
Taku Sato, sushi chef

Proof on Main—2006

Chef
Michael Paley, Fontainebleau
  Miami Beach

Mai House—2006

Chefs
Michael Bao Huynh, Max
  Hospitality
Spike Mendelsohn, PLNT Burger

Corton—2008

Chefs
Paul Liebrandt, Crumpet
  Management
David Toutain, Restaurant David
  Toutain—Paris
Fredrik Berselius, Aska
Victoria Blamey

Bâtard—2014

Chefs
Markus Glocker, chef-partner,
  Koloman
Kevin McGinley, American Brass
Doug Brixton, The Golden Swan

Pastry Chefs
Julie Elkind, Citi Field &
  NY Mets
Adrienne Odom, The
  Golden Swan

Nobu Downtown—2017

Chefs
Matt Hoyle, current
George Tang, current
Ryo Hasegawa, sushi chef

Pastry Chef
Michele Goldsmith, current

Note: This is not an exhaustive list—Myriad has also opened restaurants in Tel Aviv, Israel; Memphis, Tennessee; Nantucket, Massachusetts; and Moscow, Russia.